THE PHYSIOLOGY

The Physiology of Faith represents a highly original contribution to contemporary theology and offers a new definition of "Christian faith." John W. Dixon, Jr., contends that the "physiology" of the Body of Christ—that expression of the totality of vital processes carried out by the Christian community—constitutes the reality of our faithfulness to Christ; conversely, the reality of Christ is manifested in his influence on the way Christians shape their lives.

From this starting point, Dr. Dixon argues convincingly that the ongoing commitment to Christ is the only authentic basis of Christian theology and makes possible a radical reaffirmation of the divine initiative, the Resurrection, and redemptive love. Such conceptions also necessitate crucial redefinitions of such theological terms as soul, sin, forgiveness, and grace.

Here is the foundation for a deeper understanding of the relationship of theology to the history of religions, to the arts, and to the sciences and the groundwork for a hopeful vision of a revitalized humanity interacting significantly with the Creator in the ongoing process of creation.

Dr. Dixon's wide-ranging approach resonates with the work of Ricoeur, Buber, Cobb, Barfield, Hoerkheimer, and Jaynes, and has a particular relevance to liberation theology. At the heart of *The Physiology of Faith* is a joyous affirmation of human wholeness and God's sustaining love.

By JOHN W. DIXON, Jr.

Nature and Grace in Art
Art and the Theological Imagination

Profound thought, exhaustive research, and fresh perspective are wedded to clear, impassioned writing; this groundbreaking work sweeps the reader along with its forceful arguments and grand design to a vision of mankind fully reborn and transformed in Christ. All who take the religious quest seriously and who are dissatisfied with inadequate modes of theological investigation will find *The Physiology of Faith* stimulating and profoundly moving in its visionary contention that "faith is not belief, but the life of love in the wholeness of being human, which is, finally, the Kingdom of God."

JOHN W. DIXON, JR.

The Physiology of Faith

A THEORY OF THEOLOGICAL RELATIVITY

Published in San Francisco by Harper & Row, Publishers

NEW YORK / HAGERSTOWN / SAN FRANCISCO / LONDON

1817

FIRST EDITION

Designed by Jim Mennick

Library of Congress Cataloging in Publication Data
Dixon, John W.
THE PHYSIOLOGY OF FAITH.

Bibliography: p. 337
1. Theology, Doctrinal. I. Title.
BT75.2.D59   1979   230   79–1782
ISBN 0–06–061925–0

79 80 81 82 83 10 9 8 7 6 5 4 3 2 1

To Vivian
For whom it was done

. . . if man is once more to possess intent in his life, and to take up the responsibility implicit in his life, he has to comprehend his own process as intact, from outside, by way of his skin, in, and by his own powers of conversion, out again.

CHARLES OLSON

Contents

To the Reader

Writing a book is a great presumption. Writing a book that speaks of what things are is a presumption of such magnitude as to overshadow the further presumption of advising the reader as to how it should be read. Presumably, authors have their rights and responsibilities, but when their work is done, the umbilical cord is cut, and the book goes forth to make its way on its own energy. Readers have their rights and responsibilities, too, and one of their rights is not to be hectored (or, to alter the form of the verb to something more positive, to be not hectored) by authors. Nevertheless, authors, like parents, have their misgivings.

The format of this book is not so innovative as to carry instructions for its reading on its face. Yet it is sufficiently unconventional that a normal linear reading could be fatal to the achievement of its purpose. It is divided into a linear rational argument (here usually designated "An Essay") of the conventional kind, and a number of other things which serve a different purpose. Each requires a different type of reading, and still another type of response is required to put them together into the whole vision the book is intended to convey.

The essays are to be read as all traditional linear arguments are read: I have marshaled such evidence as I can bring to bear on the issue, assembled references, cited authorities, arranged footnotes. The first five of these (the introductory essay and the essays for Parts One–Four) may be read as any scholarly essay is read; I considered myself in writing them, as responsible for evidence and logic and for sobriety of statement as I would be in any essay submitted for the judgement of a learned audience. The genre alters somewhat in Parts Five and Six, for, by that point, the assertions are too dependent on preceding argument to be subject to the normal canons of scholarly work. They are, nevertheless, essays.

The rest of the book is made up of matters (such as most of Part One, described as "A Vocabulary") as subject to argument and demonstration as the materials of the essays, but which can be dealt with properly only in a book considerably longer than this one. Nonetheless, they are matters essential to my case, so I have set them out in schematic form as assertively as I think their importance requires, in hopes that they will make their contribution to what I judge to be essential—a reordering of our conventional sense of our place and function in our world.

Then there are those parts that are labeled *meditations*—together with a series of highly dogmatic assertions that, despite their assertiveness, should be considered as meditations. All forms of both meditations and assertions should be considered descriptions of a landscape from a particular position. I might be wrong in my description but you won't know that so long as you are standing over there looking at the landscape from a completely different place. Finding error or illogic in the essays is a way of saying "you ought not to be standing where you are if you want to see the landscape accurately and fully." But, if the argument developed in the essays and suggested in the schematic sections is reasonably sound, then the only way to prove me wrong in the assertions and meditations is to join me where I am.

Thus the proportioning of genres—as well as their melding—itself represents an epistemological assertion. I have no intention of participating in the currently fashionable repudiation of "rationality," even though I quite agree with the description of the damage it has done. Rather I want to save conventional rationality by re-placing it within its somatic context and relating it to the other modes of rationality. I am concerned with the nonrational and the irrational necessarily, but only peripherally. I am primarily concerned with the whole of rationality, not only the form it takes in verbal propositions. Since words are my language, I use them propositionally, but also in other modes as ways of stimulating the other processes of rationality.

The actual proportioning of the text does not represent my sense of the relation between the several modes of rationality quite accurately. Exigencies of contemporary publishing required shortening the manuscript and some of the nonpropositional material had to go. The principle of proportioning remains.

I should like, therefore, to think of this book as much on the model of a painting as on a linear argument. There is an intended compositional order from beginning to end and that order can be used. Equally, it is possible to dip into it almost anywhere, providing this or that detail is understood not only in its own right but as deriving meaning and function from its relation to other parts.

In fact, I encourage the reader to move freely through the text. Part Five, for example, has little meaning if detached from the analysis of human experience found in Parts Two–Four while, at the same time, the earlier parts are collections of fragments if detached from Part Five. I would feel most secure if the reader were looking at all these parts simultaneously.

All repetitions in the text are intentional.

The frame of a painting may be simply ornamental or an integral part of the work. My frame should be considered the latter. The quotations which I have placed as epigraphs at beginning and end are concise and rhythmically central summaries of the case I wish to make.

Those who care to look first at the compositional center of the presentations will find it in Section 1 of Part Five, "A Meditation on the Christ."

Looking at that section first has its usefulness in setting out the primary intent of my "painting," and also in dramatizing the dependence of that presentation on earlier sections, since parts of it are quite unintelligible without definition. The problem of vocabulary is always difficult for anyone who wishes to offer a new case to his readers. I am usually offended by an author who presumes to require me to learn a whole new vocabularly that is private to him (as Whitehead did in *Process and Reality*). On the other hand, to confine oneself to the traditional vocabulary is to place the argument in a context that is not altogether faithful to it. Since I am not rejecting, but trying to build on, the tradition I do use some standard terms in my own way.

Certain terms—*structure, process, energy, metaphor*—I use with what I think is considerable correspondence to ordinary use. Each one receives, necessarily, a distinctive coloration and, in the case of metaphor, considerable extension. Unfortunately for me, both *structure* and *process* have become the special preserve of well-known schools of thought that have little to do with the way I use them. I *need* the words and can find no acceptable synonyms. I can only ask that you lay aside all associations with Levi-Strauss and Whitehead.

Both *morality* and *theology* are used here ambivalently: sometimes conventionally, sometimes to refer to the different content I have tried to give each one.

Duality, dualism, monotheism, polytheism are used with their conventional definition as well as with an extended definition that makes them into types of the soul and of the intent of cultures. *Trinity* and *Trinitarian* represent my own attempt to make sense out of that enigmatic principle; thus, each use of them is with my definition.

Geometrics and *dramatics* are attempts to use well-known terms to convey ideas that go considerably further than the normal reference. *Telics* is my own coinage. Together, the three terms should be considered a scheme for the intelligible account both of personal and cultural psychology.

The key term in the title, *physiology*, is intended to be entirely conventional and literal; referring to the nature, structure and functions of organisms. Obviously, my use of it is entirely personal and represents the most radical assertion of the text. The definition is present, implicitly or explicitly, throughout the book. It is set out in greatest detail in the essay for Part Three, "The Metaphoric Transformation."

In this context it may be helpful to comment that, as I worked on the book, it increasingly became a reflection on that extraordinary statement of Paul, ". . . it is not I who live, but Christ who lives in me." We have had no psychology, no anthropology, no epistemology, no metaphysics that makes any sense at all of that assertion, yet it is altogether critical. I could sum up my intent in writing this book by saying it is my attempt to provide a language and a structure of principles that can give meaning to that statement.

Thus I have two books, interlocking and interdependent. In effect, there is a metaphysics and an epistemology which can be considered apart from theology. Conceivably there might be some who would accept the epistemology and reject the theological conclusions I reach on the basis of it. Nevertheless, the theology seems to me demanded by the epistemology. If I am right, it might be possible once again to see Christianity—not Christendom—as part of the order of things. At the moment our minds are captive to other structures which make Christianity into a private devotional system, or into an instrument and weapon of politics. I am most distressed by the latter. A great deal of contemporary theology seems to me to be precisely like the casuistry of the Jesuits resident at the courts of seventeenth and eighteenth-century princes, which gave those noble names, *casuistry* and *Jesuit*, their bad connotations. Its function was to provide reasons and justification for the prince to do whatever it was he decided he wanted to do.

Many (not all) of these causes are ones that I, as a political man, am committed to; but to develop a theology in order to achieve a political purpose is to make a falsehood of Christianity. Theology has political consequences—but theology ought to be something other than a weapon for political causes, however worthy.

I should, perhaps, be most gratified if this work could be seen on the model of the iconographical program of a middle Byzantine church. The lower ranges, almost within physical reach of the worshipper, set out the life and conditions of this earth. The presentations of Jesus as type and model run the full range of event, to final suffering, tragedy, and fulfillment. In the cupola, over all, there is the Christ, majestic and serene, sometimes terrible, the Pantocrator, the Lord of Creation.

Prelude

Faced with the dissolution of its mythology, a culture finds, despairingly, that it has lost its methodology as well. Method is inseparable from myth.

The despair is understandable; without myth, without method, there is no way to find a place in the world. But then despair becomes a myth and creates its own method.

A method that grows from the myth of despair is a method that can only destroy. It would be better to seek the origin of the dead myth in order to understand the world that is lost, as well as to understand the making of myth. This process, however desirable, has never before been available for use. By a singular felicity, it is now available to us, if we have the courage to use it.

Our myth and method is traceable far back, to the delta of the Tigris and Euphrates, to the height of Jerusalem and the wilderness of Judea, to the Acropolis in Athens and the hills of Rome, to the Celtic plains and forests of northern Europe. But the modern myth in its singularity began in the fifteenth century, when Brunelleschi developed the principles of linear perspective.

More than any other device, linear perspective established the sense of human control over the environing world. In itself, perspective only established optical control; the world was ordered from the point of view of the spectator. (I see, therefore the world is.)

Those, however, who lived according to linear perspective, failed to note that, in ordering the world from the point of view of the spectator, they moved the world behind the picture frame. The world became something other than the spectator. It existed on the other side of the surface of the picture.

There was no place left for the spectator to stand; there was only place for an eye.

Since there was no place for the spectator to stand, obviously there could be nothing of importance to stand there; man could be reduced to pure intellection; Descartes became inevitable.

Every important movement in modern art since Cezanne has been devoted to restoring the relation between spectator and art work, thus replacing man in his world.

The only fitting task for a theology in our day, a theology that might claim allegiance to the Christ, is not to describe the world or prescribe a solution to its problems, but to set out in as many of the human and humane languages as possible the order of a faithful experience that can enable the faithful to live faithfully in a world that belongs to them.

Variations on the Theme

To Awake From the Dream of Descartes

The creative processes of a great man are never easily accessible to the rest of us, even when he does us the courtesy of describing them. What happened to Descartes when he was shut up in that stove? Even to him it was a vision of certainty that transported him beyond the range of experience, a vision that reality was ultimately geometrical and logical and that his awareness of his own reality depended on the act of thought.

What in his own history, in the weight and act of his own flesh, the events of his own life brought him to such a conviction? I planned once to try to reconstruct the inner life of Descartes as a man, but laid the project aside; the great are entitled to their mystery and their privacy.

But the thought still remains. It was a cold, bleak winter in a dull German town. "I found no society to interest me," says Descartes' account. He had, after a studious youth, rejected or passed beyond the world of learning and had turned to an incongruously active life. But this too he passed beyond. " . . . I entirely abandoned the study of letters, and resolved no longer to seek any other science than the knowledge of myself, or of the great book of the world. . . . But after I had been occupied several years in thus studying the book of the world, and in essaying to gather some experience, I at length resolved to make myself an object of study. . . ." And so he passed outside his own involvement with the tangibilities of the world. When, subsequently, he speaks of the work of his senses, it is with the tone of an observer, detached from the occasion for his observation.

Yet, even Descartes' life was lived in the flow and continuities of the common life of this earth. As the wind blew snow across the fields, piling it against the hedgerows and around the dead stalks of vegetation, it was to the specificity of the warm tiled room that Descartes fled, from the inert streets and dull people. He fled to the study of himself and his detached mind, but what did he think as he passed through the cold, draughty corridors or felt the icy rim of his chamberpot against the straining of his bowels?

No hermit can escape the workings of his own flesh or the swarming presence of sensation. What asceticism could persuade a man that the definition and demonstration of his existence could conceivably abstract him from the uses of this earth?

Yet Descartes did, and we are now paying the price. If my reality is my act of thought, then reality itself is that which can be thought about. Descartes could draw on the storehouse of twenty-two centuries of developed skills in the art of thinking and add to it the extraordinary skill that he himself brought to the enterprise and encouraged in those who followed him. Thus there emerged the great dream of Reality that has obsessed our philosophy and our science; a structure vast in scope, intricate in structure, fruitful with ideas and invention.

This dream of Reality claims to explain me. But it doesn't need me. Others think better than I do—so they are closer to Reality than I am and describe lineaments of it that I do not see. I persist in thinking that my passage through the rain, the voices of my children, the dim gracelessness of my classroom, the weight of my flesh on the stairs have something to do with the reality of my life. In fact, the coldness of my body, the tensions of my muscles, the snow drifted in the corners of my walk, are more real than the unimportant and inconsequential thoughts I may have about Reality. But this is a measure of my failure as a Cartesian. The great crystal palace of Reality grows ever more complex before my eyes. And I become ever more unimportant to the crystal palace.

Humanly, what response is possible to the nightmare of Descartes? Some become inert: reality is what it is, whatever I may do. Some seek to escape: I can only seek fulfillment for myself outside the world that is taken away from me. Some despair: against the vast edifice of thought, what hope of purpose is there for me? Some turn to frantic and purposeless activity: against the serene structure of thought without passion, only energy demonstrates that I am.

But it may be we can wake from the nightmare of Descartes, now that the dream is becoming a nightmare. It is not simply that the crystal palace is being built at too great a cost; if it were no more than that there are many who would judge that no cost is too great in the search for Truth. But if truth itself is offended in the great dream of Truth, then the dream has become a nightmare.

A Reality that reduces persons to apathy, rage or despair has, indeed, offended against truth, for reality is the actuality of persons in their transaction with the world. A Truth that destroys is no truth, but an offense against the order of things.

Thus the measure of our despair is simultaneously our hope. A Truth that takes from me my place in the world is no truth. We have a right to be here and have a place that is our own. Therefore the despair, the alienation, are in themselves a revelation that the fault is not our own, but is the failure of the great dream of rational order. The dream become nightmare might now become part of a new dream—man, alive, in his own flesh, alert, in the world of his things, loving.

Introductory Essay: Relativity and Relativism

Very few achievements of the human mind can be considered permanent. Perhaps the achievement of our day that most nearly deserves that claim is the realization that the intellectual and moral structure of an age is not determined by the answers to its question or the institutions that emerge from the answers. Who we are is determined by the questions themselves, the structures of thought that determine the questions, and the methods for treating them.

There is seldom any return to the questions that once engaged the attention of men.

The questions themselves may have remained important; it is our attitude toward them that changes. It still makes a difference whether the earth goes around the sun or the sun goes around the earth. But no one is any longer called before the Inquisition to answer for either opinion. "What shall I do to be saved?" will passionately concern the simple and downtrodden. But it is not a question that shapes our common life. Philosophers rarely any longer ask questions like, "what is Beauty?", "what is Truth?", "what is Reality?"

Then what is our problem? Suzanne Langer identifies it as the problem of symbols. She is probably right for intellectuals, but it is not the way most people would describe their problem. What they feel, even in the integrity and continuity of their own physical existence, is a sense of isolation from the world that is the world of their experience.

Our question is: where am I in my world? What are the things of my world to me and me to them?

Where do I really lead my life? How much of my day is truly spent in careful concern for the ultimate questions that once gave life to our culture? "I think, therefore I am," says Descartes. But how much of my time do I spend in thought as Descartes defined it?

In truth, not very much and that very badly. Instead I wake in the morning to the sound of my alarm. My senses come alert slowly, out of a dream, to the weight of my body against the mattress. Through the window the trees are a net of black lines against the pale grey of the sky. There is quiet, with the crackle of stiff branches, a few tentative sounds from birds. The floor is cold on my feet. I hear the click of the thermostat, the low hum of the furnace fan. As I lie again in bed waiting for the house to get warm, my muscles are less limp, my body is cohering into its organization for the day. Now more than senses come awake. I hear my wife's breathing beside me; she and the children are also part of memory and feeling; I am the only one awake in a house that contains who we are as a family.

Then the others wake and there are sounds in the house and odors and tastes. And this is the way my day goes, in the sights and sounds, the smells, tastes and feelings, the memory and desire of ordinary life.

This, indeed, is *who* I am. *That* I am is shown to me in the mingling of my self and my world. I do not know that I am because I think. I know that I am because it is my body that moves through the halls and stairwells and open spaces of the campus. I know that I am because a high-school girl hugs me after I have helped her with her history lesson.

Reticence withholds the full reality that is present to me. But what I have described is, in principle, the day of all people. For this is the way our lives are lived, in the acts of our flesh, in communion with objects, in passage through the common space, in the concreteness of the earth, in constant interaction with others like ourselves.

This, our common life on the earth, is not so simple as bare sensory experience, for every range of our awareness of our world is shaped by who and what we are. Spaces are not simply geometrical but emotional, saturated with feelings. They are charged with emotion because of their tonality; they are gracious or serene, or cramped and mean, or terrifying, or charged with emotion because this or that event of our personal history was enacted here.

My clothing is a sensory experience and a shaper of sensory experience. I feel the world as I do, the air, light and heat, because I wear clothes and do not go nude. I experience the interplay of my skin with the shape and texture of my clothing. It gives a characteristic rhythm to the interplay of my body with the world; the greater variety and flexibility of the emotional life of women has much to do with the incomparably richer and more varied tactile experience of their clothing. But clothing as a sensory experience interacts with clothing as the enactment of body image and role. In part, I become what I am because I assume the uniform of the role I choose to enact.

And so is established the infinitely varied interaction of myself and my world, an inextricable interweaving of the senses, the emotions, the will, the drama of my participation in the common life.

It is not that these are simply things that happen to me as incidental to my being alive. These things are me, are my life. To deprive me of these things is to deprive me of who I am. This is my world, the world as my reality.

No question has so burdened the mind, the hopeful intellect of man, as the nature of reality. We speak of the search for truth, meaning those things that can be said accurately about reality. We speak of the worship of the sacred, meaning those acts and things that place us into relation with the real. But the real that our philosophy, our science, our religion, holds up before us is never the reality of the life we actually live. It contains the cosmos, but not the cold hardness of the floor under our feet in the morning. It contains the structure of the atom but not the rustle of leaves on the front walk. The reality of the philosopher, of the scientist, is separate from us.

This image of a separate reality has been built up in three millennia of heroic effort. It is one of the great creations of the human spirit. Slowly over the years it has grown, with generation after generation of men tirelessly adding their bit and passing on while others succeed them.

And so it grows, in all its grandeur, severely indifferent to me, not needing me, the great image of a capitalized Reality. When I think of the grandeur and static character of that great image of truth, I begin to understand a little better the Cartesian act of abnegation. It was not simply that Descartes grounded his sense of his own existence on his thinking. Rather it was that he could approach the great idol, Reality, only by an act of thought. Therefore, it was necessary for him to strip away all those things, all those humane, those ordinary human things that did not suit the act of thought, and by an ascetic sacrifice unparalleled in human history, define himself in the act of thinking. Ever since, the intellectual enterprise has followed his lead. "Reality" is outside myself, other than me, accessible only to thought and to the techniques that have emerged from this kind of thought.

For intellectual ascetics it has been a noble vision, but most of us are not intellectual ascetics and have no desire to be. So we have the chilling sense that our world has been taken away from us, that what we are hardly matters in the face of the majesty of Reality. Reality does not need us. It exists without us.

Suicide becomes more intelligible when one has sensed the profound separation between the person and the world, between the self and Reality. Thoughts of suicide may arise most intensely from entrapment in insuperable difficulties, a sense of personal uselessness, a sense of deep shame, or many other private miseries. But running through that concern is the sense that I am unimportant in my world; that in the world that is the habitation of my flesh, I have neither use nor purpose. And so there follows all the suicidal symptoms of our culture: the obsessive and compulsive organization of time, incessant activity, inert passivity, the contemptuous or indifferent destruction of the earth. What, then, can we do to replace ourselves in our world?

We are where we are because we have paid too little attention to the fundamental intellectual paradigm of our own day, or have paid it the wrong kind of attention.

This may be inevitable. There can be no conscious and creative use of intellectual paradigms until we learn what paradigms are like. The Quantum Theory, the Theories of Relativity, were worked out in the first decades of the century. They transformed physics and reshaped our world. But they were of no use to the rest of the intellectual world until we learned how they affected the forms of thought rather than the contained assertions.

This work is not yet complete. We cannot use physics properly by undertaking a direct transfer of vocabulary. Intellectual disciplines of waning prestige are tempted to shore up their disintegrating structures by stealing the terminology of the dominant disciplines. Thus some try to use wave mechanics to prove the existence of the Holy Spirit, or field theory to validate descriptions of Eastern mystics. Yet when terminology is used without a firm grasp on the intellectual structures that created it, the terms become no more than cheap ornament.

Thus it is with the principle of relativity. The theory of relativity suffers from misunderstanding more than most scientific theories, because its name and superficial explanation inevitably confuse it with relativism. It does indeed intersect with that name and principle. But the true relation between these principles can only be grasped by knowing that relativity is not relativism, but a return to the real and absolute in a wholly new modality.

The proper reference of relativity is not relativism but *relation*.

Relativity is not a denial of reality or denial of the possibility of knowing reality. It is a way of being related to reality.

Men have held that there is a reality, that it is knowable and that such and such a doctrine is the true representation of reality.

Men have held that there is a reality, that it is essentially unknowable and that all doctrines claiming to represent it are a vanity and a striving after wind.

Men have held that there is a reality, that it is knowable in part, in pieces, better or worse, partially, relativistically.

(There have been—are—those who hold that there is no reality; such a conviction is hardly functional in our culture.)

Absolutism is the refuge of the very brave or the very weak. It creates all the dogmatisms. These can maintain themselves only by force, for the system that looks so securely like the real to those who believe in it looks partial and limited—at best, relative—to everyone else.

Skepticism is an austere faith, sustainable by only a few. It acknowledges the presence of reality, but denies the validity of all attempts to define it. The sense of reality sustains the skeptic but the absence of an account of it requires his retreat into an inner involvement with the structures of the self.

Relativism, apparently the most sensible of all these approaches, is the most difficult to sustain. Relativism affirms not only the existence but the presence of the real, but it is a presence that is frustrating, tantalizing, incomplete, a shifting, miragelike reality, an unreliable truth, a sandy foundation, a Reality that is like Kafka's castle, broodingly dominant, overpoweringly present, but inexplicable, giving no instruction, direction or inspiration, the source of despair.

Relativism liberated man from the tyranny of dogmatism, but delivered him to the tyranny of the isolated self.

It is one of the amazements of modern culture that so many should have thought that the theory of relativity, one of the few major creative acts of the modern world, should teach so obvious a truth as that known to men from the beginning of thought: we are finite and limited and see the whole world from our own point of view, or that physics could be transformed by any such foolish statement as "truth is relative to me." To say "truth is relative to me" is to destroy logic, for the statement is clearly false at the heart of reasoning.

Relativity described as a three-dimensional spatial box moving through the fourth dimension of time is pure Newtonian physics. Does anyone seriously suppose that Newton, Bernini, Kant, or Aristotle, did not notice that time is a dimension of human experience?

The one point of intersection between the theory of relativity and the processes of imagination is decisive for the condition of man. To both, reality not only exists but is knowable and the knowledge as knowledge is absolute but reality is known only in its relation to the particularities of its involvement with specific reference points.

Obviously truth varies as the reference point varies, but only a stubborn misreading of Einstein could interpret this as a denial of truth or a definition of truth as exhausted in any one reference point; "truth is relative to *me.*" In relativity theory, the principle is less the reference point than the relation of which any reference point is simply an integral term, a vital part but a part of a whole, not separable. Thus an event from any single point of view can be known truly only as it is known to be seen from this point of view and not another. But so known it is truly known. There is no object or event in itself apart from its relations. The object or event is not definable outside these relations. Relation is always a relation *to something*. So the definition in relativity theory is always thing-relation-thing or person-relation-person or person-relation-thing. It is not so simple a matter as person-plus-person-plus-thing-plus-relation, additively, for this both Newton and Descartes saw. It is a continuity, personrelationperson, or personrelationthing.

Care on this point is vital, else we are delivered to relations without terms, or isolated terms without relations, or structures without forms, or forms without content, or experience without purpose, relevancy without anything to be relevant to, communication without anything to communicate; or, in short, to all the idols and superstitions brutalizing the modern world.

This brutalizing of the common life finds its reverse in the intellectual life. Intellectuals are less tempted to become savages than to become mandarins. Thus does scholarship and the work of the mind become ever more arcane, precious in style, private in vocabulary, impenetrably intricate. The development was made inevitable by the peculiar development of the modern mind. Earlier ages lived within a felt structure of relation and took it for granted. Our age has become far more intellectually self-conscious about the existence of relations, but, lacking any living structure to sustain a whole life, there is nothing to hold things together, so there is nothing left but to contemplate things in themselves, unrelated to anything else: relations empty of all content. But meaning is the wholeness of relation; an art or a philosophy that studies things without relation or relations without things can only be an essay in despair.

Yet despair is a human act, not built into the nature of experience. An end to false understanding and therefore false use of the theory of relativity should—must—become a major task of the intellect, if the human arts are to re-place man in his world.

The theory of relativity does not hold that truth is what is seen from my point of view, that truth is relative to me (or to you). Relativity does not hold that reality is in the relation. Rather the theory of relativity holds that reality is in the whole, the self in relation to the other. The self is never isolated from the other, nor are objects ever outside relation. There is no form without content, relations without terms to be related, content without form, or terms (persons and objects) outside relation. The observer cannot stand apart from his own web of relation or excise the lifeless body of evidence from its place in the whole.

There is no reality apart from me, excluding me. My relation to the experienced world, in so far as I maintain integrity, is both reality and truth. It is not all of the truth. There is a real world that focuses on me, that coheres in an infinite web of relation that relates me to the things and persons near me, and through them and their relations, to the outer reaches of the cosmos. That reality is absolute. It is true.

But the person (or the thing) over there, stands in a different part of the web and grasps, absolutely, a different reality of which I am now a part. I can know that reality in so far as I can participate in living relation, in the truth of that person's deepest experience.

This does not mean that I merely "believe" his explanation of his world. It means that I stand in his place and see the world with his eyes. I experience it with his nerves and his symbolic structures. I can possess reality only in so far as I can participate in the web of relations that make up the human community.

Each of us in his life-experience constitutes a vital and irreplaceable part of reality. If one of us shirks his responsibility by turning his back on his world or destroying himself, a part of reality is forever gone. To break the community of persons is, to that extent, not only to insult the person but to deny the real and the true. For each of us has custody of a portion of truth that is ours alone for the common good and the common work.

Community is not simply a pleasant association but the only fundamental instrument for knowing the world. He who would share his world with me, speak truth to me, cannot do so by telling me what his world is like. He must set it forth in forms—of thought, of art, of conduct—that I can live within and so grasp the sensibility that could produce such forms. If I would seek his truth I do not inspect his opinions. I place myself, actually, imaginatively, within the structures of his experience so I can see the reality of the world that he sees.

Each person's experience of the world is true, an aspect of reality. Each person's opinions are false, even to himself, for opinions are froth on the surface of experience, a collection of debris that falls on the surface from outside as well as from the genuine parts of the experience itself. Yet even opinions become part of reality, for they represent the way this person falsifies his reality and denies his truth. Our falsifications, too, are part of our world.

Thus, reality is not the crystal palace, built up in the sacrifices of human ascetism, indifferent to those who built it and come to it. Reality is the relation. Reality is the whole relation. No mode of accounting for reality nor of giving body to the experience of it can claim to be decisive, not philosophy or theology or physics or art, or in contemporary idiom, sex or the ecstacy of drugged nerves. Yet each of these is a window opened onto reality by some one or another group of persons and each sets forth a reality that is not to be found in any other way.

The abstract thought of ascetic Cartesianism is neuter, ageless, free from rooting in time or place or occasion. But *I* am only specificities and have no place in such a structure. Thought is enacted as though there were a truth which white, middle-class males have access to; others are admitted out of condescension. But women—and each person who is a woman—have access to a part of the truth, and without their truth the truth of men is thrown off-balance. And so with blacks, and the young and the old. To kill a Vietnamese peasant is to close a window on reality that can never again be opened.

These are definitions, and definitions are useful only as they function. This definition of reality defines the task that is now the work of the mind. If I, the whole self, am a window on reality, then to think about reality means to think about the modes of my relation to experience. It means that thought depends on, is inseparable from, *is*, knowing the interaction of our flesh in the time of our space. It means that thought is knowing the way the experiencing self engenders the forms of its experience in the human languages. It means that thought is knowing how to participate in those languages to enter into the wholeness of truth. This, then, is the way to refind ourselves in our world.

Thus the matter of experience and the process of explanation join. Explanation has been judged by the Cartesian to be the image of things *sub specie aeternitatis*, the observer suspended in a physical or moral space outside the objects and events, emancipated from space and time. Thus explanations are judged to be true and therefore intolerantly authoritative. This idea of explanation has been so powerful that the only way to achieve human tolerance has been to retreat into skepticism and relativism. But the price of this retreat has been loss of the power of explanation and isolation in purposeless experience.

Emphatically, the theory of relativity does not confirm this loss of the power of explanation, but rather redefines it. Now explanation exists only within the things and events of experience. No one symbolic speech, not mathematics, verbal propositions nor art, suffices as authoritative explanation, nor can one single person or system do all the required work. Rather explanation is, ideally, the whole life and work of the community. There are no privileged or authoritative symbolic languages, only irreplaceable functions. Arid abstractions and fecund particularities become enlivened structures and purposed energies in the workings of coherent community. The traditional languages of explanation—philosophy and theology—assume a new role no longer so brutally authoritative but, for all that, no less vital. Philosophy can represent the emergence of common experience into the symbolic speech of verbal propositions. It is not so much thinking *about* something as thinking that thing in the wholeness of the flesh, until it emerges in the systematic and controlled particularities of a specific mode of symbolic speech.

Theology is, in part, philosophic, and subject to the stringencies of that language. But theology makes certain claims for itself that cannot usefully be dismissed as ordinary arrogance. The task of theology is both like the task of all the languages, and unique. It is unique in the claims it makes for its subject matter and, if the claims are true, unique absolutely, for it claims to give an account of God. But it is like all human languages in the stringencies of its occasions and its limits. Either in assumption or in actuality the object of theology's study is absolute, but the object of theology's study cannot be an object. The logic of the debate about "God-talk" is obviated by religion: by elementary definition, God cannot be touched by human speech, but can be known only in his relations and acts. Here I am not saying "God is relative," for I have just now rejected the possibility of saying any such thing. But what God "is" can be known, if known at all, only in relation to things within the range of human symbolic operations.

Relativism and its various subjectivist descendents would make men into the creators of God; if the automobile is going sixty miles an hour as measured against me, it is very easy to think that I am determinative for the speed of the automobile. Even the most absolutist of theological assertions paradoxically resolves itself into this relativist assertion; what I am and think is legislative for the ultimate order of things.

In a theory of theological relativity, sacred reality is knowable only as it is manifested through, and by means of, the engagement of particular persons and particular cultures with that reality. Each such relation, each such engagement with reality, is "true" because it is a *relation* to reality. However false its formulations, they too are a part of one term of the relation and are, therefore, revelatory of it.

Sacred reality is not identical with nor exhausted in the particularities of any single engagement. Sacred reality cannot be known or stated apart from such particularities.

Thus, the theologian, working within a theory of theological relativity, cannot simply add another calculation to his argumentative description of reality. It is not enough simply to add a fourth dimension of time to the three dimensions of space that fixed the image of God into the likeness of a static object. A changing object or changing views of an object both inhabit Newtonion order. It does not even represent much progress to arrive at the point of recognizing the partiality and time-rooted quality of our images and dogmas. Absolutism is false but it gives a structure that can be lived in, however unpleasantly; relativism is just as false and leaves people isolated and alone.

A substantial redefinition of both the nature and the responsibility of theology is involved in this case. Older definitions make a straightforward assertion about the nature of the work; "Theology is the science of thinking about God," or about the nature and authority of its products. "The business of the theologian . . . is not to construct or invent a philosophy or religion, but to exhibit clearly, systematically and intelligibly for his own age the genuine content of historic Christian faith." Neither of these will do any longer. Both thinking and the products of thought are undergoing so drastic a redefinition as to make such definitions as these impossible. The theory of relativity presented here involves its own definition. In the first place, negatively defined, it denies the use of words or ideas such as "thinking *about*" or "making statements *about*," both of which presuppose a distinction between the thinker, the object of his thought, and the product of his thought. If thinker, thought and object are a continuous event, a relation in which each term conditions the others, then a definition would have to look something like this:

Theology is the manifestation, in an appropriate symbolic language, of an experience of and a relation to a reality which it defines as sacred.

This definition has a number of consequences. *All* theologies are "true," in that all theologies represent the embodiment of a relation. Differences among theologies grow out of differences in any of the terms. People working on them are different, with differing histories and styles. The languages are different. The particular aspect of "reality" is different. Normally several or all of the terms are different. Any judgment of validity, then, will depend on the method of correlating these varied relations. To insist that only one has general validity is the most grievous form of human arrogance.

Under this definition then, the judgment that would correspond to a judgment of "truth" is not a judgment at all, but a commitment. The commitment is not empty, for it is testable against its consequences. Again, the evaluation of consequences is itself a commitment; it is not logically demonstrable that general good takes precedence over individual good, that peace is better than war, love than hate. Consequently, the only role for argument is within the community of commitment. The role of argument for those outside the commitment is presentation, demonstration. This carries with it the obligation to endure the demonstration of other commitments, which is why Jesus, not at all a meek man, should have taught so insistently the need for meekness and submission. Only through demonstration can a commitment be known fully, as a whole. "By their fruits you shall know them" is not an ethical measure although it contains an ethical dimension; it is an affirmation of a total, whole statement as distinct from argument and opinion. Now theology can exist only in the wholeness of the embodied statement. The language of traditional theological statement is only a function within the whole. If it claims to be more it falsifies the whole.

To qualify as a theory of theological relativity, a theological theory must account for the position of the theologian, both symbolic and historical. This does not mean simply correcting for the position of the theologian as the hunter makes allowance for position, distance and speed by aiming ahead of the running deer. It must, rather, account for the relation in its completeness, and in that completeness neither subject nor object exist any longer in those terms. For subject to be subject, for object to be object is to deny the relation and so put the investigation back into a Newtonian order. It is only in the wholeness of the relation that reality is defined.

"To describe the object" is a mode of symbolic speech. As such it is a part of the relation. But the wholeness of the relation is in whole persons, not in elements of their symbolic languages. Thus, all theological understanding depends absolutely on grasping the accessible terms of the relation. The only truly accessible term is the experiencing person, alive, in the flesh, clothed in a sex and a culture formed by symbolic structures, reaching out into the world.

What such a person reaches is an act of faith. What he can describe of what he reaches is an act of faith. But it is real only as it is whole.

THE PHYSIOLOGY OF FAITH

PART ONE

The Physiology of the Imagination: A Vocabulary

The Elemental Theme

In a complex and sophisticated age, there is a powerful temptation to think that the achievement of a simple statement is somehow equivalent to laying hold on the primal order of things. But there is an even greater temptation: to think that our complexities are somehow bringing us closer to the complexity of ultimate order. This has been the basis of intellectual triumphalism, that we proceed, age to age, in triumphal progress toward the conquest of Reality.

Yet our sophisticated complexities fall so far short of the overwhelming and fragmented multitudinousness surrounding us that we despair of reaching the goal that once seemed so close and so attainable. Worse, the labor becomes that of Sisyphus; the closer we come to the goal the heavier the burden becomes until it rolls again to the foot of the hill. Variously, theology, philosophy, mathematics, history, sociology, even art have seemed to be the highway to human fulfillment. Physics has been the great dream of our own age. Now our consciousness withdraws from them all. The way to still further despairing futility is to offer yet another system to act as a lever for this huge burden of responsibility.

Rather we should retrace our path to our beginnings. It may be that it is our method, not simply our solutions, that is in error. It may be that we must, once more, ask the elementary question that only the sophisticated can ask, to set the simple problem that only the complex mind can use.

We do not, cannot, know when human life became problematic to those who lived it. We do know that when the elementary and elemental problems did begin, our ancestors had neither the tools nor experience to deal with them. We owe them no condescension; their intelligence and courage were equal to our own. But we have one advantage they did not have—their work and the work of the generations that followed them, their achievements and their failures. So, when we go back to their problem, we can, if we are humble, go chastened and enlightened, not with a sense that we are wiser or better, but with a sense of all that has happened since. Then we can, again, ask the ancient and elementary question, the question they could not ask articulately because the language for asking the question could only emerge from the experience of the question itself.

The only hope lies, not in the profundity of our asking, but in its simplicity. If we are too proud to be elementary, if we do not take the elementary answer with complete seriousness, then we will be no better off than we have been. But if we are faithful to what we now know, out of the sacrifice of those who have gone before, we might develop a new vocabulary and a new method that, for a time at least, would enable us to contend with the complexities of our experience.

The initial question, the generating problem is like the generating axiom in Euclidean geometry. It is itself unprovable, but all else emerges from it.

The generating problem is the problem of human identity. It is not the question of origin or purpose, cause or effect. It is simply: what am I that I should be other than the rest of the order of things which seem so like myself? We have called ourselves minds and wills; knowing and doing according to our knowing. Yet we carry the terrible weight of a different knowing; that we act to purposes we do not choose, choose an end and the means to that end, only to see our means serving other ends. Or we think we know, and the will fails, so intention is paralyzed. Or the possibility of purpose fades in the despairing and desiccated will.

What, then, is the nature of the human?

Given what we know now, it is no longer possible to ask this question in isolation from prior questions. 'The human' is not separable from the body of the human, so the humanistic question depends on the physiology of the body. We are animals and organisms, so the physiological question cannot be detached from the biological. Organisms are matter, so the biological question cannot be detached from the chemical and physical. All these questions are prior to the theological question. Thought is somatic. Faith is therefore an act of human physiology.

This is still undemonstrated assertion. But this demonstration should not be required to fit the pattern of the older argument. Rather it requires a new point of origin, a new procedure and a new vocabulary.

The new point of origin is no longer logic, but physics. If thought is the act and energy of matter then an awareness of the nature of matter is indispensable, which is the proper function of a humanistic physics. If the act of matter requires a structuring of forms, then the language, the vocabulary, of those forms is inescapable.

The pages that follow sketch an outline for this demonstration, and try to suggest more than can be said.

THE FIRST PRINCIPLE OF A HUMANISTIC PHYSICS

All thought, all systems of thought presuppose a "physics," a sense of what things are made of and how they are ordered. It has not yet been possible to order much of our thought according to contemporary physics.

> . . . high energy physicists conceive of the world as consisting of inter-acting particles. That's all there is in the world; there's nothing more. And if you understood what particles there are and how they interact, you would understand the world.
>
> So far there is no evidence that there is anything that happens that is not particles which interact with each other.
>
> BRUCE WINSTEIN[1]

As laymen in physics, we humanists, trained to a metaphysics of substance, think of particles as things. Our sense of analysis breaks things down into smaller and smaller things: molecules, atoms, protons, neutrons, electrons, sub-nuclear particles. But they are not things, they are particular concentrations of energy. Analysis takes us down through the stages of matter, through smaller and smaller units until at the end there is nothing, nothing but energy in rhythmic concentration.

The core of things is not substance but rhythm.

The fear of reductionism is the fear of a very real danger. But the fear of reductionism can be paralyzing it if leads us away from the elementary statement that is also elemental. Winstein did not say that all that happens is "nothing but" the interation of elementary particles. He said that everything is the interaction of elementary particles.

When we understand what elementary particles do we can, perhaps, discover ourselves again in the world.

> Thus the art of the last half-century may well be schooling our eyes to live at ease with the new concepts forced upon our credulity by scientific reasoning. What we may be witnessing is the gradual condensation of abstract ideas into images that fall within the range of our sensory imagination. Modern painting inures us to the aspect of a world housing not discrete forms but trajectories and vectors, lines of tension and strain. Form in the sense of solid substance melts away and resolves itself with dynamic process. Instead of bodies powered by muscle, or by gravity, we get energy propagating itself in the void.
>
> LEO STEINBERG

This is not intended as a redefinition, even of science. Rather it is intended to see science as it really is, in the hands of the best scientists, as a receptive and creative meditation on the order of things. It is the analytic mode of science combined with the image of masculine purpose as control that has made so much science a true enemy of the humane. Our need is neither to overcome science nor even to transcend it but use it as it best is, a communion with the mystery of the earth.

THE ARCHITECTURE OF MATTER

Today we can see, forming under our hands and eyes, the possibility of a reunified view of matter and life. And this is so first because our fundamental assumptions about matter have at last gone beyond both Aristotle's and Newton's. For us, matter is intrinsically neither developing nor inert: potentially, it can be either the one or the other. The chemical elements, as such, are neither organic nor inorganic: they have it in them equally to form gases and crystals, viruses, DNA and cells. And this reordering of our ideas is based on no mere quibble: our theories of matter have been transformed down to the very root. Classical nineteenth century science was still in crucial respects a Demokritean system: it treated the atoms of matter primarily as "bricks," and left unsolved the atomic problems of coherence and organization. There is no such Demokritean bias about contemporary wave mechanics. The physicists' fundamental units are no longer bricks: they are now *dynamic* units, defined by characteristic patterns of energy and activity; and they join together not in single chains or aggregates, but by forming out of their separate wave systems stable "concords" or harmonies, which have new capacities and activities of their own. Thus the principles underlying matter theory today are neither teleological alone, nor mechanical alone. Instead, they are *architectural*—going beyond the old distinctions between form and function, structure and activities. We find in nature a hierarchy of active forms, which run from sub-atomic wavicles, through atoms and molecules, nucleic acids and viruses, the cell-parts and cells, organs and complete organisms. (The sequence is not closed at either end.) At every level of analysis, from protons and electrons up to living creatures, the objects which nature is composed of have to be characterized in terms both of their structure and of their activities.

So the distinction between living and non-living things can no longer be drawn in *material* terms. What marks them off from one another is not the stuff of which they are made: the contrast is rather between systems whose organization and activities differ in complexity.

If humans and animals are capable—as they manifestly are—of mental and vital activities, their material organization must, as surely as that of the solar system, be of a kind that makes these activities possible.

STEPHEN TOULMIN and JUNE GOODFIELD[2]

Therefore:

1. All thought must be understood as the activity of elementary particles, i.e., energy in rhythmic relation.
2. Equally, all that is thought about is the activity of similar concentrations of energy.
3. There can be no detachment of thought from that which is thought about.
4. There are no privileged modes of thinking. Thought is an act of the whole organism.
5. There are no privileged languages for the statement of thought. True thought requires all the languages.
6. The architecture of thought involves both the elements and actions that are ordered and the principle of their ordering. Relation is as real as substance.

FUNDAMENTAL POSTULATES OF
A HUMANISTIC PHYSICS

1. The distinction between matter and energy is false and now useless. When "matter" is analyzed into its components they are found to be concentrations of energy. It is not possible to distinguish form and function, structure and process, for they are different aspects of the same thing.

2. These units of energy can never be isolated nor assumed to exist alone. They exist only in rhythmic tension with other units, a tension which creates the wholes, the larger units which have the properties of matter. Thus, the fundamental unit of reality is neither matter nor energy, but relation, the order that holds together the tensions of energy.

3. The fact that no unit exists alone is not limited to the discrete wholes that we call "objects" for every whole is a component of a larger system, a larger whole. "Things" are systems or structures of energy, each a part of a larger system or structure. Thus, reality is an increasingly complex hierarchy of structures, subsystems held together in energetic tension to make larger systems. There are certain important characteristics of these systems:

   a. Every whole is a system of subwholes which have semi-autonomy within the larger whole. The subwholes are themselves the same kind of system.

   b. Each system acts as a whole according to its own semi-autonomous structure. No system can free itself from its relation to its own subsystems nor to the system or structure of which it is a part.

   c. No system can act directly on a system that is not at the adjacent level, only by way of the intermediate system or systems. (Therefore, the place of systems of explanation such as philosophy and theology must be found before their use can be determined or their practice properly described.)

    d. Each system acts as a whole according to its own (semi-autonomous) structure. Its action is released by a trigger from another system, often a trigger of very slight force.

4. The distinction between mind and body is, in this scheme, useless, nor does this principle reduce either to the other (which cannot be in any case, since they are not different things). While we know very little about what this means, the activity that we have labeled *mind* or *thinking* must be a characteristic of these systems. Or, to put it the other way round, *material organization* must be of a kind that is properly characterized by such activities. Thus, the hierarchy of structures is continuous and, in the fundamental principle of organization, uniform.

5. Although the hierarchy of structure is continuous, there are crucial boundary divisions:

    a. The first of these is between the inorganic and the organic. (since, in the Toulmin-Goodfield presentation, the atomic structure is the same, the difference lies in the principle of organization, not in 'material'). The inorganic system is closed and subject to entropy. The organic is open and subject to *negative entropy* (Schroedinger's *negentropy*).[3] Negative entropy creates the possibility for evolution, which is not controlled solely by chance but by possibilities within the organism.

    b. The second division, within organisms, comes at the place of the organism which possesses self consciousness—man.

    c. There may be a higher division. Traditional history and anthropology have made the crucial division at the point of human culture. Probably, the question of culture must be divided in two itself. In the first place, culture is present from the beginning, since culture is an immediate product of consciousness and shapes subsequent evolution. In the second place, the 'high' or 'historic' cultures are not simply different in degree of complexity from their primitive parents, but are different *in kind,* in effect, an organism that had not existed before.

A fully developed and presented theory would be required at this point to set out two fundamental processes:

1. What is a system or structure? What are its characteristics? What is the nature of its action?
2. How are these structures related to each other?

Against the limits of space I can only make assertions. A structure is a collection of substructures which cannot be analyzed into its substructures without loss, nor accounted for finally by the system of which it is a part. It preserves its continuity of form to the extent that it has a continuing identity. It has some autonomous control over its own activity.

Since a structure is a collection of substructures without material addition, its distinguishing characteristic is the mode of relations that exist among its substructures as subsystems. Since it possesses identity, continuity, and semiautonomy, the relation is not static but tensile or energetic. To break a structure releases the energy (which is only more dramatic and instantaneous, not more destructive, at the atomic level).

So far the account has proposed a certain limited but indispensable vocabulary: system or structure, hierarchy, form, rhythm, relation. This vocabulary provides the core from which the metaphysics of this book is engendered.

How structures are related to each other at the self-conscious organic level is the primary concern of this book. Nevertheless, since I am claiming a continuity of principle throughout the whole system, it is necessary to add two more to my list of assertions (there are many others):

6. The lower down in the hierarchy (or the closer to the center), the simpler the forms, the more nearly they are closed sys-

tems, the less are they open to change and the more subject to entropy. Obviously the converse is true.

7. When one system is brought into relation with another that is not in its immediate hierarchical order, each reacts according to the pattern of its subsystems. Following assertion 6, a low-order system can respond only with fixed patterns, with the likelihood of an increase in entropy. A high-order system, still acting according to pattern, can do so with a higher degree of openness, an increase in possibility of forming new patterns and an accompanying increase in the possibility of negative entropy and constructive evolution. Entropy leads to a dispersal of systems into lower-order systems, which is at best cyclical (plants and animals into earth, into plants, etc.) or, at most, into undifferentiated systems (plants into coals, into heat, into gas) and finally dissolves everything. Negative entropy leads to increasing complexity, the establishment or engendering of new and more inclusive structures. At the highest level, the complexities of systems are such that there is no certainty at all of negative entropy but only the possibility of it, depending on whether or not the constructive, creative process is *understood* within the whole action of the organism. It should not be necessary to point out that "understood" has to do only in small part with the verbal intelligence but is a commitment of the whole organism.

A SCIENTIFIC FABLE

Knowing our own history we look back at the past, imagining it as it would have been if it looked like our reconstruction of it. Similarly our reconstruction is based on the assumption that a man like ourselves, with our vocabulary, our knowledge, our intellectual paradigms was present in the past, looking at it and describing it. Neither of these assumptions is true.

Before the human there was a vast, rhythmically pulsating web of interacting particles, nothing more. There were no trees and plants and animals occupying 'space.' Space that can be occupied is a human construct for human purposes and "space" is the human name for that construct. We cannot rightly imagine space but only, at best, a lesser density of particles, a thinning of the pulsating web of structured energy. There was no 'color' for color is a name and concept for the interaction of certain kinds of particles with other particles we call the rods and cones of the eye. There were no rocks and trees and dinosaurs, only clusters of particles with greater or lesser density, greater or lesser mobility and perhaps, greater or lesser choice. Rocks and trees do not choose. They have a history, but their history is their nature. No plant 'reaches' for water in the anthropomorphic terminology of popular botany; the cells of its roots expand and multiply in the presence of moisture. An animal may choose to eat this or that, or not to eat at all. Yet its choices are no more than an ordering of particles, for they do not affect the history of the animal, which is the fulfillment of its own being.

CHOICE AND POSSIBILITY

And yet its choices are not particles, but a mode of interaction of particles. Therefore, the animal is, a little, unlike the stone which makes no choice: it has possibility. It has no names and thus it lives in the flow of particles with no sense of division, no sense that anything is other than what it is.

There is no time in that world. Time is a human construct to cope with the meaning of continuity. Without time there is only flow and repetition.

But at a certain point, an animal did what no animal had ever done before. It became aware of what it was doing. In becoming aware it stood apart from its world, its place in the nameless flow and continuity of particles. Time and the human began.

MEDITATIONS ON A HUMANISTIC BIOLOGY

If this is, indeed, a minimum essential of physics, it remains to move into biology and take hold of hierarchies at the level of sentient organisms. My primary concern is with self-conscious organisms (man), but self-consciousness is itself so crucial that it must be dealt with separately. What I have to say here does not depend on self-consciousness and we probably share it with the animals.

The next step requires attention to perception. (Perception is a process common to all organisms, not just the conscious or self-conscious ones, but I shall confine my discussion to what we all know and can check: perception in ourselves. I shall limit the argument further to one or two paradigmatic cases.)

The first of these is the problem of the upright vertical. It is a matter of general, if not seriously noted, knowledge, that when we look at a vertical line—say the frame of a door—and then turn our heads on their sides, the vertical line remains upright. There is much that we don't know about any act of perception, but there are conclusions we can fairly reach about this one. It is extremely difficult to formulate a purely positivist or materialist view of perception that can account for the fact that the vertical remains upright. Comparisons between the eye and the camera break down on this problem, for the perception itself remains quite constant through many changes in the projected image on the retina. We can conclude that the brainmind contains an image of the doorframe which is triggered by the image projected on the retina, and which remains constant through many changes in the nature of the stimulus. The image in the brainmind is not identical with the image on the retina and certainly not with the immediate doorframe. This accounts also for the peculiar nature of recognition. Once I saw, about one hundred yards away, a man I had known for only a few months, with his back to me, wearing an overcoat and holding the hand of a small boy. I knew instantly who it was. I had never seen him in that part of town, nor had I ever seen his small boy. The recognition was not additive or incomplete, but instant and total. Very weak, camouflaged signals triggered a whole image.

There are other observations. First, there is John Platt's question; How do we perceive the straightness of a straight line using a curved retina, and his response, "We do not see objects, but relationships."[4] While Platt, in speaking of relations, has in mind the relations existing in the things that are seen, he and many others go on to account for perception as a relation between the perceiver and that which is seen. This is truly the only way our transaction with the world can be rightly understood. All our experience of the world is a transaction with it, a relation to it, in which who and what we are is an indispensable and inescapable ingredient.

I, as an isolated subject, do not see the tree as an isolated object. That which I call a tree is "really" a particular coagulation of energy in a certain rhythm of relations. "I" am a similar condensation of energy. These two forms, or structures, as energy systems, impinge on each other, engendering an alteration in the tuning of the rhythmic patterns of both. While a fuller treatment requires consideration of both attention and naming (by attention, I isolate one or a group of systems and name it or them), it is also necessary to realize that the one—the tree—is an element in the whole, which is "world". It is not true that I make my world—although there are some rhetorical advantages in putting it that way. Rather, world as it emerges in my experience is altogether inseparable from the possibilities of my whole nervous system.

"Tree" is one thing to me, another to the bird, to the squirrel, to the chimpanzee. It is one thing to me, another to the lumberman, the hunter, the painter, the farmer, the city man. It is not good to say that it is the same tree seen differently, which is only relativism. It is truly a different tree. Also, each tree is true, although there can be false relations to trees. In the words of Ortega, "In the old relativism our knowledge is relative because what we aspire to know, viz., space-time reality, is absolute and we cannot attain to it. In the physics of Einstein our knowledge is absolute; it is reality that is relative."[5]

At this point it is necessary to make another great leap in the argument. Again, there is a great mass of material to draw from. I shall confine myself to two illustrations, Thomas Kuhn's use of the word *paradigm* and Benjamin Lee Whorf's work in linguistics.

Too briefly put, Kuhn demonstrates that physics, so far from developing according to the traditional patterns of scientific method, (i.e., observation, hypothesis, experiment, conclusion) works according to certain patterns of thought and of "seeing" the world, certain "paradigms" that determine the nature of observations, the limit of theory, what is, indeed, possible. Progress is never continuous except within the limits of a paradigm. When a paradigm is exhausted, there is no further progress possible, no matter what the expenditure of time, energy, cash and patience, unless there is a new paradigm.[6]

Whorf's case[7] is put succinctly in the words of his master, Edward Sapir. " . . . the 'real world' is to a "large extent unconsciously built up on the language habits of the group." Basically, Whorf is saying that we "see" (understand), the world only in the forms made possible by our language.[8]

Whorf's case is marred by the excess characteristic of the pioneers and particularly the amateurs. Since we think in a great many ways other than the verbal, it is not true to say that we dissect the universe in ways made possible by language only. I would ammend the case only by making *language* plural. We think only what is possible to think in one of our languages and in the forms, the paradigms, laid down in those languages, or in the new paradigms that generate a new language.

There is an inescapable origin of language; but languages also develop through human creativity. Thus the patterning of our nervous systems that makes perception possible is paralleled and completed by the patterning, the structure, of our modes of thought (the paradigm), and of our languages.

Vital as it is to get on to the content of these paradigms, it might be well first to undertake a brief summing up:

We are particular concentrations of energy in rhythmic interaction with other systems of energy concentration. We are a hierarchy of semiautonomous systems, each responding to the action of the next higher and next lower levels in the hierarchy. Each system has its characteristic pattern of response which is more fixed at the lower levels of the hierarchy, more open and complex at the higher. The patterns are patterns of structure only at the lower levels; patterns of action (particularly language and thought) at the higher levels. Because each system is uniquely patterned, the world that proceeds from each system is unique. Since systems are similar in structure and since their structures overlap, their worlds are similar and related.

It remains now to look at the content of the structures.

A HISTORICAL FABLE

In the film *2001*, director Stanley Kubrick designed a fable of the beginning of man: An anthropoid was idly playing with a bone, pounding other bones. Suddenly a vision of possibility came to him, almost palpable on his face. The scene shifts rapidly to the killing of a pig with the bone used as a club, and then to a group of these hominoids—no longer simple anthropoids—driving others like themselves from the waterhole.

A history and metaphysics of substance would define this as primitive man inventing the club and using it to kill and secure control of the waterhole. But there was no man or bone or club or waterhole, only a complex web of intricately structured particles. Rather, this creature, this concentration of structured energies, in a single act focused on the bone, grasped possibility. In the bone he sensed food and power, grasped the whole in a stupendous act of imagination.

A thing was seen in terms of complexity of operation, a thing was seen as a link between things and acts that were not itself. Thing and function were linked. He had created metaphor.

The act, the discovery, the invention were simple: person, object, purpose were fused into a single event, which had never happened before. This act became then a new structure, reordering the structured energies that had filled what we call millions of years. This structure engendered new structures; the anthropoids became a human society, joined to a common purpose.

In the long slow process of the nonhuman past, the structures of energy that we call matter had undergone vast and consequential changes into new structures, that were in all parts like those from which they emerged. Now, suddenly, there were new structures unlike any others, for they had emerged from the purposeful creativity of one of the old structures. Yet these new structures were true structures, ordering segments of the rhythmically pulsating web of structured energy that was the real. The new structurss were real and parts of reality, not simply ways of acting on the real.

And the new structures had consequences far beyond the immediate: in generating metaphor the anthropoid became man. One structure in the myriad concentrations of structured energy grasped thing and act to conscious purpose and, in grasping conscious purpose, became conscious. To be aware of thing and purpose outside the self is to be aware of the self that had purpose. In the achievement of consciousness, an animal became self-conscious and thus became something other than it was.

In the metaphoric process, the structures of the human came into being. Human history came into being; by the metaphoric process, the creative power was preserved and extended, held in memory and record. The slow unfolding of human possibility began.

CULTURE AS THE STRUCTURE OF THE HUMAN

The metaphoric process produces structures which, so long as they are adequately vital, preserve and extend the linking process of metaphor.

The principle of structure makes it possible to dissolve the distinction between physics and biology. If matter is indistinguishable from energy, if matter becomes energy when analyzed into its smallest units, then the critical aspect of matter is precisely the relation among its units that prevents its dissolution. The relation that then exists is energy in tension, creating a structure that is not so passive as that word might suggest, but is saturated with energy. Since this characterizes everything we call matter it follows remorselessly that the decisive element of reality is the type of structure—which is simply a way of referring to the rhythmic mode of tensions that hold the energy into coherence.

The first levels of structure are those holding energy into the ordered tensions we call matter or substance. With choice, there entered a new dimension of structure—behavior. Behavior is a mode of relation quite unlike any other, but as a mode of relation it should not be considered as something other than the systems of structure that is merely added to them. Behavior itself is part of the structural hierarchy, an ingredient of it, a mode of relation. Or, directly, real.

The nature of reality can now be grasped only as it is understood not as "substance" but as relation. Thus, something—relation—which is, ordinarily, thought of as an abstraction and, therefore, unreal, is actually taken from reality because it is of the very substance of reality. Clearly animal behavior is limited and, beyond certain restricted limits of freedom, patterned, so that it is with an illusion of freedom the animal carries on the courses of nature. Thus behavior and freedom of choice are not intrusions into the order of nature but modulations of the patterns of relation that characterize the natural order.

In all respects, humans are—or were—animals and live in the

rhythms of nature as animals do. But into the structured energies of nature, humans inserted a new process, the metaphoric act, seeing a thing as act, the act as function, the function as achieving purpose and, therefore, seeing things and purpose intricately linked and impregnating each other with desire and achievement.

Human act turns repetition into time. The cycle becomes the line, for every such act relentlessly requires other acts. Kubrick's fable went further than depiction of the original metaphoric achievement. His humanoid next appeared at the front of a group of his fellows, each armed with a bone. Organization and leadership had been achieved, achieved through the metaphoric power of the bone-club.

Once begun, this process has its own life, for every achievement creates unavoidable possibilities and problems. So simple an event as the one in Kubrick's fable contains in miniature all the ingredients of human society—power, leadership, organization, a physical center. Each of these created psychic possibilities—jealousy, rebellion, adoration. Each created numerous physical and social possibilities in a process that has no end, a process which can never be suspended, for every attempt to control it or stop it creates a different set of possibilities and problems.

What are the consequences of this analysis? What is the relation of these structures to reality?

There is no doubt of the answer of traditional scholarship: the creatures who developed these elementary social acts and relations were essentially like ourselves, minus the knowledge we have accumulated over the ages. Ignorance has consequences, of course, but, as human, these creatures are supposed to have possessed the same will, the same desire for knowledge and control. Their achievement, therefore, would have been exactly like all human achievements, something made that is external to the basic reality of persons and things. Culture is considered external to the human, essential perhaps, but something other than the primary reality.

We are no longer in the area of fable and guess but in the area of knowledge; the evolution of culture did not follow the completion of the evolution of man. Culture is not something added to and created by a completely evolved human. Culture began long before the completion of human evolution and shaped that evolution. The human is inseparable from culture. Culture is as much a part of the reality of the human as our nervous system. It is not, obviously, a matter of a particular cultural form, but that system of relations which basically constitutes a culture.

Thus, to the systems of energy that constitute reality a new system has been added. Negative entropy, negentropy, has done its work; reality has been enlarged.

The cultural system, these symbolic structures, are systems like all systems that constitute the real. Thus they are inserted into the hierarchy of systems that constitute reality. At one end of the scale there are the atomic systems, particles of energy in rhythmic tension; at the other end the cosmic order, made up of the infinite series of hierarchically structured systems. At an appropriate place in the hierarchy, the structures of human culture take their place, acting on the other systems, being acted on by them, according to the postulates laid down earlier.

Equally, these systems, these structures of the imagination, these symbolic structures are not external to ourselves. As an ingredient of ourselves, they are parts of the reality of the self—and they are the decisive parts of the self in its intercourse with the world. Perception is not simply a matter of stimulated nerves; it is the response of the symbolic structure of the self to its interaction with the systems of the environing world. And that response constitutes the self's world.

"World" without the human is rhythmic flow and interchange, the intricate reverberation of hierarchically ordered systems, without name, without distinction, without memory, without purpose, a vast, rhythmically pulsating harmony of energy in tension.

In this vast web of interacting systems, one system or one series of systems acquired or was granted a capacity none other had: by being aware of its own process it was able—indeed, compelled—to create a new system that became part of the whole, a functioning part interacting with the others in the same way. Thus it was an addition to creation or the order of things and, at the same time, a functioning system whose function is unlike any other, to name the parts of the world and thus bring world into being.

Thus, "the physiology of the imagination" is quite literally part of human physiology; the symbolic structure that constitutes the self is a system of relations within the organism, functioning as a part of the organism exactly as do those systems of relations we call the nervous or the circulatory systems. Equally, these symbolic structures are not held within the envelope of the skin, for they are inherited from the work of the past, shared by others and embodied in the work of culture.

The self, the person, is not inserted—or thrown—into a neutral or alien order of things. The self is ingredient to the order of things, functioning within it, constituted by it, constituting it, always in interchange and interaction with it. The neutral and alien pronoun *it*, becomes wholly inadequate for such a relation, which places the "personal" and "impersonal", the "organic" and "inorganic", the "objective" and "subjective" into the single rhythmic harmony of interacting tensile structures. The self, the person, constitutes the world. The world is ingredient to the self. The only way to know the self is to know its world. The only way to know the world is to know the self that constitutes it. The beginning of all knowledge is the process of interchange of the self in its world.

And yet the self is never at ease in its world. Intimately involved in the world, intricately interacting with it, the self always feels alien to the world. The beginning of wisdom is the understanding of the self's distance from the world which is part of itself.

THE ORIGINAL DISTINCTION

The plant is born, grows, dies, decays back into the soil that bore it. It does not think, it cannot act to a purpose. It does not know that it is a plant.

The animal is born, grows, dies, decays into the soil. It thinks, it acts to a chosen purpose. It feels love, fear, desire. So far as we can tell, it never thinks of itself as being an animal.

A human being is an animal who is born, grows, dies. Sometimes he tries to resist his decaying, sometimes he goes joyfully back into union with the soil. He thinks, he acts to a chosen purpose. He feels love, fear, desire. He also feels hatred, lust, despair, hope. He is aware of himself as being human. He is aware of himself as being a man; she is aware of herself as being a woman.

They are not the same. Both plant and animal can act toward each other according to the usage of being male or female; they do not think, "I am male and therefore——," or "I am female and therefore———."

All things that humans are and do, animals are and do, except those things that issue from the original human act—the awareness of being human.

CULTURE AND SELF CONSCIOUSNESS

Being human is, primordially, self-consciousness.

Being human, therefore, is, elementally, the act of *distinction*.

The act of distinction generates certain kinds of awareness. Out of that awareness there emerges certain kinds of desire.

1. The world is something other than I: there is the self and the not-self.
2. The not-self is made up of others who are like me and others who are not like me.
3. Where I am is here, where the other is, is there.
4. Either here or there is the better place to be.
5. I am related to the not-self in one way or another: equality, domination or subordination; friend or enemy, etc.
6. This distinction is good and should be preserved, or bad and should, in one way or another, be overcome.

All culture is the creation of systems and institutions out of the combinations of responses to these problems.

CONSEQUENCES OF THE DISTINCTION

Who can truly know the world of the animal? Who can truly know the world of the human who first became aware that he was a self, yet had no language to give body to his selfhood? All we can do is make schemes and hope thereby to make some suggestion of the mystery of our own selfhood.

There is no more important imaginative act than the attempt to project ourselves into the world of our first ancestors. It is a false pride that separates us too sharply from the animals for they are flesh of our flesh. The distinction between the human and the animal is small and the continuities must be respected. But, however small, the distinction is crucial.

With distinction, the consciousness of being a self, there enters the sense of ordered space.

With distinction, there enters the consciousness of event, the interactions of the self and the other.

With event there enters the sense of ordered time.

Event, action in ordered space and time, carry the sense of purpose, the intent to which space and time are directed.

Thus, the act of distinction is manifested in three interrelated forms:

a. *Dramatics*

There is a self and a not-self. The two are related to each other, they act, react, and interact. The operative model is choice and decision in the intentions of morality. The effect is process, and the dynamic; time. Dramatics is the organization of energy.

b. *Geometrics*

There is here, where the self is, and there, where the not-self is. This side, that side, this and that, now and then, inside and outside. The operative model is structure and the effect is geometric and the static; space. Geometrics is the organization of structure.

c. *Telics*

Dramatics requires purpose; structure implies valve. The interaction of dramatics and geometrics generates purpose and value. The operative mode is reason and the effect is instrumental.

Telics is the implication and consequence of dramatics and geometrics.

There may be a "correct" ordering of these. If so I do not know what it is. I prefer to see them in a circle rather than in a causal or hierarchial order. Telics is the definition of purpose but the purpose may emerge from the dramatics or the structure as well as existing determinatively prior to them.

These three engender each other. To speak of them separately is only a device for speaking at all.

TELICS

Dramatics and *geometrics* between them define the shape and energy of human experience. *Telics* defines the direction and purpose of that experience. The full study of geometrics and dramatics describes and ultimately defines the particularities of a human situation. It constitutes the proper work and true mission of history. But, taken alone, geometrics and dramatics can be altogether misleading categories for they do not exist apart from a purpose toward which they are directed. Their purpose is defined within the essential condition of human self-consciousness.

We are animals. As animals we are part of the harmonics of the natural order, the rhythmic interaction of harmonically organized hierarchies of energy. The prime characteristic of the natural order in all its variety is precisely these harmonics, and this unity. All its systems find their completion in unity.

We are self-conscious animals. As self-conscious, we are separated from the unity that is of our nature and subjected to a remorseless and inescapable duality.

By nature we are a part of nature. By nature we are apart from nature.

In the process of abstraction which is humanistic logic, the prossibilities of movement away from this remorseless duality can be laid out as a scheme.

1. Duality can be affirmed as the controlling principle of human affairs. It is the origin of all dualisms.
2. Unity can be sought, either in opposition to or in harmony with the primal unity.
   a. Unity is sought as the domination of one principle over all others, the origin of all monotheisms.
   b. Unity is sought as the absorption of all units into the oneness of things, or a balanced equality of all things, the origin of all polytheisms.
3. The separation among things created by duality is accepted

as governing all things and thus generates the great dream of anarchy (which cannot, by definition, have any control of power and, therefore will always succumb to one of the others).

4. The paradoxical situation of the human, caught between unity and duality is accepted as constituent of the order of things. This can take two forms:

   a. The Hegelian thesis-antithesis-synthesis. Insofar as there is a final synthesis ending the process, this is another way of resolving duality back into unity.

   b. The Christian Trinity, the engendering from the duality.of a new unity which sustains and enhances the distinctiveness of the elements of the unity, without either domination or obliteration.

If these categories are understood as analytical and interpretive tools rather than as labels, they can, in a loose way, characterize all purposeful human action and thought. The actual course of history is much too complex for any one label to serve for any institution or system of either thought or act. Nevertheless, religions have a center of gravity or a governing purpose that shapes their general course. These require comment.

MONOTHEISM

Quite late in human history, the drive toward unity took the form of monotheism, the affirmation of a single force. Since the state of being human is inalienably dualistic, this affirmation could only be political; monotheisms are intolerant. Warfare is a consequence of duality, not of any particular reduction of duality, so all religions can be used as instruments of power. Generally it is monotheisms that propogate religion by force.

DUALISM

The primary distinction, self–not-self, is the source, not of the dualisms themselves within which man lives, but of duality, which, in symbolic awareness, becomes *dualism* and the problem of dualism—night and day, the self and the other, knowledge of good and evil.

Psychologically, dualisms seem to be nearly intolerable. There is incessant pressure in one direction or the other. (The seemingly dualistic religions and philosophies look forward to an eventual unity, whether apocalyptic or evolutionary.)

POLYTHEISM

Multiplicity is the source of all polytheisms and represents an attempt to create order (itself a unity) within variety. As religion (not necessarily as nations holding the religion) polytheisms are tolerant and emphasize fertility and union.

ANARCHY

Chaos is a value-laden term intelligible as such only from within one of the first three. The first three all presuppose *order*. This does not. A better, if more technical term is *gestalt-free* form.

Gestalt-free religions appear in two forms. On the one hand there is the undifferentiated cosmos of the modern bourgeois type in which no place or thing has special value or meaning. On the other hand, there is the religion represented by the "theology of the secular" movement, an attempt to find meaning without sacral order. The rapidity of the disappearance of this movement suggests that it was more a dream of a religion than a true religion. (But the inability of human beings to sustain a dream does not prove its invalidity.)

TRINITARIANISM

One's inevitable misgivings in the use of a dogmatic term arise from no sense of its inappropriateness but from the implied authority it grants Christianity. Indeed, only Christianity has proclaimed a true trinity, but it achieves it rarely and perhaps to no greater degree than have other people. The usual form of Christianity is monotheistic (the source of Christian dogmatism, intolerance and imperialism) or polytheistic (Christolatry, Mariolatry, etc. The saints and holy figures in Mexico are functionally Aztec gods; in the Mediterranean area, Mary is functionally the mother goddess, etc. In American religion, the church is essentially an organization of the nodal points of natural and social energies).

The natural state of all organisms is unity.
The inalienable state of being human is duality.

There is no resolution of this fatal paradox, nor ever will be. It is the nature and therefore the tragedy of the human. It is also the source of all creativity, all that is most characteristically human.

GEOMETRICS

Geometrics is the inclusive term for the study of *structure* as fixing the image of relation.

The term geometrics is more inclusive than its ordinary use suggests. It includes all relations which are represented by geometric order and figure. Thus, geometrics includes political order which engenders control of political act, which is a part of dramatics.

The primordial distinction establishes the categories of telics and formal purpose and so is inherent in all human thought. The primordial distinction is felt most strongly as *spatial:* this side–that side, inside–outside. To be in the garden is the primordial unity; to be expelled from the garden is the primordial duality. The fall of man is the awareness of self as not the other, which is the source of his humanness The consequence of his fall, inherent in humanness, is his displacement from the center of meaning.

The fall is not understood so long as it is defined solely as moral. It is also logical and geometrical.

The fundamental categories of space are:
a. Direction
   Vertical, horizontal, diagonal (skew, spiral).
b. Figure
   Point and line, square and cube, triangle and pyramid, circle and sphere, radial forms (star, swastika), web and labyrinth. Radial forms introduce movement into figure.
c. Time
   Considered as a dimension of space rather than history; experienced as one or another figure and direction.

Direction and figure are the determining modes of *relation* which in turn becomes the primary political category, when integrated with modes of energy. The categories of space become manifest as structure, which is the determining logic of relation. Structure is experienced and formed by body image, containers, houses, streets, formal architecture, cities, territory, cosmos.

Direction and figure in time produce all forms, organic and inorganic, through the logic of crystals and the biogeometry of cells.

The custodians of the spatial categories are the arts of tangible matter, primarily architecture and the making of containers (pottery and basketweaving), secondarily the other arts. (Contrary to earlier understanding, music is also a spatial art.)

ARCHITECTURE

Buildings involve all the spatial categories—direction, figure and time. A building is both container and contained. Thus it is the primary image of the human body and the body's place in the cosmos. It is even a primary image of the body's orifices and organs. It sets out the basic directions and establishes the goal of processional which is sacral movement through time.

SCULPTURE

The image of shape, tangible matter and the human body. Begins as idol or as the condensation of a dimension of architecture, or both.

PAINTING

2062465

The place of intersection between the two-dimensional world and the transcendent world of the third dimension of space. Objectivity and subjectivity are defined in the tension between plane surface and depth.

ORNAMENT

Figure extended in space.

CONTAINERS

Both useful objects and the image of the female body. In many (but not all) cultures pottery and basketweaving are the responsibility of women.

MUSIC

The shape of time. For true musicians music, which establishes the symbolism of time, is a single, shaped movement in space.

The arts are not ornaments either to a willed or a thought existence. They are the primary mode of consciousness and, therefore, the first forms of true thought.

DRAMATICS

Logic is applicable to both structure and process. Geometry is structural and static. The origin of nature is geometric (its cellular structure), but it is also organic and therefore dynamic. Therefore, the primordial distinction is not only geometric but vital, the awareness of the self and all that is not the self. Thus, the primordial separation is, in origin, *dramatic*. The terminology of *dramatics* is:

DRAMATICS

Dramatics is an inclusive term for the study of energy as determining the purposeful interaction of persons.

ENERGY

Organic energy: the essential life of the natural order—which is the source of all dramatic interaction.

Mechanical energy: the means for human transformation of the natural order and control of natural energies. Mechanical energy forms the imagination both by determining the context of human action and by its own action reflecting back on the sensibility of the user of it. The tool shapes nature to the intent of human purpose; it also shapes the hand and mind of those who use it.

POWER

Energies exist and work as ingredients of the natural order. Energy controlled to purpose is power.

It is a dream of the humanist intellectual to have a human existence without power, but this is a false and deadly dream. All humane construction is, finally, the ordering of power. The kingdom of God is definable as the state in which power is replaced by love.

EROTICS

Erotics is the science of attraction, desire, love. Erotics is the definition of purpose and, therefore, of power and politics.

DECISION

To act with any purpose beyond the maintenance of the organic balance is to decide, to make a choice. Decisive and consequential choice is the only origin of true personality.

POLITICS

The structure of power is the origin of politics; politics is the science of power, the arena for the enactment of the structures of relation. Politics is a pattern of relation actively defined as dominance and subordination.

HISTORY

History is power used for purposeful change in time. Therefore, it is defined by politics and erotics, and not by either alone. Politics without a developed erotics is not history, but simply a succession of events. Politics motivated by mere love of power is purposeless energy. Thus a revolution that merely shifts the administration of power to someone else is not true politics and is not, therefore, a historical event. The obsession of historians with the conflicts of power—political or military—falsifies their own discipline. The conflicts of power are historical only when they serve to redefine purpose.

NARRATIVE

When an event becomes, in consciousness, more than a simple response, it takes on conscious succession and the possibility of purpose.

MYTH

Myth is the original narrative which establishes the shape and ordering of relation, thus setting the conditions for defining the nature and direction of both erotics and politics.

All human energies, of whatever kind, are shaped by the myth, long after the narrative has been reduced to tale or forgotten.

DRAMA

Narrative as lived rather than recounted in myth is simply a succession of events. When the motive force of narrative is purpose (erotics), the interaction and conflict of different purposes creates *drama*.

Drama is the true locus of being human; it defines the condition of duality within the immediacy and particularity of the situation. If the duality is not resolved it is bad drama—melodrama or sentimentality.

PLACE

The intersection of the natural energies, human creativity and a particular geography create the sacred place. This place both creates and shapes the god. Thus the sacred place, the holy city, is 'revelation' in as valid a sense as law, propositions or mystical vision and has equal or greater status in reality.

Gods are not made in the image of man but are generated out of man's experience of structure and vitality. This does not explain away the gods; it is the only way men can respond. There is not, in Delphi, the possibility of denying Apollo, for Delphi is a creator of Apollo—and of the Dionysiac power that is part of the Apollonian energy. Athena is a creation and therefore a summation of the Acropolis; the builders of the Parthenon made manifest the image of Athena that is implicit in the Acropolis. Yahweh is not as close to nature, but is not understandable apart from the Sinai, Judea and Jerusalem. The gods, or God as the summation of the gods, are co-terminous with life. To say that God is dead is to do no more than affirm an antiquated metaphysic.

ICON AND IDOL

The point of intersection between value (meaning and purpose) and geometrics is the investment of a particular thing with sacrality. If the thing contains the sacred it is an idol, if it gives access to the sacred it is an icon.

RITUAL

The custodian of the dramatic categories is *ritual*, which involves the primary art of the body (dance and music), and the primary art of words (myth). Developmentally, the enacted myth is analyzed into epic, drama, music and dance. Later, as in the other arts, these become reflective and, therefore, philosophical (e.g. the novel and lyric poetry are the reflective modes of the impulsive arts of epic and ritual drama just as the string quartet is one of the reflective modes of music).

Ritual is always enacted in space, thus creating or recreating the sacred place. The ritual is always enacted with objects, thus creating or recreating the idol and icon. Developmentally, the place and the idol are analyzed into architecture and art. Easel painting is the philosophic mode of art.

PRELIMINARY NOTES ON THE CONSTRUCTION
OF THE SELF

We can, thus schematically, outline a structure for the description of our world. As a description it would be more inclusive and more comprehensive than most descriptions. Yet, left as it stands it is still a description, which presupposes an observer standing apart from the object of observation. True description, true analysis is a good deal more complicated than that for in a world so described there can be no separation between the observer and the observed. We observe by means of the very instruments of our observation. We are ourselves part of what we analyze.

By our observation we become, differently, a part of what we observe and this in our involvement remake what we are.

> . . . method constructs the mind at the same time it constructs the constructions of the mind.
>
> ELIZABETH SEWELL

> . . . we are ourselves both the instrument of discovery and the instrument of definition.
>
> CHARLES OLSON

So far the scheme by being analytical does not permit the account of this self-making. For that a different analytic category is required.

RHYTHM

There is a category that can only in a very old-fashioned terminology be termed a category; it is an ingredient to all the others and both could and should be listed under each. It cannot, however, be considered totally a part of any. This is *rhythm*. Rhythm is the link between direction, figure, time and energy. It fixes time into space (figure). It enlivens figure into time (energy). It controls the translation of space–time into purpose (direction), and so is an ingredient of morality.

The elements of rhythm are:

a. Tempo
b. Interval
c. Proportion

The sources of rhythm are:

a. Organic. The human body and the natural order.
b. Inorganic. Inorganic rhythms are regular and geometrical, one of the sources of ornament, which condenses energy into patterns; e.g. crystals.
c. Human creativity. These are the rhythms generated in the search for meaningful order. They represent a distinctive and unique fusion of organic and inorganic rhythms with symbolic rhythms.

Duality is inherent in distinction and the primordial separation. Isolated, duality is defined by power in the desperate search for unity; thus the condition of man is enmity. Persons are structured into dualisms.

But rhythm is chiastic—what goes out can return. Thus rhythm makes possible *exchange*, and all community is built on exchange. Dualism is the suspension of rhythm and, therefore, experience.

Exchange is, as all things are, subject to telics. Dominated by duality it is directed toward unity or multiplicity (or "multiple unity"). It then becomes *transformation* or metamorphosis: this becomes that.

In trinitarian logic (and the concept of the Trinity is usable as a theological term only as it is understood as a mode of imaginative logic), *this* in exchange with (communicating with) *that*, becomes *the other* which is more than both this and that, includes this and that but does not obliterate either, and exhausts neither.

The primary instrument of trinitarian transformation is *metaphor*, which is the embodiment of the transaction. Metaphor extracts the common structures in different dramatics. (When metaphor deals only with common dramatics in different structures or, worse, a coincidence of inconsequential appearance, it is a figure of speech and not a primal imaginative act.)

In the chiastic rhythms of metaphor, whatever person or conjunction of forces shapes the myth shapes the structures by which we experience the world.

THE WORK OF RHYTHM

There is no single custodian of rhythm. Music is the most public, perhaps the most influential, but equally powerful is the disposition of forms in space. Rhythms are too much a part of the common life to be subject to any single control.

Breath, heartbeat, physiological rhythms, days and seasons, plants and animals, the logical rhythms of duality, trinity, multiplicity are all the context of our natural and passionate life. Human life is the ordering of rhythms within our space and purpose, and the ordering of our national rhythms into constructive social purposes.

When, in sleep, motor functions, and therefore the political action of the body are cut off from the brain, the mind operates without regard to consequences. Images adhere to the nodal points of the structure and, therefore, make the structure itself visible. These images are the functional material of the dream and the myth, but the structure of their order and their transmutation are decisive for the grasp of their dramatics. Dreams are the functional metaphors of the individual, whereby the structure and logic of the individual's experience of reality are embodied in a different dramatics. Similarly, myth (the collective dream) is the functional metaphor of a people, whereby the structure and logic of the people's experience of reality are embodied in a different dramatics.

ANALYSIS AND RHYTHM

Ultimately, the purpose of analysis is the apprehension (not the description) of the essential rhythm of a phenomenon. The primary act of analysis is the description of structure, which is for the most part accessible to our analytical tools and our languages. ("Structure" is here considered the organization of relations in time and space, according to a determinable logical principle and purpose.) Yet, however accurate the account of structure, to miss rhythm is to make a living phenomenon, in man's case, into an android. It may look alive, it may even act alive. But it has no soul.

The death of God is neither metaphysical nor historical, but is a term that corresponds to the death of rhythm. It is a true death and not a metaphor or a rhetorical device.

Sacrality is inseparable from a common rhythm.

He who possesses rhythm possesses the universe.

CHARLES OLSON

MORALITY

Morality is given a separate place here, because it is neither an element nor a condition; morality is an achievement.

There is nothing in the scheme proposed so far to prevent man from being defined as a very complicated animal. Indeed, for most people most of the time even complex acts are not freely chosen but are responses to complex situations. But to be human it is not sufficient simply to have a purpose. Rather the purpose must be chosen according to a standard of value. If the origin of the human is in the original distinction that is self-consciousness, then the fulfillment of that distinction is the intentional choice of purpose. The finally decisive human question is, then, the judgment to be made on the intention. That is morality.

As long as decisive choice is directed toward a particular figure of relation through power, it is political. When decisive choice involves a judgment of *value*, of "better" or "worse," it is moral. Judgments of value do not emerge naturally at this stage of either analysis or experience; there is no such thing as natural morality (or natural law) since even if morality is defined as conformity to natural order and purpose, this is not a judgment any natural organism ever makes. It is a judgment in history, and is consequent on the symbolic structures that emerge as the particular manifestation in time and place of the elements here presented as a theoretical scheme. Thus, finally, the question of morality is not separable from the question of the workings of culture.

CULTURE

A true culture is intentional event structured to moral purpose. Its geometrics, dramatics and telics are not worked out in the abstract, but in all its creations. For example:

Drama is the ideal shape of a culture's narrative; what is, in the mode of what ought to be.

History is the shape of a culture's narrative in the mode of contingency; what ought to be, or what is desired, in the mode of what is.

Art is the shape of a culture's geometrics in its ideal mode; what is, transmuted by the structure and energies of what is most desired.

Physics is the shape of a culture's geometrics under the conditions of concreteness; what is desired or dreamed, ordered and compelled by the conditions of what is.

Therefore, history is understandable only as the analysis of drama gives access to the categories of interpretation. Physics is understandable only as the analysis of art establishes the shape and direction of the understanding sensibility.

Art and drama both analyze and shape the responding sensibility; history and physics analyze and determine our form of what is responded to.

Knowledge and Will: An Essay

The vagaries of the human mind are such that, when we find ourselves faced with an insoluble problem, we are more likely to sink
into hopeless despair than to admit to ourselves that we have formulated the question badly. Yet every act of human thought is
shaped finally not by the answers it produces but by the way the
problem was originally stated.

We are encouraged in this vagary by the inescapable fact that a
false or inadequate statement of the problem by no means leads
necessarily to false conclusions. The history of science is full of discoveries that were made while the scientist in question was at-
tempting to solve some other problem, and of answers that demol-
ished the question that gave rise to them. At a deeper level, any
people's symbolic structure gives rise to problems—whose solution
would satisfy the needs of the symbolic structure quite as much as
it would yield any validating experience of reality. Thus, an insoluble problem is not simply a riddle without an answer; it im-
perils the very grounds of psychic existence. A symbolic structure
is what a people experience *with*; if its questions, its problems,
cannot be formulated correctly, then it is *itself* called into question, which is something very few people are capable of doing. Instead, they give way to a sense of hopelessness and failure. Their
sense of meaninglessness is well-founded, for they have called into
question the very grounds of their meaning and have recourse
only to despair, to eccentric comfort in the transcendental or to
energetic activity.

It normally takes someone not as committed to that symbolism to suggest the obvious resolution. If the problem is insoluble it may be a false problem and the problem must be reformulated even at the expense of reordering the symbolic structures out of which it grew. We have reached that point in our attempt to grasp the meaning and purpose of being human. We are no longer able to formulate answerable problems. *We* have become the gravest of all problems to ourselves and, as a people, we have degenerated into eccentric mysticisms or purposeless activities. We are the victim of our own false premises.

It is not so simple as saying that we have been in error, for the premises that have created our problems are also the premises that have created the world we live in. So we are not entirely without reason in holding so desperately to the image of man that has dominated our common enterprise, particularly since it is an image integral to the realities of history.

It is, for example, reasonable to imagine that our earliest ancestors first became something other than nature, when they first became aware that they were something other than nature. If this was the beginning, the next step is logical to the point of inevitability. People became aware that, as something other than all that which was not themselves, they could act on that which was not themselves, altering it to their own purpose. The next step was equally logical, equally inevitable; acting was itself a kind of knowing, and generated knowing. Knowing increased the effectiveness of the action, and gave the actor control over the act, so that desire or purpose and will became more nearly one. It became possible to think of man as decisively controlled by will and knowledge.

Yet the greater part of human experience is remorselessly a part of nature. Most of human history has, finally, been controlled by the authority of nature. Without a developed technology, human existence is necessarily at the mercy of the natural order; knowledge and will are used to bring the common life into some acceptable equilibrium with the natural energies and the controlling image of man is shaped around other principles than our own. All such cultures had an ample supply of both will-full and knowledgeable people but it was not they who engendered the dominant image of human nature and purpose.

History is not cyclical; in the obscure economy of human affairs there is accumulation and development. For undiscernable reasons this slow work made it possible to shape an image of man around the dominant principles of knowledge and of will. Toward the end of the second millenium B.C. this image and its necessary symbolic structures began to emerge in the eastern Mediterranean. By the time of Augustine, the image was basically fixed, shaping the image of man in Western culture, and has remained so until our day.

The situation would be sufficiently difficult even if we were able to say simply that this history burdened us with an inadequate definition of our humanity. (I say "inadequate" rather than false, for we undoubtedly do know things and we undoubtedly can act, willfully.) But its difficulties are compounded by the inevitable consequence of the attempt to organize the human around its willfulness.

In so far as we can imagine ourselves back into the attitude of our earliest ancestors we can guess that their sense of causation was decidedly limited, and not very much involved with themselves. Things did happen, but not much happened as a consequence of their own acts. Thus their energies went into bringing themselves into harmony with those forces that did determine events. What they themselves could cause to happen played little role in their sense of the ordering of things.

Quite complex cultures were built up on this image of order. Early cultures had their own schizophrenia: urgent enterprise is begun and carried to completion by human causation and there must have been many a man who knew quite well that he was not simply the agent of causes outside himself, but had himself caused the result; he could have been altogether cynical about the mythology that absorbed and explained his work. But his secret and cynical knowledge did not determine the mythology which was his culture's functional equivalent of our "explanations".

It is not necessary to know why and how the shift came about but only to know that it did come about: the image of the human was organized around the principles of knowledge and will. What matters at the moment is less knowledge (which is a condition of will) than the idea of the will, for it shaped the image of culture.

Will is known only in its effects. Will determines acts and the acts have consequences. An effective will causes something, must cause something or it is not effective and man could not consider himself, decisively, will.

Thus the image of man as determined by knowledge, and will of necessity generated an image of the order of things dominated by linear causality, for one presupposes the other. A philosophic and scientific explanation became a psychological necessity. A psychological definition became determinative for the scientific image of order.

This interaction engendered a distinct interpretation of morality: however differently defined, the truth is known; thus failure to abide by the known is proof of ignorance or of a weak will. The crucial energy of moral training then goes into education, exhortation or penal discipline. Conversely, as the hold of linear causality in scientific theory weakens, the reverberations are felt in the sense of personality and, finally, in the sphere of morality. There is either an abandonment of morality, a paralyzed will, or else a frantic emphasis on schools, desperate exhortation or angry, cruel, intensifications of punishment. What seems psychologically impossible is to accept the consequences of this situation and conclude that the motivating image of man is wrong.

The problem becomes still more complex, for knowledge and will, determining an obsession with causality, reach out into politics. What has been said already, suggests the origin of intolerance; if the truth is knowable and if we have the power to act on what we know, then a failure to know and act according to the truth is proof of immaturity (requiring direction), or of error (requiring education, forcible if necessary), or of evil (requiring correction or punishment).

It provides, too, a theory of politics. Since every willed cause has a predictable effect, then every effect must have a willed cause. Thus, every situation, however reprehensible, must have been caused by a knowing and willing agent. Since obviously we do not will our own failure, any failure we suffer is caused by someone else; if we do not know who that is we can assume a conspiracy. (All "liberation" movements are as burdened with the conspiracy theory of history as is the so-called "establishment".)

If this view of causality creates the conspiracy theory of history it also creates a technological conception of all social action. All situations are problems and all problems have solutions. Thus culture and counterculture alike look for the technique that will solve the problems that face us.

The dual tones of knowledge and will resonate as at least the ground bass in all the dominant themes of western interpretation. Even those who call into question one or the other terms of the formula do so on the assumption that knowledge and will are the normal modes of definition of being human; the absence of one or the other is felt, definitively, as an *absence*, fully as defining as its presence. The skeptic, for example, may deny in various ways the possibility of knowing; but then it becomes the duty of man to determine what act or attitude should proceed from the will—in light of the failure of knowledge.

The emphasis of the interpreter may fall on that which is known, which places thought in the arena of metaphysics. Or it may fall, variously, on the possibilities or limitations of knowledge, which centers thought on epistemology. Or it may center on the knower, which is psychology. Or it may center on what the knower should do with the known, which is ethics.

It is the various treatments of these central areas, and the manner in which they are related, that gives names to movements of thought and interpretation. There is no need here to attempt any summary of those movements, particularly since their various formulations as often as not undercut their own overt assertions. The most extreme skeptic who still remains within the discourse (obviously we know nothing about those who remove themselves from the discourse) is still saying, in effect, "We know that we do not know; therefore, we ought to act in such a way." ("Therefore" is a word bridging knowledge and will; "ought" is a word within the province of the will.) We not only know that we do or do not know, we know that we ought to act in such a way, on the basis of what we either know or do not know.

Yet, in fact, the human race is not definable within the coordinates of knowledge and will. It is possible to treat some limited situations as though they were amenable to knowledge and will alone, but such situations arise only under certain conditions—and the conditions only conceal temporarily the price that will be paid later. Part of the price is the malaise of our own day. At a time when our knowledge appears (deceptively) to be at least theoretically unlimited, our confidence in the will has been seriously undermined. Partly this is the result of experience. We are beginning to learn what serious observers have always known, that in human affairs serious action rarely produces the intended and desired result but something altogether unforeseen. Partly it is the result of modern knowledge itself: Freud, Marx and the sociologists of knowledge have clearly demonstrated how complex is the act of willful decision, how bound up it is with matters quite beyond the control of the will.

Yet even those systems that indict the will in this way still act on the overpowering assumption that man is essentially "known" as knowledge and will. Psychoanalysts are not noticeably reticent about asserting how people *ought* to behave in the light of what analysis now enables us to *know* about them.

A clue to the problem begins to emerge from consideration of the strange situation of Freudianism and Marxism in the modern world. Instead of being seen as an account of what human action *is*, in the reality of experience, they became systems of explanation. Systems of explanation, in our culture, at least, are inevitably considered operated by the motor of cause and effect. Freudian and Marxist literature are saturated with the terminology of causation. Thus poetic or prophetic visions are turned into systems of knowing.

It is time, therefore, to accept the fact that it is incorrect to analyze man as determined by or defineable by the coordinates of knowledge and will. Man must be otherwise defined.

In this change, there are two particular dangers to guard against. In the first place, it is essential not to fall back on any attempt to make a new account of knowledge and will. It does not appear unreasonable to conclude, observing the litter of corpses on the battlefield, that all possible strategies have been tried. Rather, it is essential to start at some completely different point. In the second place, it is vital to see that knowledge and will cannot be eliminated. But they can be placed in a different context. Little good would be accomplished by any attempt to recapitulate the innumerable and intricate debates that have arisen out of the inherited definitions; the philosophical literature is full of such summaries, normally accompanied by valiant attempts to resolve the conflict. The attempts are valiant but they are futile. On the level of debate, there is always evidence and argument for each position, equally substantial evidence, equally convincing argument against each position. There are some people who are irrevocably committed to one specific position. People not so committed tend to feel that we clearly know too much for skepticism to be more than a style of life, yet obviously our knowledge is too limited, and itself too shaped by style for the old confidence to survive. Similarly, we are too clearly able to act willfully and our acts are too consequential to permit belief in determinism—yet it is equally clear that our acts are inextricably involved in forces we cannot control and our free decisions have consequences quite other than those we wanted or intended.

Philosophy has, by and large, abandoned the attempt to resolve these problems and has retreated into an examination of its own tools. The other traditional hermeneutical discipline, theology, has either followed the lead of philosophy or simply surrendered. There is either a better way of doing things or there is no refuge from skepticism or despair.

To propose a new way is not nearly so presumptuous as it sounds; it does not necessarily mean, "I am going to solve the problem that has baffled the finest minds for centuries," because the whole point of the new idea is that it starts from a different point altogether. It is no great source of pride to me to say I see a landscape scene better than a great man does, if he is behind a wall trying to guess from an assortment of confused clues what the scene is like while I am sitting on his shoulders looking over the wall. The analogy will break down fairly quickly (no "new way" will ever enable us to see *that* clearly.) But at least it is a new start and if it ends by simply providing us with a new set of equally frustrating problems we will at least have learned some new things along the way.

Since the enterprise is not so simple as climbing a stepladder to look over the wall, or walking to the corner to look round its end, what clues do we have? There are many, if we only learn to see them, but the clue to use at the moment is the one already mentioned—the tenacious hold over both our minds and our acts of patterns, forms, structures of relation, habits of mind, systems of classification, modes of thinking about thinking. It is the compelling force of these that determines the ordering of our life and thought more powerfully than the asserted subject matter. Thus Freudianism may function as a major idea, but cannot function as it should, because it became amalgamated into the structure of thought which it had done so much to dissolve.

Every profession, even less well-developed occupations, has its own pattern of work and thought. Apprenticeship (e.g., the training of graduate students) is a matter of forming these patterns; teaching information and techniques is simply a means to that end. Institutions which ostensibly belong to one structure of thought may, in their essential shape, be determined by another. Even those intellectual disciplines that are supposedly "objective" are dominated by patterns of thought which I am not qualified to trace. I mean here the deeper matters of the "paradigms" that Thomas Kuhn has so sensitively described, but also the tonality of thought that is more diffuse in its working, but probably just as powerful. There is no reason to think that by nature science participates in the powerfully masculinized sense of the frontier hero–myth. But scientists themselves, as well as their publicists, speak of "pursuing" the solution to a problem, or "pushing back the frontiers of ignorance," or of "conquering" a disease. Intelligent will is attributed to organisms that clearly have neither intelligence nor will; plants are described as "reaching down" to get water.

"Conquering" a disease may, in fact, be a useful example to use to condense a much wider range of illustrations. It would be hard to find a more complete example, for it contains all the elements that characterize the western habit of mind. It assumes that a disease has an identifiable causative agent and exists as something apart from the patient whose body it happens to affect. If there is sufficient knowledge (which can be accumulated by an appropriate combination of intelligence and will and now money, since the image of the lonely shaman has been displaced by the expensive task force,) if there is sufficient knowledge, the counteragent can be discovered by an act of will and the disease eradicated.

Of course in many cases, this works perfectly well. But it is apparent that the situation is far more complicated. For example, tuberculosis used to be a classic example of the conquest of disease. But it now appears that the incidence of tuberculosis has had a clear pattern of rise and fall that has had little to do with knowledge of the disease. The fall in the number of cases long preceded the discovery of the drugs now used to treat the disease.

Similarly, diptheria virtually disappeared in this country after an intensive immunization program; it disappeared equally rapidly in Scandinavia where there was no immunization program.

It turns out that organisms characteristic of many diseases are ubiquitous; some people get the diseases and some don't, but on a regular rather than random statistical pattern.

After describing the complicated factors under examination in experiments on breast cancer in mice, viruses, genetics, diet, hormones and environment, John Cassel says, "It's not one of these things. It's not even necessarily just the summation of them. It's the configuration, the pattern."[9] He is asserting that no one, nor even a fixed combination, is the "cause" of breast cancer in mice. There is much more in Cassel's brief and nontechnical lectures, but I will isolate only one other point for use here:

It appears that a central factor in the health of animals is the presence of predictable response in other similar animals, a response that is part of the ritual of communication, and serves to establish the individual's place in the community. Other studies have tended to confirm the same thing for humans. The presence of others in an understood relationship is necessary to health. ". . . that those circumstances in which an individual is not receiving adequate feedback from important others in his life, that his actions are important or accomplishing their intended consequences, those will be the circumstances in which people will be more susceptible to a wide variety of diseases." Further, if one disease is prevented or cured, another will happen, for the patient is not in a cause–effect situation but is in a disease-producing situation. If no disease-producing organisms are handy, he will make up his own by heart disease, ulcers or schizophrenia.

There appear to be two possible conclusions to these studies. First, what we have called "disease" is really a configuration of agents and forces. The second, that disease or the lack of it is itself a part of a configuration, a situation. Health is a characteristic of a pattern or structure, not a state of an isolated organism.

This work, much of which is still quite tentative, will, or should, greatly alter our sense of health and the ordering of society. It should alter our ways of thinking about the world; it should significantly diminish our reliance on linear causality.

It is equally important to remember that this understanding was developed by people strictly trained in the procedures of linear causality, who could discover complications in that causality and begin to formulate modes of behavior to meet the newly understood situation. There may be integrated primitive societies that do not have the assortment of pathologies that have emerged in our own society. But when confronted with changed conditions they have no resources of understanding to preserve their integral communities. We have gotten ourselves into a vast mess by our reliance on causality within the grid of knowledge and will. But it is knowledge and will that can discover for us the modes of action that might, or will, free us from this dependence on knowledge and will.

Equally, we should not let respect for our own characteristic (and very nearly unique) instruments blind us to the merits of modes of thought unlike our own. They were used by men of equal intelligence to ours whose different instruments may have revealed things that are no longer accessible to us, just as our own instruments discovered essential things hidden from them (maybe the medieval doctrine of the "humors" has more to say to us than we realize.)

If I am making the assertion that knowledge and will are no longer sufficient as an analysis of the distinctively human and if I am asserting at the same time that the achievements that have grown out of that definition are indispensable to future humanness, then I have incurred the responsibility of providing, for reasonable use, a model of humanness to incorporate these assertions. The design of such a model is the concern of the rest of this book. The principle at least can be asserted here.

The principle has already been illustrated in the newly emerging definition of disease. The self, the person, is not a thing isolated within definable boundaries, acted on by and acting on other identifiable things. The self is not simply a more complex structure of elements than the inherited model of knowledge and will would have it. The self is a complex structure in active relation to other structures of equal complexity. The relation is not causal but vectorial; if the word is not now lost in the popular use of *defining edges*, the relation is a parameter.

Thus the self and every event the self is in is a shifting tension of structure and forces; structures that are not fixed in an eternal shape but a transient balance of forces; forces or processes that are the tensions between structures. Therefore both self and its events must be understood using the analogy of something like a web or a woven fabric; changes in one part of the fabric are transmitted to other parts of the structure with quite unpredictable consequences.

It is for this reason that knowledge, intelligence, will, causality are by no means displaced or denied here. They are accounted for, rather, as powerful vectors acting among other vectors that are not now so clearly understood. It is quite possible, even usual, to combine knowledge and will into an act that has a causal relation to something else. If the conditions are strictly controlled and certain kinds of interactions selected for observation, then the repeated cause always produces the same effect. But in situations that cannot be controlled, in events whose elements cannot be restricted, then the same cause can produce completely different effects.

Thus causality as traditionally understood is a very powerful force indeed. But it is one force among many, and probably it would be better to confine the word to those situations, few and easily characterized as they are, that have the qualities of control and repeatability. Any other use will continue to be delusive, for the model of causality will control thinking about situations in which causality only confuses the real issue. The Black Death of

1665 was not "caused" by infected rats from a ship in Naples. The organism of bubonic plague is endemic to crowded cities right now. The Black Death was an impossibly complex configuration in which religion, diet, crowding, social strain, certainly played as large a role. There would have been no plague without the bacillus but if that bacillus had been absent something else would have happened, since the vectors had produced a situation of intolerable strain.

This is equally true of all social pathology. The principle of causality throws the study of history hopelessly out of shape. On the one hand, all great events emerge out of a complex of structures and forces that is impossible to understand analytically. It is possible to say that the causes of the Civil War don't exist. On the other hand, the study of history tends to be confined to those events that most nearly fit the pattern of causality. Historians don't confine themselves to politics and war because those make up the definition of history but because politics and war are the most evident arena for the work of the consequential causal will. The will is a powerful force. Ideas, knowledge, are elements of great power in the configuration; but they are not all.

No succesful politician works by the principle of causality. He knows instinctively what analysts have an impossible time learning, that he can cause almost nothing. He can alter conditions so that the desired result might emerge. Successful politicians look devious because they are devious and can't be anything else. Furthermore the fortunate ones die or retire early. They do not "understand" political actions with the conscious verbal mind. They have a "feel" for the situation and act instinctively. Their successful action gives them unbounded confidence in their instincts. But the action itself alters the situation so that instincts shaped in one configuration of forces no longer respond to the new configuration and the bewildered person loses his touch. Kings have it harder than presidents; even Queen Elizabeth I was irrelevant before she died because of the vastly changed situations her own actions had engendered.

Just as important as the patterns and forces involved is the timing, the rhythm of the act; an act today is one thing, tomorrow it will be something else. Or a situation produced by one kind of action today will require a very different action tomorrow to produce anything like the same effect.

Then, too, the definition suffers from its own terminology. "Patterns" or "configurations" or "structure"—well, perhaps. But why "forces?" Yes, the word is appropriate to many situations; a situation is the consequence of the interaction of forces varying in direction and intensity. But this is still comprehensibly causal. There may be more going on than we can ever calculate—but we can at least imagine the calculations; presumably Archimedes never expected to have an adequate lever or a fulcrum but he asserted something important about his image of the order of things by his rhetoric. And so would I were I to be content to describe the self and its world in terms of forces. Words like "forces" are metaphors and all true metaphors link disparate things by sharing something of each. But thought ought not to be imprisoned in its metaphors.

It would be, I think, equally necessary to draw on the principle of growth. The self and a great many of its events are not caused any more than the flower is caused by the seed. Often it is not caused by the more complex array of forces that do shape it. Rather it is engendered, it grows and matures, and much that seems causal is simply antecedent.

Yet even the metaphor of growth must not be pressed too far, for it carries with it too much the sense of natural, determined completion; a rosebush subject to any combination of "forces" will never bear apples—but human beings and their acts are not rosebushes. Perhaps a musical analogy or metaphor is required. So the self in its world—our selves in our separate worlds and our common world—must be understood as a harmony (or disharmony) of like and contrasting elements, following an inherent logic, responding creatively to different conditions, growing organically from an initial principle.

Perhaps necessarily, there are other metaphors, but the multi-plication of metaphors can itself become an indulgence. The self would then be seen apart from the whole, describing the rest of the whole by a new gnosis. The power of our imaginative structures is such that they can absorb and transform the very principle intended to transform them.

For example, the great, generative principle of the Protestant Reformation was that man is justified by faith, not by works. Few can agree on a verbal definition of faith, but certainly it is not a thing produced by the will or by knowing. It is a dispositon of the soul, a mode of thought and act. Yet, within a few years of the initial promulgation of this doctrine, the identifying mark of the Protestant was not so much faith as believing in the doctrine of the justification by faith, which is, obviously, a work. This is the compulsive authority of symbolic structures that shapes all we do, including the very principles that should undermine them.

It is hard to imagine Buddha as a Buddhist, or Jesus as a Christian. St. Francis had to withdraw from the Franciscan movement in his own lifetime.

It is not useful to condemn this character of our experience as a perversity subject to the correction of the knowing will. Perversity there has been aplenty but it is the remorseless logic, the inescapable fatality, of human affairs. We do not escape our condition by taking thought or shaping up our will. We live within the conditions as they are.

For it works both ways. Buddhism, Christianity, Franciscan and Protestant Christianity may be something quite different from what their founders envisaged for them. But the world is very much different because of what they did. They are not causes. They altered the conditions, the way we think, the structures by which we perceive and interpret the world, the purpose of our acts, the rhythm, the distances of our relations. And by so doing they engendered a new world.

We inherit now not only the good but the destructiveness of our obsession with the knowing, causal will. But to rest within our ruin is not only indulgence. It is cowardice. It is an offense against the order of things. Since we now can know what other men's will has done, our knowledge can inform our will to a new grasp of our own processes.

The function of knowledge and will within that process determines what we think about morality. I have asserted earlier that our sense of what morality is does not derive from the presence of a known moral law, which remains only to be obeyed and accurately applied by the instructed will. It derives rather from the unexamined assumptions of that statement: we are able to *know* the difference between right and wrong and have only to *will* the right in order to be able to do it. Thus, our morality does not truly rest on the moral law. Whatever the ontological status of the moral law, our morality rests on the two pillars of knowledge and will, which are the only means of access to what we think we know of the moral law. Therefore, if knowledge and will are not properly the foundation of our relation to the world, the foundation of our present moral order has been wrecked.

This argument has a certain force in the abstract. But so serious a matter as morality is not safely left to deductions from arguments based elsewhere. It is better, with morality as with politics, to find the internal evidence. The evidence is there. It is both internal and external.

Internally, we know what Paul knew when he said, "I can will what is right, but I cannot do it. For I do not do the good I want, but the evil I do not want is what I do" (Romans 7:18-19). Thus, Paul has laid out an accurate description of the way we behave, if we are honest with ourselves. We can know what is good, sufficiently to know what we should will; we can will it; but willing is futile. We do what we do not will; we will what we do not do.

Paul has described the futility of knowledge and the paralysis of will. So what else is left? Paul completes the bafflement by going on, "now if I do what I do not want, it is no longer I that do it, but sin which dwells within me." Exegetical confusion here reaches a kind of ultimate. What is this "sin" that is "within" me doing something through me that I consciously will not to do? I have no idea what Paul meant but certainly we have had no vocabulary for dealing with things like that.

Paul appears to reinforce our intellectual prejudices when he talks of "the flesh," "the law of sin which dwells in my members" as though the limits of our body were evil. I suspect he knew what he was talking about, but his vocabulary, whatever it meant to his readers then, only compounds our problem. His description undercuts our deepest faith about ourselves—and yet is remorselessly accurate. His resolution is not much help, either, to many of the intellectually serious; to say that, somehow, Jesus delivers us from this body of death is a chant of considerable use to the innocent but there is nowhere in our serious vocabulary for it to be of use to us.

The result is fatal. Were we to take the analysis seriously, the result could only be despair. Since few people like to despair, they stop taking it seriously. Since we have had no way of making sense of it anyway, it has slowly dropped out of consciousness. There moral law atrophies and we are left to our natural impulses.

Externally, consequences are equally bad, for the very definition of morality becomes subversive of morality; since, by the definition, failure to live morally (by this definition) is a failure of will or fatal ignorance. If the moral law is something to be known, it lies outside, therefore conformity to it can be enforced. Enforcement is a category of power. Although power may be a political necessity subject to morality, it is not itself a moral category. Yet the reality of human conduct and the definition of morality make power a necessary part of the moral order. Inevitably, of course, what is enforced is conduct dictated by what I or my group wills according to what we know. Morality then becomes relentlessly linked to the knowledge and will of a particular group of people, its only operative instrument force. Thus morality disintegrates, not simply through evil wills but through the good who work evil in the intent to be good.

It is not a coincidence that so many of those who have rebelled against this transformation of morality into power, should have rebelled against other assumptions of the traditional moral code as well, particularly those dealing with sexual matters. Yet it is too simple to see only the rebellion and not the forms the rebellion takes, for it is the forms that are symptoms of the originating situation. If the moral law is objective, existing there as if by nature other than ourselves, for us to conform ourselves to, then it is in the dualistic relation to us and sets for us the pattern of dualism, to know and to will obedience. Thus we are set apart from the order of things, isolated and alone. Those who recoil from the consequences of this morality in its destructive and oppressive power escape from it usually, not by the generation of a new morality but by retreating from will into instinct. They redefine knowledge as harmony with things as they are, will as a yielding to the harmony. Some sexual activity is, of course, an attempt to obliterate the self in something larger than the self but often it is probably a more serious attempt to retreat into the natural harmonies.

For we are by nature natural, and in nature there is only process, not morality. By nature no act is moral or immoral. Good and bad are not natural categories. The decision about what is good and what is bad must be made on some basis other than nature. The expectation that human beings act morally only creates disdain and despair, for most people most of the time have little opportunity to be other than what they are by nature.

Yet human beings by nature are other than nature, and the conscious search for the natural act is, by nature, artificial. This is the tragedy of being human, and the old moral codes, the morality originating in knowledge and will, were necessary (in lieu of anything better, still are) in order to put fences around the tragedy of the natural. Within the enclosure, people could learn how to bear the heavy burden of their individuality, for individuality is first defined by knowledge, then developed out of the choices made in the knowing will. Such historical movements can be sustained only by the vitality of their purpose and the integrity of their assumptions. At the same time that faith in knowledge and will was dissolving, morality was bogging down in the rigidities and cruelties of selfish, lawful, moral power. Redefinition of "the human" requires, therefore, more than finding an acceptable substitute for knowledge and will; it requires, and must generate, the redefinition of morality.

Morality is an achievement, not a command. It is a relation, not a limit. It is a means of communication, not a fence or a prison.

Casuistry cannot be abolished with causality for there will always be as much need of relating a general process to a specific occasion, as there was in the old morality of applying a general principle to a specific problem. There is always a need for the intelligent will. But always the process and relation are prior to the act; no act, in its isolated self, is good or bad. It is good or bad according to what it does.

Here, again, restraint and balance are in order. Human situations are rarely unique, decisions have often to be made in a hurry, and a learned body of rules is essential to an ordered life. But rules are not the ordering of morality; they are the deposit of moral energies, for morality is not in the acts but in the process. Not the isolated act but what is generated out of the act is, finally, decisive.

The judgment of acts is not, therefore, a mechanical application of rules. Neither is it enough to say that any act done in love or to further love is good. Rather, it is the wholeness of the occasion, the consequences beyond the immediate, the web of relation within which the moral drama is enacted—these are the measure of morality.

It is not even enough to say that the moral act is the act that generates community. It sounds good and free and liberated. But it still defines morality in terms of the causal will acting toward a known end.

Love and community are the proper touchstones of the essential discipline of casuistry. Most decisions are contingent and local, and it is inhumane to teach that every act is done in the context of eternal purpose. So self-conscious a life would be the ultimate in artificiality. Nonetheless, that is the only true definition of morality, and the guiding star of creative moral thought. The truly moral life is the generation of an order, an engendering harmony, within which a fully human life can emerge.

At this point, the argument returns to the point of its departure, the knowing will in the whole person. If we can, again, come to terms with our knowing, we may hope for a rebirth of a sustaining and creative order.

Thus, the task of our knowing begins to emerge. It is defined by the terminology that has appeared in this discussion. On the one hand, there are structure, configuration, pattern, relation. On the other hand, there are process, change, transformation, energy. Yet these are not new coordinates to replace knowledge and will. They are, rather, two modalities of a unified whole. Our task, then, is to understand them as clearly as possible, determine their elements and their modes of operation, determine how they have appeared in historical embodiments.

After that, we may know a little better how to order our own acts, to let process once more flow in us and make our lives again intact.

A Note on Authority

Every assertion implies an authority because it is implicitly based on that authority. This principle, although obvious, is often treated with disrespect. What is less obvious is itself an assertion: the authority which an assertion is based on is more important than the content of the assertion itself.

Under many circumstances, this is not difficult to accept. To say "It is the will of God that——" is to make an assertion whose content is clearly less important than the authority of God. This is equally true of "Science tells us that——", or The experiment has proven that——" or "My calculations show that——" or Logic demonstrates that——". In each case an assertion is made on the basis of an acknowledged authority larger than the content of the assertion.

The trouble is, the assertions are not really in the statements indicated by the dashes. The assertions are in the initial clause. The assertion is not, "Thou shalt not kill," or "Water is composed of hydrogen and oxygen." The assertion that matters is, "It is the will of God," and "The experiment has proven." Thus authority in these statements lies, not in the authority of God nor the authority of the experiment, but in something implied, but not truly examined. The true authority in this statement is the authority for making the statement itself, not the authority (now a subauthority) within the statement. How do we know what the will of God is? How do we know whether the results of an experiment are true? *That* is the real authority, not God or the experiment.

The two assertions have a somewhat different reference (there is an empirical check for the experiment, but there is not one so clearly about God). But it is not to our present purpose to talk about the nature or the limitations of scientific method, but about the nature of authority.

The difficulty with examining authority, or at least one of the reasons why it is so rarely truly done, is simple. Any instrument that can be used to examine authority is thereby superior to that authority and is, therefore, the authority. It is no good saying, "The unexamined life is not worth living." Quite aside from the point that many unexamined lives are obviously worth living, what is the instrument for examining the examination? If that, too, is not put to the test, then the act of examination is no more than an act of blind faith.

What is the authority for the examination of the examination? Clearly we are up against the problem of infinite regress, a logical problem that is empty of use. It would be better to accept more immediate conclusions: the authority for our assertions about the world lies within ourselves and is, finally, neither testable nor demonstrable.

Perhaps it is not possible to evade totally the question of scientific method, for the experimenter will object that his procedures demonstrate that water is divisible into hydrogen and oxygen. This is undoubtedly true; as a boy, I did it myself in a bedroom chemical laboratory. But this is not the authority for making the statement; it is the test of the statement and its proof. The authority lies elsewhere.

First of all, authority lies behind the assumption that the word "water" shall apply to a pure liquid composed only of hydrogen and oxygen, eliminating its sweetness, saltiness, its mineral content, its algae, in fact, all other things found in water. Pure water exists only under laboratory conditions. Water "is" a multitude of liquids in various places, under various conditions and uses, including the imaginative and symbolic. An extraordinary act of asceticism isolated one mode of water (its chemically pure state) as authoritative for the word—that act is the one emerging from the true authority.

Such an act itself is not only defensible, but necessary. It is the foundation stone of the modern intellect. Any attempt to get us away from it would destroy us as surely as the experimental method itself might; which does not in the least justify the unexamined dogma that lies behind the experiment. Rather its position in the modern world is like that of the man working on the Sabbath to whom Jesus is apocryphally reported to have said, "Blessed are you, O man, if you know what you are doing. Cursed are you if you don't."

That the experiment does something humanly vital is obvious. What is not so obvious is the status granted to what it does. Science has striking empirical demonstrations; rockets landed within a few yards of their target on the moon, so obviously somebody is doing something right. But the act that initiated the process—the isolation of one substance from another, the isolation of certain acts from other acts, is not validated by those results. It remains an unexaminable act of commitment, with other consequences just as important as touching down on target on the moon.

Thus, after all, science is ultimately not so different from theology. There are even overtones of Pascal's famous wager that it is more dangerous to gamble that God does not exist than that he does. We are gambling that what we undoubtedly learn by scientific asceticism is more important than the dangers we undoubtedly run by cutting our lives into fragments; we are gambling that the isolating method is somehow closer to truth or to reality than any other method.

Theology's final authority is just as easily demonstrated. Whatever the claim, its authority is not God but whatever makes it possible to speak of God. Thus all theologies find their source in something. Traditional theologies go back to an authoritative scripture or myth, either directly or as transmitted and interpreted by an institution, or they go back to direct revelation. Whichever it is, the question still remains, how do you know this scripture is authoritative, or how do you know it was God who spoke to you? It is an unanswerable question, for the answer to the question then becomes the true authority.

More recent theologians have lost confidence in scriptures, institutions or revelation. Therefore they ground their theologies on personal experience, on autobiography or, significantly, on myth (I do not know why they should retain any more confidence in myth than they do in revelation or scriptures). Generally, they are not relativists, and not rigorous solipsists, so they are left with the same unanswerable question, "What gives authority to your experience?"

From that point on, both traditional and more modern theologians work in the same way, transferring authority to the process of logic, and working deductively on the basis of the initial assumptions. Since the authority of logic is nowhere demonstrated (because it is undemonstrable), again the enterprise becomes an act of commitment. Therefore, the choices before a scrupulous person seem clearly set out:

1. To accept without question whichever undemonstrable authority seems most convincing. This is the route taken by all scientific, political or religious fundamentalists, desperately asserting some basic dogma.
2. To be convinced that every person is isolated from every other person and "the only world I know is the one I build." This is solipsism.
3. To be convinced that there is no sure authority at all, that all opinions about reality are relative to the position of the speaker and have no status beyond that. This is relativism.
4. To do nothing serious, lapsing into sloth or purposeless energy.

Our traditional understanding of authority has brought us to this condition. It has considerable consequences in our response to the world.

Many people are fatefully disposed (perhaps as a part of our cultural tradition) to identify a condition or a result as a cause. Thus a discipline that is an integral part of an imaginative vision is interpreted as a cause of that vision and the discipline is distorted from its original role.

This is peculiarly and incongruously a part of the rebellion against inherited cultural tradition. Many people are attracted to eastern religions or primitive religions. Seeing the disciplines that are a part of those religions, they assume that the admired state of mind is caused by the discipline. Thus a discipline, which is contingent on a commitment, is treated as a technique. But a discipline which is integral to one context is not the same as a causal technique and, as a technique, it produces quite different effects. This is basically a confusion of authority. The controlling vision of Zen Buddhism is a state of the soul as part of a vision of cosmic order. The authority, the controlling vision, of those who would adopt Zen Buddhism for other purposes is technology in causal relation to a desired effect. These are two very different things.

Now it is required of me to set out the authority for this writing. It makes assertions; therefore it too is based on authority. What, then, is the authority? The answer is, there isn't one. The whole work is predicated on the assumption that there is no authority to call on, only commitment.

There is neither choice nor thought except in the act of commitment. We do not stand outside those positions, deciding which (if any) to act on. We *are* one or another of them. To change commitment is not to alter opinions but to remake the self (to be "born again").

The standard of choice does not, and clearly cannot, lie outside one of the logical destinies. We might dimly sense the differences between dualism, and monism and trinitarianism. But their proof is part of themselves. The authority for judging one is drawn from within a commitment to another (as I judge trinitarianism to be the most human), and so is self-serving. There is no final authority to appeal to.

Since this commitment is by nature total it cannot be relativistic. Since it is consequential it cannot be solipsistic. To say "Man makes God" or god, or the gods, is to say what now can be *known*. But it does not say that therefore there is nothing out there corresponding to that great metaphor, "God." It is vital to know that all we say or think on the subject is generated out of our own symbolic encounters—but the encounter is with a genuine reality. Therefore the commitment is not a commitment to a chimera of our own imagining; it is a commitment which we make, which we must, unavoidably, make.

It is, therefore, as Pascal knew, a wager. But not so cold-bloodedly trivial as our reading of Pascal tends to make it. It is from our commitment that we generate a self. It is our commitment that places authority where it belongs, within sacred reality, and not in our own instruments. It is commitment that does not give us authority *over*, but places us in living relation to; commitment which might, finally, make us human.

PART TWO

Structure

THE ELEMENTS OF STRUCTURE

Structure is shape and ordered relation. *Process* is first of all communication among structures, then the reshaping of one structure into another, the transformation of one by another. Therefore, it is false to separate structure from process for any reason other than convenience in clarifying analysis.

Axioms of structural analysis:

1. All forms, organic and inorganic, natural or man-made, have their own characteristic structure.
2. Elemental structures are those given universally in the natural order: organic and inorganic nature, weather, landscape, given conditions of food production, etc.
3. Derivative structures (those engendered from or made out of the elemental structures) are generated from the interaction of the elemental structures and therefore participate in them. They can be understood only by the prior understanding of the elemental structures.
4. No structure exists apart from its manifestation. The most extravagant idealist attempt to presuppose or achieve a structure without an embodiment, still must do so in some form of image, language or logic.
5. Not only things but images, languages and logic have their characteristic structure, which conditions, limits and generates the structures which come to manifestation through them.
6. Elemental structures (including man-made structures such as tools, which are products of man's intercourse with natural reality in the grip of necessity) are shaped and determined by natural necessity. Derivative structures are shaped and determined by meaning and purpose. (This obviously does not preclude structures that possess both necessity, and meaning and purpose.)

7. *All* experience is structured. There is no such thing as a direct and accurate experience of reality, for the experience is always mediated by physiological and cultural structures.
8. Therefore, no analysis of any experience that isolates one structure as controlling, decisive or normative can ever be true; for structure is known (therefore "exists") only in relation to other structures.
9. The only true access to a person's or a people's meaning and purpose is through an analysis of their structural forms; the only purpose of structural analysis is the apprehension of meaning and purpose.

HUMANISM AND STRUCTURE

The secret of being human is the ability to transform structures (which is process). Animals have appropriate neurological structures, and therefore psychological and cultural structures, that are both intricate and attractive. But they have almost no capacity to modify those structures, to modulate from one to another.

It is not at all accidental that the well-known contemporary forms of "structural analysis" should either be totalitarian in intent or ascetically despairing about the death of "man" and the end of the humanistic enterprise. Structure without process is fixity, death.

Humans who respond with fixed and closed structures have suspended their humanity.

AN OUTLINE OF STRUCTURE

1. *Abstract*

   Abstract structures are relational and, therefore, are at the heart of all other structures. Geometrics is the study of abstract structures.

2. *Natural*

   a. Crystalline forms of inorganic structures.

   b. Characteristic structures of living creatures, including the structured acts and relations that are consequences of (and, in evolution, create) their structured forms.

   c. Rhythmic (therefore structured) forces of the natural order—light and dark, seasons, storms, the sea, etc.

3. *Cultural*

   a. Techniques

   Techniques are an extension and consequence of tools.

   b. All acts designed to orient man in the natural forces, i.e., ritual.

   c. Institutions, including customs and manners appropriate to the institutions

      1. Personal-family, etc.

      2. Political

      3. Economic

   d. Symbol

   Symbols are objects or acts that condense and concentrate some range of meaning, purpose, structure.

   e. Metaphor

   Metaphor is a symbol that connects other symbols; revealing one in the other, transforming one into the other.

   f. Language and logic

   Language and logic are partly given in the order of things and therefore "natural." Partly created, or, perhaps better, specified, in the creative act of persons.

1. Poetry

   Including all nondiscursive or nonimperative use of language, not just verse.

2. Concept and proposition.

   The systematic, discursive and self-conscious embodiment of the metaphoric act.

g. All "made" things that function variously as explanation, control, participation, etc. This would include the structures of thought, the arts, etc.

4. *Relation*

   The system of relations has a reality apart from the things being related. This is not idealism.

5. *Rhythms*

   Rhythms are the spirit of life breathed into the nostrils of a structure which otherwise would be only a coagulation of dust.

6. *Symbolic structures*

   Symbolic structures are those orderings of objects or acts that make perceptible the sense of structure in which a people live. Symbolic structure is the ordering of all the elements, but without the sense of the enspiriting rhythms there is no apprehension of the symbolic structure.

THE CONDITION OF STRUCTURE

The perpetual temptation of the academic intelligence—and, for better or for worse, this is an academic work—is to consider a systematic analysis the reconstructed equivalent of the thing or the state analyzed. Systematic analysis has its indispensable use, else we flee into mystic awareness outside consciousness, yet systematic analysis can identify the structure but not the structure as symbol. The condition of a symbolic structure is the rhythm that holds the elements together. To know the symbolic structure as true symbol, it is not enough to describe the elements. It is essential to apprehend the rhythm.

The elements of rhythm can be described analytically. Rhythm itself can only be felt somatically.

To feel the rhythm of another people's order is to participate in the reality of their world.

True knowledge, therefore, is never objective; it is participatory. What we call "objective" knowledge is a material and inalienable condition for true knowing.

. . . fact as the place of the cluster of belief. . .

CHARLES OLSON

MAKING THE WORLD

Every symbol system makes a world.

Symbolic systems are to be known as human achievements, not judged as successes or failures according to their results. All symbolic systems ensure their own success; they construct a method for controlling experience and thus produce miracles, productive devotional techniques, a rich social order. Since they construct personalities according to the process of their interaction, they are self-validating. Equally, all systems ensure their own failure, since the symbolic system always creates conditions it cannot control.

To participate in the reality of another's world is to love him or her.

There is, therefore, in love an extension of the individuality which absorbs other things into it, which units them to us. This union and interpretation enables us to acquire a deep understanding of the properties of the beloved object. We see it whole and it is revealed to us in all its worth. Then we observe that the beloved object is, in its turn, part of something else that it requires and to which it is bound, and as this is indispensable for the beloved object, it also becomes indispensable to us. In this way love binds one thing to another and everything to us, in a firm essential structure.

ORTEGA [10]

A final condition of all structural analysis and, therefore, a final condition of all true scholarship, is love.

PERCEPTION

Perception is not simply the channel for information; it is the ordering of human physiology, chiefly the nervous system, which places a person in the natural order (according to his controlling image of direction and figure in time). It is traditional, if somewhat deceptive and misleading, to divide perception into the *senses* and treat each sense as though it were a tool. Perception, however, is an activity, not a thing; its work can be variously done. The senses are *systems* which cohere into a whole perceptual *system*, which is conterminous with the whole somatic activity; that is, proprioception.

Perception is not a physiological act to be examined and explained by the thinking mind; it is ingredient to mind, a condition of thinking. It is the primary, the elemental, mode of being and acting in the world.

Light is the first condition of primary perception. No perceptual system is solitary or irreplaceable, but the visual system has always maintained an imaginative primacy. "I see" = "I understand." Light is also a condition of signs and therefore, of language.

Sound is a second condition of primary perception. Probably the first modality of language. A condition of spatial orientation and a determiner of the emotional timbre of space.

> . . . with reference to Africa, that the non-literate rural population lives largely in a world of sound, in contrast to western Europeans who live largely in a world of vision. . . . Whereas for Europeans, in general "seeing is believing," for rural Africans reality seems to reside far more in what is heard and what is said.
>
> J.C. CAROTHERS[11]

Touch is the experience of intimacy. A condition for determining if a surface encloses.

The "counter-culture" shifts from the visual to the tactile, the intellectual to the sensual. "I see" is transformed into "I feel."

Odor is both a condition for receiving certain kinds of information and a modality of emotional character.

Taste is a minor sensory system in most immediate perceptual acts, but nevertheless a shaper of emotional response.

Proprioception is the coherence of all the perceptual systems to generate the awareness of a self as a nodal point, a ganglion, within a whole. No longer rightly to be taken as that vague activity, the perception of one's internal workings.

The eye is a part of the mind.
LEO STEINBERG

Perception is not a true job, depositing information in the brain. It is coterminous with the body's activities, its life in its circumstances. We *are* our interaction with our world; the eye is a part of the mind. Names such as "perception," "thinking" give the illusion of distinct substances to processes that are inseparable, even indistinguishable. In the process of bringing the human into being, perception is central.

VERBAL STRUCTURES

The ordering of words is a controlling factor in all the above, as well as its own independent world. Words can shape a world, define the experience of things, the experience of persons. There is no escape from the order of words. Thus it is vital to find the source of words and the structure of their ordering. For words emerge from:

the world of things and persons as engendered by experience;
other words, as engendered by the structure of words themselves.

The second of these is the origin of most human delusion, error and wickedness for things and persons are thereby subjected to the order of words rather than words emerging from the life of things and the relations of persons.

Words, too, are living things and can engender further life by their intercourse. But once the connection between word and thing is severed at any point, all that grows after is a poisonous weed.

Speech is the realization of our humanity. Speech is also our fatal disease. Speech is the manifestation of our self toward the other. Speech is also the surest means of concealing our self from the other and, therefore, killing the soul.

Words will remain our surest humane language. But verbal language is now out of control. The control will be reestablished not by the discipline of words alone, but by learning to know the other languages as languages, learning how to relate them to the verbal language as making up the whole of human speech, thereby learning how language works in the whole human enterprise.

Therefore the idea of the concept, the concept of the concept, is itself a metaphor, for it is the linking of two disparate things. *All* propositions are metaphors. The forms of the verb "to be" are not, in themselves, commitments about "reality"; they are the linking terms in a metaphor.

Human thought is not merely metaphoric in operation. Itself forms one term of a metaphor.

... the loss of metaphor is the loss of language, and language is the essential instrument of the human imagination.

> Western thought through the tradition of its languages, has postulated some centre of the mind where we work in and through images; imatinatio. Einbildung. To this centre come all images of the external world and of the body given by our senses, by means of language which we superimpose on, or fuse with, them, we make sense of the universe and ourselves, and can also use the images, by virtue of the fact that words are not denotative symbols alone but clusters of allusive and metaphoric potential, for speculative construction. Metaphor is all the idiom of language untranslatable into a system of algebraic notation. By means of it we are enabled to think with and not only about, both the universe and ourselves.
>
> ELIZABETH SEWELL

Metaphor without process is allegory.

But the role of the metaphor is also priestly joining those things whose nature is revealed only in their joining.

CONCEPT AND PROPOSITION

Language is poetry, rhetoric, a rhythmic structure of images, the vitality of metaphor.

Language is also concept, and the proposition which is the embodiment of concept.

To abandon either character of language is to abandon language itself. The retreat from language is the retreat from the human into the natural. It is the nature of language to distinguish between subject and object, subject and predicate. No animal has a true language because no animal has a sense of the self as other than the not-self. Human existence cannot be sustained on propositional language alone, but it cannot be sustained without propositional language.

Yet much of our current social and intellectual difficulty arises from the abuse of propositional speech, a misunderstanding of the role of concepts, a grievous exaggeration of what happens and what can be accomplished by verbal propositions. Decades of work by philosophers, linguists and others have not yet succeeded in taming the devouring ferocity of the concept. Even those who would rebel against it or reject it make incessant use of an entirely traditional form of concept.

The fundamental error, the simple and obvious error, is mistaking the reference of concepts and of the words that make them up. The orthodox understanding of the reference of words is that they refer to things. Instead, they refer to events and occasions in our bodies. So long as we look for the reference of words in the character of things we will continue to deceive ourselves. We must, instead, discover the origin, the occasion, the character of those bodily events.

Therefore the idea of the concept, the concept of the concept, is itself a metaphor, for it is the linking of two disparate things. *All* propositions are metaphors. The forms of the verb "to be" are not, in themselves, commitments about "reality"; they are the linking terms in a metaphor.

Thus:

There is an encounter between a person and the reality of his world. The world he encounters is shaped for him in part by his languages, just as the sum total of the things he experiences make up his languages. The reality of his encounter emerges into consciousness thought and by means of the languages that are available to him. The propositional language is to some degree available to all people, even if only in its borrowed or inherited forms (thus cliché). To some it is available in a detailed, complex and variously specialized way. In either case, part of the experience emerges partly into the structure of verbal propositions.

And:

The proposition is always true as the embodiment of part of this person's experience of the world; its "truth" in any final sense depends on the adequacy of the experience, which is only in part testable by words.

The oppressive power of verbal systems does not reside in the convincing authority of the argument but in the anciently inherited power of words to evoke, engender or stimulate an image of order which has an iconic power. The scholar who offers his constructions as "truth" feels himself to be among the enlightened ones but his object is at best an icon, often an idol.

THE FUNCTION OF PROPOSITIONAL LANGUAGE

That was a shorthand statement of the work of all languages. The language of verbal propositions has unique functions, responsibilities and possibilities:

1. Communication among the languages
   It is the only one of the languages capable of talking about all the others.
2. Criticism
   It is the only one of the languages capable of relating each of the other languages to a larger context.
3. Equivalence
   It is the only one of the languages capable of restating, however partially and inaccurately, what has been done in the others.
4. Pedagogy
   A consequence of 1, 2, and 3.
5. Comprehensiveness
   Its range is greater than any other language.
6. Precision and flexibility
   Each language has its own characteristic precision, flexibility and range; none is comparable to the propositional language in having the quality of precision and flexibility over so wide a range.

The entranced discovery of these characteristics of propositional language led, not unnaturally, to a major exaggeration of its possibilities; its formulations came to be identified with truth. This has, indeed, led to terrible consequences, as false belief, false commitment, always does. The proper response to these consequences is not to reject the language, but rather the false belief about it. Verbal language can perform its proper function if it is understood properly and if it is related, as it has not been heretofore, to the whole activity of man.

As traditionally understood, the proposition is a failed tyrant. But, as a servant of the human enterprise, propositions are among the most elegant, the most powerful creations of human beings.

The proposition is metaphor, poetry. It is the only translatable poetry, for the proposition is the poetry of ideas, the metaphor linking acts of thought.

The proposition is the controlled and rhythmic dance of the mind.

The incestuous proposition finally becomes infertile, a eunuch guarding the prison of men detached from the experience of nature. The proposition in fruitful relation to natural experience becomes a means for the liberation from nature. To be human is to be a part of nature; art and science are the response to the natural. To be human is to be apart from nature; the *dance* of the mind is a natural rhythm, as rhythm is always of nature but, as the dance of the *mind*, it transcends nature.

Therefore to deny the proposition is to deny the human.

SYMBOL

Rhythm is the ordering of relation, felt but impalpable, controlling but fleeting. Symbol is the capturing, the condensing in a physical material of the essential rhythms. Thus, the symbol does not "stand for" something else; it condenses the essence, the rhythmic relations, i.e., the life, of a vital human experience. It is the coagulation of a felt ordering of structure and energy.

Thus, a symbol is anything that contains this kind of symbolic authority—a piece of music, a tree, a geometrical diagram (e.g., the mandala, the cross), a TV soap opera, a poem (by Auden or by Rod McKuen—symbolic authority is not to be identified with artistic quality), a city, a nation, etc.

A *symbolic structure*, is an organization of relations that carries this symbolic authority.

There are symbols of structure, symbols of energy, symbols of relation, symbols of purpose. Perhaps the greatest of all a people's symbols is their symbol of God or the gods.

> All of us are convinced of this much: nowhere in physical space are there such man-like beings as Zeus, or Athena, nor have they ever existed anywhere, barring lifeless statues. And yet, these mythical images express great and inescapable realities. But the realm in which they have reality is not the material outer world, it is the human soul itself. . . .
>
> The gods are not concepts, they are powers. In fact, they are the ruling powers of man's life.
>
> CARL F. VON WEIZSAKER[12]

> The gods are not stripped of their abstract, mythical character; what they were they remain—mere names of the gigantic forces they represent, forces which keep in motion the model of the world and the struggle of man.
>
> HERMAN BROCH[13]

Rhythm and symbol are so closely intertwined that one can hardly be said to exist without the other. Rhythm, indeed, is ever-present as the pace and markings in the relation of both objects and events. But rhythm so understood is simply flow. Only when it is condensed into formed actions or objects does it possess symbolic authority. Similarly, the symbol may not rightly be considered as a shorthand statement or a sign of another thing. As the condensation of the fundamental rhythm of a structure of things and events, symbol enables the experiencing mind to organize an experience that would otherwise be formless, inchoate.

Symbol gives rhythm its structure, rhythm gives symbol its energy.

When symbols lose their authority and therefore their capacity to organize human experience, rhythms become purposeless energies; our culture has been delivered over to the undefined and uncontrolled energies of technology, or the equally undefined and uncontrolled energies of the natural organism. We feel no intelligible relation between the two.

When rhythms lose their energy and therefore the authority to transmute power into purpose, symbols become empty things or inert events; our culture is burdened with the corpses of symbols that function only as talismen, weapons, badges of identification.

SACRALITY

Elements thus far have been "things", objects, felt rhythms, acts. Sacrality is not a thing but a quality, a dimension, an attribute.

Sacrality is the character of the center, that which holds everything together, the point from which essential energy radiates, the goal toward which all movement is directed. Since the sacred is felt to "exist" apart from, behind, above, within, its manifestation it is unusually (and originally) religious and the source of religion. Religions as they are known to us are the codifications of the experience of sacrality.

But the sacred is as necessary as food and air. This is why the sacred is felt as power, as independent of its occasion, as transmitted by or contained in objects but not confined to them, as controllable by magical or priestly acts. Only a modern man could think of sacrality as a quality rather than a force.

It is a matter of conviction and commitment whether things are sacred because they contain meaning and purpose or whether they have meaning and purpose because they are sacred.

When the codified religion loses, as it must because of the codification, the sense of the sacred, there are only certain possibilities open:

1. Sloth, acedia, indifference; the characteristic sin of secular man.
2. The desperate search for a new center, a new focus, a new structure of meaning; this gives rise to all those commitments that perform some of the functions of religion.
3. The rise of a new religion or the rejuvenation of the old.

Then if anyone says to you "Lo, here is the Christ!" or "There he is!" do not believe it. For false Christs will arise and show great signs and wonders, so as to lead astray, if possible, even the elect.

JESUS

Christ renders Anti-Christ possible. . . . The true Christian as an "I" faces the "thou" freely. He sees his fellow and, in this seeing freedom, loves him. When from this attitude love is stricken out while knowledge remains, then fellow-man is no longer approached as a subject. Now everything can be investigated in detached freedom. The subject now looks at an object.

But when knowledge without love becomes the hireling of the resistance against love, then it assumes the role which in the Christian mythical imagery is the role of the devil.

CARL F. VON WEIZSACKER[14]

There is, in this, one of the most terrible of all the Christian truths, that Christ not only makes anti-Christ possible but makes the anti-Christ. The dreadful sayings such as "I come to bring not peace but a sword" are literal truths which are wholly enigmatic in a metaphysics of substance. Yet they must be understood if the Christ is to be understood for the Christ defines us absolutely in our response.

. . . his death convicted us of sin, that it proved our kind to be so cruel that when goodness itself appeared amongst us we could find nothing better to do with it than kill it.

REBECCA WEST

THE WORLD AS A STRUCTURE OF THE SELF

"The world" here means all those things listed previously, now seen, as it were, from the outside in. *The self* starts from the viscera and rhythmically radiates outward. *World* starts at the edges of the physical limits and rhythmically responds inward.

The self does not create world; there is something "out there." But the self does not know the world as it is, but only as it is part of the particular processes of the self. The world "as it is" is the demon of the absolute that has for so long haunted the imaginations of men. The vain search for the world as it is has indeed taught us all we know about the world; but one of the things we now know from that search is that we can never know what "is" except in terms of our involvement in it.

World is not a mystical term; in English, it is not a word to capitalize when it does not appear at the beginning of a sentence; it is not a large, general, abstract word. "World" is the concreteness of persons and things in environing space.

No thing or person is defined for us absolutely. Things and persons are defined for us in our interaction with them. The ordering of our relation to them is our structure, our geometrics. The character of our interaction with them is our process, our dramatics. These two coordinates, enacted in space and time, define our world and set the logical purpose which irrevocably shapes our experience. No exhortation that leaves the world untouched can move a person to a new purpose, for his purpose is an inherent part of his world.

Our worlds overlap and intersect; we may to some degree or another share each other's worlds, for the things and persons of each world are in common and where there is a common humanity and a common culture there are symbolic structures—the organization of geometrics and dramatics—that can be partially shared. To love others is to participate their worlds.

Whatever exists in the world, as the world, apart from us, we can never know fully as it is in itself; we can know only those aspects of it that are revealed by investigatory techniques, those things as they are part of the rhythmic ordering of a personal world. Thus "objectivity" defeats itself by defining the whole of reality precisely in terms of those aspects of the world that are not being humanly participated in.

World exists as participated by the self, the self as it participates the world.

FORMATION OF THE WORLD

TONE AND COLOR

The conditions under which we experience light and, in the absence of touch, the character of *surfaces* and therefore *masses* are tone and color. Tone and color also establish both rhythmic relation and feeling.

SURFACE

Concave and convex, inside and outside, contained and container. Since the world is, to a very considerable degree experienced as surface, the ordering and perception of surfaces is a primary intellectual act. Surfaces are ordered as:

a. *surface of the body*
   segmentation within the self
   focus and occasion for erotic interaction.
b. *clothing*
   manifestation of role and status, determined by dramatics
   manifestation of self-image
   modulator of sensory activity
   erotic signal and stimulus
c. *containers*
   curved or rectilinear
   containers function differently depending on whether they are perceived as containers or containing (i.e., whether they are perceived from the outside or the inside).
d. *walls*
   a more intense mode of container, including the whole body.
   the surface of all objects
   sky, plain, the sea, etc.

CONTOUR

Contour is the edges of surfaces, volumes and masses. To analyze, it is necessary to see the edges of things, rather than their
binding surfaces.

SPACE

Space here is a specific experience and placement rather than a
general category. Spatial ordering is a proprioceptive act, not a
consequence of a single system (e.g. linear perspective as an abstraction of vision.)
  a. negative space is that which is between objects.
  b. positive space is that which contains objects.
  c. relational space is that which connects objects in an order.
     (all spaces are necessarily relational in their statement and
     effect, whether or not they are felt to be.)
Spaces are experienced in the abstract, if at all, only by an especially gifted few. Spaces are, for most, specific. They are rooms,
corridors, stairs, chests, drawers, closets, streets, plazas, churches,
deserts, forests, etc.

An analysis of intellectual systems which was confined to this
vocabulary of structure would be woefully incomplete—but it
would come closer to the heart of a system as an experience of the
world than prevailing attempts to judge the system as a description of reality. "History" as recounted is usually confined to a
study of a limited range of a people's dramatics. It should, rather,
begin with an account of their geometrics, the shape of their
"world", and then with a study of their dramatics, recount the
modulations of one geometric into another. Events (including
politics) are determined by structure and in their turn, as a part of
dramatics, enforce change and engender new structures.

Outline of a Theory of Structure: An Essay

All theory of structure, all structural analysis depends absolutely on two assertions:

1. Every event and thing is composed of two parts:
   a) The elements that compose it.
   b) The order and relation which hold the elements together.
2. This structure has a significance which is other than the significance of its elements.

There are further assertions subsidiary to the basic ones, but equally involved in the understanding of structure.

1. Strictly speaking, a structure ought to be understood as the elements, plus their ordering, plus the reference, the significance of that ordering. Keeping to the term itself, the analogy is not engineering—where the primary concern is the forces that are involved—but architecture, where all the elements are interwoven to make an integral whole.
2. Structure does not exist without content ("meaning") nor is there a content separable from the structure.
3. Whatever meaning or reference is contained within the separate elements, they cannot rightly be detached from the structure in which they are embodied. Nor does any element

exist apart from *some* structure; to attempt to remove an element from a structure or to treat it as though it had a separable meaning is simply to transfer it from one structure to another, thus fixing it into a new structure of meaning.

4. Each element of a structure has its own structure which it brings to, and therefore conditions with, any structure which it enters as an element. All structures are hierarchies of structures; if there is a monad or a basic structure, or even a basic logic of structure it is by no means evident at this time. If the analogy of chemistry is at all sound, the successive divisions of the atomistic elements do not lead to a monad but to energy. Thus is structure not finally reducible to an elementary base structure but to the energy of process.

5. Some structures are "natural" as a part of experienced nature. Some are man-made. Man-made structures cannot escape from natural structures. There is no man-made structure so abstract that its materials, its substructures or its constituent elements are not in some way natural. Thus man-made structures (whether architectural structures, systems of thought or music) are simultaneously and interchangeably the symbolic embodiment of the sense of meaning and the instrument of organization and control of the natural structures from which they emerge.

6. Specific conditions of the modern Western intellectual structure have produced a conflict between centripetal and centrifugal analyses. The word "structure" has been associated with an analytical procedure that eliminates all the higher or outer layers of the structure in favor of a core of basic operation. This has yielded, not a base structure, but the logic of structure. A work of architecture does depend on an irreducible minimum of relation—that between supported and supporting members—and no work of architecture can be even approximately understood unless this primitive dialectic is understood. But this, the irreducible minimum of con-

structional logic, is no more than the beginning; it is held in common; it is the originating definition of all architecture, even those forms which combine supporting and supported into single tensile forms (primitive reed huts, geodesic domes, etc.). The question that matters is, "How are the twin functions, supporting-supported, achieved?" The answer to this question is, the *whole* building, for there is no part of it that is not consequentially related to other parts.

Thus a structure is not the exclusive core of its logic but the whole of which the logic is a part.

7. There are structures that are clearly natural (the body, landscapes). There are others that are clearly man-made (art works, philosophical systems). There are still others that emerge from human work, but are not describable so clearly as natural or man-made. These include mathematics and also music. Music appears to be man-made but is built on a series of relations that may be described as discoveries. Mathematics appears to be a discovery but has a style that is a consequence of human expression. Not only art but philosophical systems have a spatial, and therefore geometrical, order emerging from a geometry that is either a discovery or a human creation. This is probably a question not to be settled theoretically but only in the hard cases of analysis.

8. The word "structure" inevitably carries with it the connotations of its analogical source; structure is incorrigibly an architectural term and connotes such forces as thrust and gravitation acting in a spatial ordering. This connotation is all to the good, for the cosmic image that is finally at the core of meaning and purpose is, of necessity, spatial; a disposition of persons and things in a meaningful order. But the analogy, however apt, ought not to dominate the reference of the word; structure is also a word properly applied to sets of relations that are not so tangible and spatial. Rhythm, for example, is a vital aspect of all structures. There are fatal in-

adequacies in Lévi-Strauss' use of the word "structure;" nevertheless it is perfectly proper to use the word to include the constructional logic which he finds at the origin of structure.

This much said by way of preliminary hypothesis, it is necessary to look next at the various kinds of structures and the ways in which they interact with each other. Here, the body is useful as an illustration, but also as the instrument by which all other structures are known. If the body is unknown or falsely known, all the others are falsified. The body illustrates, further, the extreme difficulty of talking about structure apart from energy; so many of the bodily structures "are" what they do.

Structures of the body, then, are dynamic and static, active and passive, projective and receptive. These can be separated, if at all, only for the sake of analysis. Even the senses are not passive receiving-instruments but are active probes into the environment.

The choice of where to begin outlining the body's structures is quite an arbitrary one. Perhaps the senses are the most useful point of origin for an investigation; by them we experience the world, and thereby they either determine or powerfully influence what we *do* in the world.

None of the senses can be understood as a conduit through which floods an undifferentiated mass of sense data. Rather each serves, even at its most passive, as an instrument for screening and classification. Each is limited, and therefore selects from presented data (sense impressions), but each is varied in its pattern of sensitivity. Human hearing does not go beyond 18,000 cycles per second. Middle-aged hearing may go no higher than 10,000 cps. But more is involved than simply limitations, for within the range of hearing the ear is patterned in its areas of sensitivity. Therefore a sound structure (say music), striking the ear, arrives at the brain only after being repatterned by the physiological structure of the acoustic nerves.

These patterns (still, perhaps, too elementary to be called structures) are both physiological and cultural. There are sound structures we must learn to hear. In the absence of learning, what we hear is not a strange structure but noise.

A complete theory of bodily structure would have to include something that is still only slightly understood: that the senses are no more isolated from each other, than they are just conduits for information. Rather they interact with each other in extraordinarily complex ways. It is this interaction that makes possible a structuring of the nervous system that is not just a single structure but a hierarchy of structures. The structure at one level is not transmitted *exactly* by the nervous system. Rather it triggers the operation of the next higher structure and reverberates through adjacent structures. This process not only accounts for apparently inexplicable responses, where conduct seems unlike the stimulus, it is also one of the refutations of behaviorism. A very slight, weak, or even distorted signal from one structure, can set off the full operation of the next, just as a very powerful signal might equally be controlled by the restraints of another structure. This incommensurability of stimulus and response is ultimately the source of freedom of action and of creativity.

Again, these structures are both natural and cultural: the relative proportioning of the senses is culturally determined or at least culturally rooted.

Much of the physiology of this is entirely unknown. What is known would fill another book.

Outward activity follows the same principles, and participates in the same structuring, with its roots comparably in nature and culture.

So, there is a hierarchy of structures making up the process of reception and action. There is, further, the structure of the body itself, the system of its weights and acts, its solid areas and its movements. There is the structure of the body which is shared by all humans. There are the structures that distinguish the sexes; the patterns of concave and convex, of hard and soft (the rhythm of relation and act are decidedly different in a man and a woman). There are structures of bodily action that distinguish nations and (probably to a lesser extent), races. (Historical films that were convincing in the 1930s now are quite out of phase, for the actors so clearly move with the rhythms of the thirties. The Williamsburg, [Virginia] reconstruction owes as much to the Bauhaus as it does to old Williamsburg.)

But the body never exists—cannot survive—in isolation from all the other structures of its context, both natural and cultural. The earliest of these, still perhaps the most powerful, are those of nature herself. Some of these are only slightly felt as structures, but more as rhythms. The pronounced but delicate changes of day and night, seasons, weather, are felt as rhythmic process. But rhythm is felt, finally as a shape in space as well as time, and so becomes a structure. What effect these structures have on the structure of the body and the imagination no one now knows.

Earth structures are more obviously structures. What effect they have on the body and on the imagination is no better known. These are the conditions of "natural" man, in his flesh, on the earth, in the context of light, air, space, night, wind, rain.

None of these structures are inert, for among them there play the incessant workings of need and desire. The fulfillment of either need or desire requires a technique of some kind, but both need, desire and technique require ordering the inchoateness of experience. Ordering is a part of living and lived structures—the articulation of the body, the shape of the earth, the rhythm of weather and seasons. But technique is choice and decision. The satisfaction of needs and desires requires hierarchy and pattern.

Needs and desires inevitably include both propitiation and the yearning for understanding, for the context of life is not only the necessary and desirable but also the fearful and mysterious. Thus human creativity begins to engender orderings of things which include their relations, as well as their origin and purpose. Thus are born the great symbolic structures that fix for us the flux of experience, define shape and direction, so that we can construct a human life within the measureless expanse and variety.

These structures are, as themselves, never felt or seen. But neither do they exist without concrete embodiment. There is no evidence that the creativity of men ever can hold them as pure abstractions. Rather they are known, even to those who are engendering them, as they are incarnated in the physical material. This, then, provides a further clue to structural theory, for there begins to emerge a sense of the elements of this process. These are:

1. The creative intelligence of the person.
2. The instruments of that intelligence, including:
   a) The body-mind; for example, the trained hand of the artist, the logical intelligence of the philosopher.
   b) Tools.
3. Language; words, in their discursive or poetic form; logic; stone, etc.
4. The contents of the language occasion. Poet and philosopher are always writing about something, the engineer has a particular river to bridge over, the painter paints a deer in a cave, or a crucifixion on the altar.

No one of these is separable from another. And each has its own structure which conditions its interaction with the others. It is not true that we divide and order reality according to the structures of our verbal language; we have too many different languages for our commerce with reality and too much ingenuity in the use of too many different kinds of tools. These combinations are finite, and each language, each tool, each subject, contains its own characteristic structure, which both limits and conditions the workings of the others. This is why all creativity has a quality of the uncanny, for it involves structures and energies beyond the reach of the conscious, calculating intelligence. Practitioners of the art of each language claim the right to authority for their language; but reality is far more complex than that.

Each language must be known distinctly in its structure and energies, insofar as it is possible to think of them separately. But this is difficult, for the languages exist apart from their actions only ideally. Their life, their vitality is in their commerce, their interchange, with each other. What we do know are the products and occasion for these engenderings. To know languages as such is to know possibilities only. They are truly known only in their consequences, their products, only in their fruitful relation. It is by seeing what they do with each other that we can know what they "are."

What are these "consequences," these "products?" Simply—all the things human beings make, including all the patterns of action they have established for doing their work and their mutual exchange. To "make" here refers not just to objects but to systems, structured thought, rhythmic procedures, institutions with their formed and forming processes, manners and social forms, art works, tools, systems of production, styles of clothing. Insofar as man makes himself, "making" includes his body rhythms, the pattern of his dreams, his neuroses.

Reciprocally these made things are truly known only as the consequences of a process of engendering; they cannot be grasped in themselves, as somehow independent of reference to the process that produced them. Each receives its characteristic structure out of a process of creativity, each is sustained and enlivened by that structure. But the structure is not created out of nothing; it is at the confluence of the exchange between all the structures that have engendered it.

Much of this is accepted already, as far as certain of these manifestations are concerned. Dreams for example, are rarely any longer taken seriously "in themselves." Rather they are symbols of something much more fundamental in the psyche than the apparently arbitrary and senseless jumble of exchanges, transformations and juxtapositions that make up the dream as such. Further, serious students of dreams know that dream elements have no detachable meaning, no dictionary meaning, but only the meaning of their function within a particular symbolic whole.

Insofar as other structures lend themselves to comparable analysis, some scholars will accept this model. But the symbolic expressiveness of dreams is an inadequate model for many structures, for the very reason of its characteristic revelatory importance. By dropping below—or out of—conscious control, the dream is isolated from the whole process of exchange, cut off from the structures of tools, techniques and language, from the disciplined encounter with matter. A dream is the free play, and therefore revelation, of the creative mind. A dream gives indispensable and irreplaceable access to psychic structures, but it is no apt model for human creativity.

Feeling this, most (not all) scholars reject the use of their material as another form of symbolic expressionism. It is necessary that they do so, for it is the only way they have of protecting the integrity of the objects they are responsible for. But an adequate theory of structure should enable us to see how all human creations emerge from and reveal the structures and the creative processes that are characteristically human.

An exhaustive treatment of such a theory could not avoid the question of causality: the image of cause as operating one-dimensionally, in a line, inevitably reduces the structuring process to simple expressionism. It is quite true that a dream can reveal latent homosexuality, for there is a direct, unmediated causal relation between repressed desires and the association of dream images. There are certainly other direct causal links of like nature. But to say (as I have heard said) that Shakespeare's *Richard II* is nothing but a study of Richard's homosexuality is not only to destroy the play but to destroy the possibility of understanding human creativity. Shakespeare's Richard is clearly homosexual. That is one focal point for the play's energies. But the play itself is the intersection of a number of structures: (1) Shakespeare's psychic life, of which his sexuality is a part; (2) the structures of English history as Shakespeare knew them; (3) the structures of Tudor policy; (4) the structures of human personality (as distinct from the unconscious processes of Shakespeare's own psyche); (5) the structures of English poetic speech; (6) the structures of the English countryside, weather, social institutions; (7) the structures of the theater.

Such structures are not animate; to speak of them as engendering a new structure is a figure of speech. What happens is the apprehension of all these structures by the perceptual equipment of a creative intelligence; the engendering is a human act. In a limited intelligence the causation may be limited, and the play (or the bombing policy), may be an expression of suppressed sexuality. But the simplest action or object is enacted under the condition of a variety of structures and the final result is a consequence of them all and participates in them all.

But the result is not reducible to any. The thing itself has its structure and is known by grasping its structure. Knowing that it is a product of the processes of many structures, we can carefully feel our way outward to those others, treating each for what it is— not a separate thread but part of a fabric of meaning.

Implicit in this analysis are two things of major importance: If every structure, every system, every representation, is engendered from the creative interaction of a number of structures, it follows inevitably that no structure is ever, or ever conceivably can be, an authoritative equivalent of another. It may reveal more or less of another which has been made the particular object of attention. That revelation depends on the relative weighting of the participant structures, and is never a complete or authoritative statement about any. Therefore the demon of the absolute is exorcised: "This is true," "This is the will of God", "This is the nature of the real". Those are false gods, demons that make us restless in the night.

Thus, we can never know "reality" directly; we can only know the structures that emerge from our experiences of reality. Nor are any of these permanent achievements. So long as they are held tentatively, as an achievement, in the freshness of their creation, we can sense those structures that engendered them. As soon as we withdrew from them, set them up as authorities, use them as weapons or measures, they go inert and deceive us.

For as we become different, the structure that was once the occasion for a living intercourse with reality becomes something different also. This is the second major implication and consequence of this theory—we can experience structures only by the complex structures that make up our body and history. Since that body and that history are private to me, the reality engendered from my experience is only mine and not replaceable by any other. But even as mine, it is never fixed or still. The structure engendered from my experience changes me as a new part of my world, my reality. Thus the structures by which I apprehend the world, participate in reality, are different, and the world I construct becomes subtly (and truly) different.

Thus structure modulates into process, which is the control of the energies of being alive and human. And this whole discussion is falsified because it addresses itself only to half of what is a complex whole. Yet there are dangers, terrible dangers, in the premature search for energies, because it is only through structures that energy is controlled into process. Our culture may now be dying of energies uncontrolled and misunderstood. Only as we know structure can we safely try to know energy.

If we can know only *by* structure, what then can we know *of* structure? If knowledge remakes us, how can we know the very thing that is transforming what we know with? The process as described makes any analysis comparable to dissecting one's own eye. In many ways it is; for the very act of analysis alters both the structures of analysis and the structure being analysed.

But fortunately the pain of this intrusion is not quite comparable to the dissection of the eye. Much can be known and if, finally, all cannot be known, by the very nature of what is known, still we can understand the generality of what is happening and, in understanding, grasp a little more of our humanity.

Structures, however complex in their individuality, are not wholly inaccessible. At the base of all structuring is a common function, a common responsibility, that of organizing human experiences under the conditions of the earth. Thus there are elementary conditions to fulfill that provide the outline of the analysis.

There are three elements in the origin of any structure:

1. The organic energies of the natural order
2. The static geometry of the abstract order
3. The creative will of man.

A structure can be described (although not defined with philosophic precision) as the organization of the three elements. For these are the basic, the constituting elements of human existence.

All persons of all times are born into the burgeoning, fecund, delightful, threatening energies of nature, felt in the passions and pleasures of the body.

Abstract order is not quite so powerfully and immediately evident, for it is just that—an abstraction from experience. Static geometry is evident in nature only in the structure of cells (which would not have been evident to most people during most of history), a few natural forms such as honeycombs, etc., and the shapes of certain kinds of stones when following the lines of natural cleavage. But elementary geometry is easily abstracted from natural experiences: the vertical from trees, the standing body, cliffs; the horizontal from the earth, large stones, etc.; catenary curves from hanging vines; trigonometrical spirals in the disposition of branches and some seed pods; cylinders from the tree trunks; rectilinear forms from stones; the intricate curves and arches of various skeletons. It is a more sophisticated act of abstraction, but a further stage in the identification of geometry, when it can be traced out along lines of force: the curve of thrown objects, the angular action of simple levers, the vertical of dropped objects, an in and out relation of movement through entrances. And so on.

The "creative will" of the person is only in part to be considered an elemental, for it never exists apart from determination by its cultural symbolism. Thus we know it only in its derivative forms. But all human structures are products of decisions and acts, so there is an unconditioned will at the center. It is a fair presumption that all culture began from the interaction of this primordial will with the elemental energy and statics. Thus culture is coterminous with being human, probably in the form of the enacted story (myth and ritual), the idol (the work of art), the circumscribed sacred space (architecture), and, elementally, technics.

All structural analysis is an attempt to get back to the heart of structure; the heart, the core of structure is the particular mode of interaction of these three under the condition of the given structures discussed earlier as the structures of the body and the acting intelligence, the tools, the material and the subject. This core is the aim of the analysis, both because it is the center of the generation of structure and because, in its centrality, it is the core of person and meaning. Finally, structure and meaning are inseparable. Rightly understood, structure *is* meaning.

The very existence of these elementals in structured relations presupposes other elementals, which are placed here in a secondary position, only because they are consequences of the basic structure. The imposition of geometric shape on energy establishes rhythms. Direction and energy determine goals; goals become the definition of value; value structured into the social order becomes the geometry of relations, the determiner of class structure and social ordering.

Described, these elements appear too linear, or too hierarchical. The elementals are never felt in isolation. They interact on each other in wild and unpredictable patterns. The image of time may emerge from the structuring of energy, but its image has a singular authority that tends to shape the image of energy. The rhythm of cities shapes the direction of energy as it moves among the static shapes. Accordingly streets are static areas connecting human acts, or they are channels of energetic movement. Stasis or movement affect the nervous system, which then acts accordingly, and so it goes. That is why the "history of ideas" is so futile an enterprise, and "eternal" truths are so transitory. An idea or a "truth" is one thing in one set of relations and something different in another. It carries with it its own inherent structure, but, always subjected to the forces of its context, it functions differently and therefore "is" something different, in each historical context.

To trace the process is ultimately impossible; it is terrifying even to contemplate it. The happiest person is the one who has found a mode of living in some degree of harmony among the various structures that impinge on him and emerge from him. Very few people succeed in that. Intellectuals usually do so only by the assertion of a limited range of structures, and the ruthless exclusion of all others (which is why intellectuals do so badly in the political world).

But all is not lost. The process is not simply activity; it is consequential. Process, structured energy, produces forms which are the definitive deposit of a continuous activity. It is by the analysis of forms, then, that structures become uncovered. Structure is the meaning of form, form is the representation and, therefore, the revelation of structure.

In the presentation of this model, moving centrifugally, the center is the essential structure, surrounded by those elementals which are an inevitable concomitant of the structure. Form, then, is the outer limit, the visible or tangible, the evident.

Structure is inevitable; the specifications of form are not. Forms are subject to accident and caprice; Mexican saints have Christian designations because of the accident of the Spanish conquest, but structurally they are often Mayan or Aztec.

Thus, a "formal analysis" is never sufficient for the definition of any work. Yet it is the only route to the structure. On the other hand, the delusion that structure can "exist" apart from form can only lead to Lévi-Strauss's structuralism which, by virtue of being abstracted from materialization, is not structure at all, but logic.

Thus we have successive "layers" (still using analogical speech) of generality and particularity. By definition, forms are particular to each discipline and finally to each person. Attempts to set up correlations among different forms are always superficial and misleading, which is what interdisciplinary studies so often are. But each successive step toward the center brings a higher degree of generality. In coherent cultures the central or essential or generative structure is common to most, if not all, major cultural and intellectual expressions.

The difficulty with such an assertion is that, in consistency with this argument, it is very nearly undemonstrable or unprovable. Structures never appear pure. They are manifest only as forms. It has been an essential part of this argument that no structure ever appears in isolation, for every deep structure interacts with other structures in the process of emergence as form. This is not so simple a matter as conceiving a pure structure, hidden or distorted by an overlay of other structures, but nonetheless "existing" at the center. Rather the central or essential structure emerges only by means of its interaction with others.

Essential structure is not to be thought of only as an abstraction emerging from successive analyses, as though there were an impenetrable center, which can be sensed only by sighting along the various special analyses. That was what Plato was talking about as an Idea; but vainly sought in its purity because, in his structure, immediacies were abhorrent.

Purity is only in the immediacies, the particularities, the concrete.

Even so, the central structure is not hypothesis, a functional abstraction, and unknowable. Its presence is pervasive and powerful. Its presence is the source of cultural coherence; its absence the obstruction of culture.

The phenomenon of the deep, essential structure accounts for many things that are so difficult to account for causally. "Falling in love" is finding the person who completes the appropriate external form of a deep structure. Religious conversion is double, either finding the forms that make possible the realization of a deep structure, or accepting a fundamental alteration in the deep structure itself. The immense satisfaction derived from this or that art work, or music, is not because of titillation of this or that part of the nervous system; it is because this work is a form of the deep essential structure. A politician might succeed and seem to shape his age, while better, wiser, more able men languish unrecognized. This is not the caprice or injustice of history; the lesser man is the means for giving form to the essential structure of the nation while the forms of the abler man are private to him.

Thus the central structure, the core structure is felt rather than described. It is finally a mode and a function, not a thing. It is known in its workings, in its effects, and thus brought into the day and into history. Plato, one of the wisest of men, was quite consistent; there is nothing to do with the Idea but look at it. But the right to look at it is bought with the price of human experience.

Plato, one of the wisest of men, knew also that he had to go back into the world of experience to lead out those who would not be able to follow him from a distance and without instruction. Thereby he made of himself a Bodhisattva. But the tragedy of Syracuse was not that it was a political failure; it was a consequence of a false definition of structure. Human life is not lived in the indulgence of King Dionysus, but it is not lived in the contemplation of ultimate structure either.

I am neither Plato, nor a mystic, so I do not know what Plato and the mystics have seen. If they have seen the heart of structure, the mystic rose, they are singularly blessed. But they are fully human only as they do not create hierarchies of illuminati or present an ideal so distant from experience, but only as they return to the world of forms, the habits and orders, the exchanges and dramas, the objects and institutions that can place all those who will in the flow of the great engendering.

Which is the definition of the creators.
Which is, more importantly, the definition of the Christ.
And the bounden duty and service of the Christian.

Thus, the deep, core structure of a culture is felt by every serious person who is part of that culture. It may or may not be "seen" by the few blessed ones, the saints. The scholar, the critic, is not likely to be a blessed one, and is required to be other than simply a serious person sensing something out there. Guarding against the danger of expecting more than his techniques can achieve, he can work his analytical way along the line till he can do more than simply sense the existence of the undefinable; he can point to it verbally with some verbal accuracy.

These analytical procedures are identifiable in outline.

1. The first stage is represented in this essay by a pregnant void; the analytical procedures are appropriate to the forms of each specific discipline, and thus develop according to the requirements of that discipline. They cannot be recapitulated here. The procedures I am proposing do not abolish these laws but fulfill them.

Increasingly, however, the sense of an isolated discipline is breaking down and disciplines appear, even in academia, not just in hyphenated pairs but hyphenated trios. This suggests burrowing beneath the surface structure, the forms, to the structures beneath that link varied forms. It suggests also a definition of study as defined by the requirements of different bodies of evidence rather than inherited methods. It has the further advantage of making this level of analysis not only useful but essential to the central analysis. For, if the generative structure is known only under the conditions of its emergence in interaction with the structures of its manifestations, then those structures must be *known*. Their potential and their limits have to be known in themselves, as possibilities. No study whose emergent form is verbal can assume that its language is transparent to an abstract truth. Rather its structure finally emerges only under the condition of the verbal language, inseparably linked to it. It is "true", not as a container for a thing, but only as it functions "truly" within the living structures of those who read it.

And so with all the limiting and revelatory structures, the body-mind, the tools, the subject, the language.

2. Once this is done (in practice these steps are probably done concurrently) analysis is carried to the stage of the secondary structures, those that stand between the deep structures and the form. The vocabulary at this point becomes, of necessity, strikingly aesthetic. For "structure" *is* an aesthetic category and rightly so. The most important, perhaps the profoundest understanding of the human psyche to be developed in our day is not the mythological symbolism of depth psychology but the sense of structure of the whole person in his world. " . . . the person and his world are a unitary, structural whole: the hyphenation of the phrase being-in-the-world expresses precisely that. . . World is the structure of meaningful relationships in which a person exists and in the design of which he participates." So says Rollo May[15] in summing up this principle.

There is an enormous amount yet to learn about these things, but enough is now understood for one to assert confidentally that the psyche of a person is inseparable from (perhaps "is", whatever that curious word means) the structure of its lived world, a structure which is an organization of space and time—rightly, space-time—with the ordering, movement, relations which place the person in space-time. These things are known in the intellectual community but casually; they are judged to apply to persons only, not to the objective occasion for the working of the critical intellect. One purpose of this essay could be summed up by saying that it tries to demonstrate that these psychic structures are not critically, intellectually irrelevant, but that they are the source of *all* forms, they are the modes of actualization of the deep structures which are, finally, the meaning of human existence. Scholarship, to be faithful to its responsibility, cannot stand apart from the world, but must truly be in the world.

Since the forms, not the deepest core structure, are available for analysis, the method of analysis is vital. Too much is yet unknown to make possible even a fully-detailed outline but it can be sketched with some accuracy.

The controlling image is *space-time*. Analytically space and time can be looked at in different moments, and certain categories seen as more related to one aspect of the space-time continuum than the other.

The categories of space include first of all the *image of space* itself, whether it is limitless or bounded, the definition of its boundaries, whether it is positive or negative (does space contain things, or is space simply that which exists between things?). There is, further, the question of *shape* and *direction*. (The resolution of direction is one of the linkages between space and time.)

Direction (or directionlessness) determines the cosmic image out of which emerges the ordering of *relation* (which finally determines the moral category of *purpose*). Neither space nor time exist apart from the experiencing person. There is no structure of space-time describable from outside of a particular structure or as existing outside the experience of persons. Thus relation is not simply an ordering of things within the spatial structure but the placement of persons in the ordering (it may, indeed, be a displacement of persons, as appears to be the case in much prehistoric religion, where the person is less important than the animal image).

This ordering of relation defines basic geometric *figure*, which in turn determines the direction of authority and submission. Thus Western space involves linear shape, vertical direction and, inevitably, hierarchical organization. Much argumentative thought is less important for its assertions, its purported description of "reality," than it is for its implied structure. It bewilders and astonishes theologians and philosophers to discover that systems which once reigned supreme now meet with indifference. This indifference is not due to any special depravity. Rather a spatial image dominated by purposeful time (which requires logical definition) has been replaced by a different ordering of relation in which logic plays no more than an incidental part.

The categories of time include *direction*, of course, as well as, in its own way, *shape*. Time receives a shape by rhythms, which translate time into space and space into time. The governing categories of rhythms are *tempo* and *proportion*.

Rhythm is not only a decisive subcategory of time. It is also a crucial aspect of the analysis, for it enlivens the structure, turning it from an inert abstraction to a living experience.

These are more than empty analytical categories, less than the reality of experience. They are the elements of structure which "en-liven" and "in-form" the surface structure, the forms, of experience. Thus no external experience can be grasped unless its motivating structures are grasped; but, equally, no structure or element of a structure can be isolated from its involvement with the other elements, the material and the structures of the material which create the final embodiment.

Thus, structural analysis is not a matter of peeling off the successive layers of experience to get at its logical core. It is a matter of holding, within the structures of apprehension, the completeness of the thing from its surface appearance to its central and most abstract core. To lose awareness of any element at any level is to falsify the wholeness of the experience.

Which is, obviously, inevitable. The initial fact is that the observer is never wholly outside the experience (object or event), but apprehends it only by entering it into his own structures of awareness; therefore, the experience is never knowable in itself but only as a part of another structured experience. The claim to truth, to knowledge, is normally an assertion of the hierarchical value of one structure over others. It is not within the range of human abil-

ity to be quite so comprehensive. Something is always lost or distorted.

Thus, structural analysis is never a final thing, but a dialogue, a
process, always open to revision, to other apprehensions.

For this reason and for others, this whole account is invalidated,
rendered wholly void, if it is not seen as one dimension of analysis
which must also include the analysis of energy, the process by
which structures are activated. Thus space and time are understandable only as the space-time setting for the acts of generation
and transformation in which the crucial category is metaphor.

PART THREE

Process: Energy and Dramatics

PROEM

There is no structure that is not involved in process; nature itself has a history; time, change, transformation, are parts of the life even of crystals. Only humans have a sense of the fixed, the eternal, the absolute, the unchanging. Structures are abstractions from experience. "Being" is a metaphor.

Fear of death creates the symbols of the absolute; the tragic fascination with what is most feared compels people to flee from change into the fixed structures that are the fatality of what is most human in them.

As organisms, we are and will forever remain subject to the forces and the structures of organisms; we are a part of nature.

As humans we are, by nature, divided from nature, subject to the telics and geometrics and dramatics that are a part of being human.

We cannot successfully resign either our nature or our humanity.

The tragedy of man is not that he is going to die but that he knows he is going to die.

As human, knowing good and evil, we have the problem of knowing what is good and what is evil.

As an organism that knows, we want both to live within organic wholeness and to escape from it. Which way of living is good and which is evil?

Divided from nature, our humanity seeks to know and to use nature.

All culture is an attempt to reproduce the wholeness of nature in a human society. Some cultures achieve, in parallel, the rhythmic harmony of the natural order. There is an incorrigible inclination to upset that balance; to use the knowledge and disrupt the harmony.

Therefore process is the act of involvement with nature, for process is the condition of the natural. But process is the act of the characteristically human, using nature in the fated attempt to escape from nature.

Process is enacted by means of and under the condition of structure.

Process is the transformation of one structure into another.

THE CONDITIONS OF PROCESS

Organisms do not act with purpose; they respond. A plant does not "reach" for water or the sun, as even professional literature sometimes has it; its cells divide in the direction of moisture or light. Purpose is a consequence of the primal division; only human beings act with true purpose. But purpose does not give comprehensiveness.

Every organism is its hierarchical ordering of structures. Every organism responds only to those stimulations that are accessible to its particular nervous system. Some have a wider range than others, and greater flexibility, yet none can perceive or act beyond what is possible in its own communication system.

Some knowledge, some responses, are inherent in an organism; the dog will scratch the living-room rug after defecating on it. Some responses can be learned according to the limit of the organism's capacity, which is a truism. All learned responses are shaped by the patterns inherent in the organism, which is not a truism. The whole study of man begins with the grasp of those patterns, those models, those paradigms.

Man, divided from and facing his world, wants to know that world. "To know" had originally little of the sense we give it now—to understand and make true verbal propositions about. Rather "to know" is to participate in, to enter with meaning, to be in harmony with.

Divided from his world, man knows himself as something other than his world; in duality is the origin of self-consciousness. Because he is separate, all his works are caught into the remorseless and inescapable energies of organicity.

Because he is an organism he knows the world only through the instruments of the organism—the senses.

Because he is a man, and conscious, the action of his senses is shaped by the telics, the geometrics and the dramatics of his humanity.

Because he is an organism, what he can perceive is limited by the limits of the organism.

The world man perceives is always a partial world.

The nervous system is not like a telephone switchboard, inertly carrying information. It is like a complex musical instrument, its response determined in part by the stimulation it receives but in greater part by the structure, the organization, the texture and the tuning of the instrument itself.

Thus to know the stimulation ("reality"), it is inescapably necessary to know the shape and the tuning of the responding instrument.

The "shape" of the responding instrument is the structure that is built up of its many structures. Its "tuning" is a part of its nature as an organism. It is, perhaps even in greater part, an act of culture.

Therefore knowledge is always and everywhere an act of culture, a part of culture. It is a culture's way of contending with and giving shape to its experience of the world.

THE NATURE OF PROCESS

Duality exists in nature, but dualism does not. Night and day, male and female, up and down, I and you, are parts or aspects of wholeness. Only man can—and must—see them as two.

Thus the tautology: the processes of nature are natural. The structures are harmoniously independent, polyphonically dependent. Structures are related to each other, or are transformed into another according to their own natural processes and the slow, determined rhythms of the organic order.

Man, as a part of nature, participates in the organic processes. But man alone (and man, alone), is aware of himself in the process, as part of it and, by thinking about it, as something other than nature. Simultaneously desiring the natural processes and fearing them, seeking to identify himself with them, to dominate them, to escape from them, he creates structures that themselves shape his relations and his transformations.

Therefore, "between" (the quotation marks because all prepositions are value laden and ought to be set apart), "between" man and his world are the formal structures that shape the world as he actually knows it. There is never an escape from the natural structures of human experience; the most fanatic yogi disciplines a human body in the attempt to transcend it; the most extreme idealist thinks in the structured logic and the classifying vocabulary of his natural language. The natural structures are both context and material, both possibility and condition, for the uniquely human structures.

These formed structures exist and are themselves known only in their particularities. Within each is a process that is inalienably human, then and now, a process which can be analyzed as telics, dramatics, geometrics.

Obedient to the principles of the primordial logic, dramatics is manifested in a narrative (the myth) which is enacted ritualistically in the geometrics of a particular place, with particular objects. This is the primordial act of being human.

The simplest drama, the most elementary ritual enacted in the clearing or a space marked on the ground, using a stone, a block of wood, or a bone are still the basic ingredients of the human consciousness.

These four—myth, ritual, art, architecture—are the generators of the human, and the means men have used to create and define their humanity.

All that is human, however removed in appearance, is a complication of, an extension of, or derivative from, these four.

THE METAPHORIC PROCESS

Metaphor is not a thing but an act; not a structure but a process. Structure alone is imprisonment, petrification, death. Energy alone is dispersion, disintegration, death. Only as structure is energized, as energy is structured, is there life. In nature, the joining of structure and energy is a natural act; objects and creatures pass from one to another in the rhythmic pulsations of their organic history. And so with natural man.

But man is not only natural; he seeks to know and to master. In man as transcending nature, metaphor is the joining of structure and process. Metaphor is the forming of the human.

Functions and types of metaphor:

1. Equivalence and classification
2. Participation
3. Exchange
4. Transformation
5. Control

Metaphor, therefore, is understandable only as relation, linking, passage. Its analytic understanding requires grasping:

1. Structure

   Which involves knowing what is equivalent to what; the basis of all classification.

2. Direction

   Which determines not only what is being classified but the order of the classification. Are the terms of the metaphor meeting in equal union or is one subordinate to the other?

The first two determine and require the third:

3. Function

   Is one term enabled by the metaphor to participate in, be open to the other? And which is which?

   Is one term being changed into the other?

   Is one term being used to control the other?

The metaphoric act appears under various forms:

1. Words
   "Metaphor" as traditionally defined.
2. Objects
   The symbol functioning as metaphor.
3. Acts
   Actions can be performed purely for their own sake as a situation requires. Others can be performed solely for their metaphoric purpose. Others, perhaps most, are both useful (even if only as reminiscent survivals), and metaphoric. Acts have style and style is a form of metaphor.

An understanding of metaphor, of 'symbol-as-metaphor,' is seriously handicapped by the arbitrary selection of one direction. Does the spire symbolize the penis or the penis the spire? It would be more faithful to the character of metaphor to see that both penis and spire are, first of all, what they are, and second, that they contain the act of engendering verticality. The phallus (the penis as metaphor) directs verticality toward its fruitfulness, the spire fruitfulness toward verticality.

Sex is a metaphor of religion as much as religion is a metaphor of sex, which Saint Theresa, Bernini and the sculptors of Khajuraho knew perfectly well.

TYPES OF METAPHOR

The great metaphors:

1. The city
2. The state
3. The body
4. The natural order
5. Geometry

Each of these contains a large number of potential metaphors, and the potentiality of a large number of symbolic acts:

1. The city
   The circle, the grid, the accidental; open and closed, horizontal and vertical, active and static.
   Does the city create community or does community create the city? Can there be community without the city?
2. The state
   An organism or a mechanism.
   Hierarchy or web. Permeable or enclosed. Power. The image of the state controls the image of the body.
3. The body
   Boundary or transition. Active and passive. Bilateral symmetry. Hard and soft. Concave and convex. The image of the body controls the image of the state.
4. The natural order
   Fertility and growth. Open and closed. Forest, plains, deserts, mountains, valleys, etc.
5. Geometry
   Direction. The shape of relation. The structure of nature. The body is a bilaterally symmetrical ordering of cylinders, cubes, planes, convexities. The state is a pyramid.

These are samples and pointers only. Their possibilities, particularly their combinations, are infinite.

Conventional education concentrates on a single symbolic act ("thinking", in the traditional Cartesian sense) and trains the individual by trying to compel memory of verbally or mathematically structured information. This process ignores the rest of the self, which is abandoned to the formative influence of all sorts of other divergent forces, most of which contradict the assumptions on which the act of education is based. Even the "thinking" is of small use to a very large number of people, since they have no symbolic structure into which this act can be fitted. So they go through the appointed motions for a given period of time and leave almost untouched by what has happened to them; their education has been determined by other forces.

Thinking is the ordering of experiences and their engendered symbols into symbolic structures, generating relations among them by metaphors and metaphoric acts. Those activities traditionally known as thinking, especially the Cartesian *cogito*, are a vital part of this process, but only a part. Isolated from the totality of the process, or—more accurately—understood as isolated from the process, this part of thought becomes a human defeat.

HISTORY AND PROCESS

What can be perceived is shaped by human history. The human organism can perceive only what it has learned to perceive. Thus the world we know is always both partial and shaped. No knowledge of the world is, or ever can be, complete and whole and true.

Neither can any knowledge of the world, beyond the simplest perception, be direct. Man has been expelled from the Garden and is forever after subject to the telics, geometrics and dramatics of his condition. These are the sciences observing our organic forces; we approach the world with an organism tuned by these elements, and our system resonates to the natural order according to the harmonies that are native to our condition.

What can be perceived is limited and also shaped by the organism; our bodies have developed in harmony with, interaction with the structures and the energies of our culture; we are what we are because those who came before us thought and created as they did. We are mammals. We are anthropoids. We are humans. We have a particular history. The shape of our perception—and those forms of perception that we call thought—is inseparable from our biology and history.

A Catholic peasant having a vision sees Mary dressed in blue and white; but never Parvati. Nor does a Hindu have a vision of the crucified Christ. This observation does not necessarily invalidate either vision.

We do not perceive *the* world. We construct *a* world, which is the only world we know.

The isolating techniques of the modern world that divide person from person also divides us from our past. We are what we are, as human, because we have been made so by those who preceded us. Community exists in time as well as space.

   . . . much of what we think of as human evolved long after the use of tools. It is probably more correct to think of much of our structures as a result of culture than it is to think of men anatomically like ourselves slowly discovering culture.

S. L. WASHBURN

   . . . cruelty and indifference are no more innate human characteristics than kindness; both have their origin in fundamental ways of perceiving and feeling.

WILLIAM J. BRANDT

   . . . the evolution of man's cortical structure could not help but be extensively influenced by a capacity for language acquired very early and in the crudest possible state. Which amounts to assuming that spoken language, when it appeared among primitive mankind, not only made possible the evolution of culture but contributed decisively to man's physical evolution.

JACQUES MONOD

It is inevitable that man should make God—or the gods or the sacred—in his own image. What other instrument does he have to communicate what cannot, by definition, be apprehended, to express the inexpressible? Similarly, man kills God only in his pride or self-hatred.

THE FATALITY OF PROCESS

Most of us can think only those thoughts, have only those feelings that are built into our organism. A few can create new patterns, or combinations of patterns and thus extend our humanity. We know nearly nothing at all about such creativity or our relation to it. We can know what we think about reality, or feel about our experiences, only by means of the somatic structures that are biologically inherited and culturally established.

The ingredients of process are the same for all people. The self faces the primal experiences—birth, death, sex, pain, hunger, cold, heat, decay, light, dark, sound, weather, etc. Some of these take on symbolic primacy or power in objects or persons—blood, Women, penis, serpent, the Old Man, the King, etc. The primal symbols are organized into symbolic structures by which men relate themselves to the world. These structures are primarily *structures*. It is not their assertions nor their representations that are decisive but their relations, all of which submit to the primordial logic. They respond to and account for unity, duality, multiplicity, chaos, giving value to one and seeking for it, in some direction and within a system of formal relations.

Each symbolic structure is known by its contained logical principle, its direction and figure, its distribution of time and energy according to its characteristic rhythm.

The elements are never known, experienced, felt, in isolation, but as part of particular symbolic structures. The study of such structures is *symbolics*.

This is the physiological or natural dimension of the symbolic imagination. But the imagination is enacted historically in a particular time and place, and the three elements disappear into an indecipherably complex human act. The primal logic is shaped by historical dramatics as well as primal dramatics. The rhythm of a particular landscape (place, figure and direction) intersects with and shapes the sense of time and energy, which are in turn shaped by the dominant fauna, the character of a particular invader, the weight and texture of the particularities of the past. And so on beyond the capacity of even schematic analysis, much less complete description.

Each people, subject to the consequences of human dualism, contending with the character of place and history, generate a particular symbolic structure or paradigm, which constitutes its world, and is the means by which it experiences "reality."

The tragic fatality of being human is that all these symbolic structures are doomed to failure and death. Faced with their natural condition, contending with it by a symbolic structure, people change their world by the intrusion into it of their symbolic structures. Since the symbolic structure could not be so constructed as to anticipate the consequences of its own intrusion, the situation becomes alien to the structure intended to deal with it. Obviously symbolic structures will vary widely in both range and flexibility (it is characteristic—and perhaps a definition of—primitive cultures that they disintegrate rapidly under the impact of more complex cultures). But the effective life of any symbolic structure is necessarily very short. The structure itself alters its context. By means of the techniques derived from the structures, men learn more than they can handle by the structure.

THE END OF PROCESS

Thus moments of unity and high confidence are short in any culture. They are followed by all the symptoms of failure—rebellion, blind and obsessive reiteration, frivolous manipulation, apathetic withdrawal.

Add to this the inevitable consequence of the variety of structures, natural and symbolic, within which we live. The accidents and contingencies that seem only the absurdity of experience, are not absurd because they do not submit to the rationality of a symbolic structure. The only absurdity is the presumption that the stars in their courses and the natural will of persons order themselves according to the instructions consequent on one of the temporary shelters of the human symbolic pilgrimage. And so human history remains subject to both natural and human contingency.

Both the fatality and the contingency of symbolic structures lead to their own characteristic consequences. When a man discovers that there is a reality unaccounted for by his symbolic structures, he goes inert or he goes mad. When a culture discovers it, it disintegrates.

It is not an easy thing to read the signs of the times; much that is thought to be quite creative and new is no more than the consequence of the remorseless logic of history.

Even sin is different at different stages. The characteristic sin of a coherent culture is pride, of a disintegrating culture is despair or acedia. The form a sin takes is itself revelatory of the characteristic form of that culture.

When the trinitarian logic of Western culture broke down, the consequences were quite logical. The primal dualism reasserted itself and social order became dominated by power or sensuality. Power manifests itself as polytheistic anarchy or monotheistic authority. Sensuality is manifested in promiscuity or the orgy—an attempt to recapture primal chaos and the natural unity. Or, when love is present, it is manifested as informal polygamy or polyandry—an attempt to recapture polytheism, unity through multiplicity.

Most establishment politics and epistemology is a consequence of the failure of the trinitarian imagination, and results in a sterile monotheism or ordinary power, without imaginative structure. Most counterculture politics and epistemology is a desperate attempt to revitalize primordial unities and Eastern polytheisms, or a turning loose of unstructured organic energies.

CONSTRUCTION OF THE SELF

The "self" has its structures and its interaction among structures, as all things do.

1. Telics of the self.

   There is the sense of purpose, however inchoately felt, that provides the orientation of the self's structures and the direction of the self's processes.

2. Geometrics of the self.

   The self is organized in relation to others and to things, to others as others or as things, to things as things or as others.

   This relation is pattern and direction. Neither pattern nor direction is understandable without the other. Nor can the self be understood without grasping its pattern and direction.

   Pattern establishes the ordering of the relation; direction establishes the nature of communication and authority within the relation.

   Pattern potentially includes the cosmos, the natural order as world, all living creatures, the human race, a particular race, nation, tribe, family, work groups. The account of the pattern of a particular self requires grasping which of these groups are in the pattern and which are not.

   The pattern has edges which are hard or soft, rigid or flexible, open or impenetrable. The character of these edges with a particular direction goes very far toward the establishment of the public personality.

   Divisions of the pattern have, at their edges, areas of transition and transformation, entry, change and exit. One of the principal functions of myth and ritual is instruction in the nature of each division of the structure and the proper effecting of the passage between them.

3. Dramatics of the self.

Structures of the self, as all structures, do not exist except in act and relation. The self is defined, too, in the character and quality of these acts.

Public narrative, as myth and history, is the source of common order, the shaping of the corporate acts.

Personal narrative incorporates the self into the particularities of the public narrative. The personal narrative includes the private narrative, the quality of the self within the corporate drama.

Education is the forming of the structures of the self. There is no self without these structures (the "natural self" which, with other fantasies like the Noble Savage, dances like will-o'-the-wisp before so many). Whoever and whatever shapes these acting structures is the teacher of a culture or a person, for the self is its rhythm of act, relation, transition, figure.

When a culture fails to teach, when its models of act and relation no longer carry authority and sufficiency, the person is thrown back on the private narrative or a concocted and often bizarre public narrative.

MEDITATIONS ON THE CONSTRUCTION OF THE SELF

The self's structures are themselves so varied and so variously involved with divergent structures that it is nearly impossible to construct a self that is a complete and adequate whole. Most who are successful as persons are so as partial structures. Most of us make do as best we can with a mixture of incompatible structures and patterns of actions in confused and uneasy accommodation.

But alter the mix too drastically and the self disintegrates. Much urban crime grows out of the destruction of the spatial image of so many people.

The self is subject to stresses and breaks as well as new or false integration. In the absence of a compelling public structure, American soldiers in Korea succumbed much more quickly than Turkish soldiers to Chinese "brainwashing" (which is not a psychological mystery, but a remaking of personal geometrics). Similarly there are structures latent in every nation, language, person that can remain invisible for a long time, only to be suddenly activated by an event or person.

The self has extraordinary resilience. In some brainwashing the body has ceased before the self's structures can be broken. In others, the structures gradually resume their former shape. The profoundest lesson of the Attica prison riots is that men subjected from babyhood to the most brutalizing experiences and often guilty of brutal acts, imprisoned under obscene conditions, could yet emerge with a sense of their own human integrity, set out with a crude and simple eloquence far greater than the moral emptiness of their well-intentioned governors. The brutalized spoke and acted as persons in the fullness of a suffering self. The sleek, clean spokesmen of authority were empty words.

Efforts to understand the self are plagued by the demon of linear causality, which has the self emerge from single and simple causes. Even Freud and Marx, to whom we owe so much that is essential, finally succumb to the fallacy of simple causation. For linear causality leads finally to "nothing but," and the arrangement that makes of man an indecipherable mystery when what is happening is that a living person is making some private accommodation to the intricacy of his structures.

Determinists select this or that pattern (which undeniably exists and works) and arbitrarily term it the determiner of the self. The variety and the independence of the structures of human involvement make possible the decisions from which selfhood grows.

Thus "construction" is not building a static structure by organizing creative energies. "Construction" is a process, and the process that engenders the self is both condition and purpose of all culture. For the self is ordered, and related process is the condition of eternal life.

THE PROCESS OF THE SELF

That great mystery, the self, is a mystery because it has been defined as a thing and not a process. It is vainly sought in the intricacies of the body. The self is a process that begins with those instinctive and automatic structures clustered around the brain stem, and extends to the outer reaches of communication and fantasy. Whatever the center of gravity of the self's action, it cannot be extracted from this totality, nor analyzed as though it were apart from it and not in constant interchange with all the structures of its context.

The self, then, is the particular pattern of relation subsisting among the structures within which this person is placed. Some of these structures are neurologically or logically given: there is an undeniable minimum of organization of the human body, certain inescapable types of relation within community. Some of these structures are inherited biologically or culturally. Some of them are made. The pattern itself is the source of the distinctiveness of personality: the center of gravity of selfhood can be found within the person, within the community, within things, etc. There are complex patterns of circumstances (causality) out of which this patterned self emerges and a good many decisions and choices to make among structures and relations.

Therefore, the self is understandable only as a particular pattern within a whole context, structures and energies disposed distinctively, a narrative history and a myth to give shape and act to time, a structure of bodily and social relations in space, a rhythm of relation, a direction of acts, a collection of defining metaphors, various gaps of sensitivity, blockages of transition. Structures can be rich or meager, fixed, flexible or spongy; energies can be disciplined or loose, diffuse or concentrated. This or that element may be isolated but *there is no self without the whole.*

The infinite variety of selves arises from the infinite range of possible structures and their relations. We are our circumstances.

But even shared circumstances are subtly altered from different points of view. The structures into which we place the immediacies of our circumstances are given shape, rhythm and tonality by a history that is ours alone. The choice of one set of structures for development can lead to the fatal neglect of others (in either a person or a culture). A structure or process at one point of experience can appear plausible, entirely convincing, yet destroy other structures (as I judge to be the case with the argument for the primacy of "self-realization"), and, in that destruction, destroy the self.

No structure, particularly those that define the self, is ever a discrete thing; it is the momentary suspension of an activity of relation. Transferred to another context, another complex of relation and act, it becomes another structure. The new structure overlaps the old and can bring the old into the new relation; the Parthenon does link us to the ancient Greeks. The new structure may function validly in the new relation; shorn of its original liturgical and psychological function, the Parthenon remains one of our great assertions of religious humanism and is, now, one of the major essays on the intercourse of the vertical and horizontal in environing space.

Thus, are our selves related to history; history is an inescapable dimension of the self.

THE FUTURE OF THE SELF

Which of the great structures and processes are essential to the formation of the self? Some are given in nature and are, therefore, inescapable. Others are found only in the forms of a particular culture, but may be as organically necessary.

Is ritual essential to the human self? Is the degeneration or disappearance of ritual a cause or an effect of the dispersal and discontinuity of the self in our culture?

There is a temptation in our culture to say that because something is, it must be good. Because "modern man" (a mythical creature at best) is secular, and has "come of age," then religion must accept the conditions of the secular. But secular man may stand only for a pause between ritualized symbolic structures. For the self is not constructed of dogmas.

A metaphor (and that enlarged metaphor, the myth) cannot be demythologized nor can its contents (the reference beyond it which is not accessible without it) be translated into a more palatable figure. As the theoretical authority fades, its imaginative authority must not. Rather we focus on the distinctive energies "beyond" it, which are formed in the structures of the metaphor, focus with an entranced concentration, a receptive contemplation, which may enable these energies to stir into life a new metaphor which may carry in its own structures the homeless energies of a dying structure. If the concentration is intense enough, it may engender not only a new carrier of former energies, but more comprehensive structures that give form and focus to new energies, hitherto unfelt because unembodied, unmanifested and uncontrolled.

There is hope but there is also danger. History is not determined by impersonal forces but emerges from engendering choice, and we have the real possibility of choosing the death of the self, thereby losing the power to choose.

There is pathos and the possibility of tragedy in the attempt to revive the rituals of another people. Whatever American Indians may have meant by their invocation to the spirits of earth and sky, the invocations functioned in a particular structuring of human energies. Transferred to the wholly different physical and symbolic context of our own culture, such rituals are not only irrelevant, they block achievement of the very purposes they were originally intended to serve.

Recapitulation: There is a core self, a consciousness with the capacity for intentionality, a self that can act among the extensive structures of consciousness. But the self is not, is never, definable as the isolated core of its structured activity. Rather the self is a web of relations and energies which extends from the deepest unconscious bodily acts, the automatic acts of the organism, the deep layers of history and fantasy entangled with the instincts of the organism, through the intentional consciousness and the determining symbolic structures that make up the conventionally designated self, through the objects, acts, and institutions that make up the self's involvement with others and the world. The web of relation is inescapable in actuality and description. The self, the person "is" the particular pattern and rhythms within this web of relation.

The potentialities and pathologies of the self are to be found only within the wholeness of this intricate web of relation. The major single source of both error and misunderstanding in training and therapy lies in the search for single causes within only a small part of the self.

The self is an intricate structure extending far beyond the boundaries of the traditional self; it is also an infinitely delicate rhythm of relation, interaction, communication among these structures, a process of transformation and exchange. Thus activities within one structure may require completion or manifestation in another. Or the fulfillment within one structure may require the human skills that may be learned only in another.

The structured energies of the self require a context of the human community for fulfillment and enactment; this is known, and therapy often directs itself toward the family and interpersonal transactions. What is less known is that the energies of the self need an ordered space for their enactment. If there is no appropriate spatial structure available, if it is not possible to generate one, if the compelled spatial context is alien to the self's energies, then those energies break out in destructive forms or are dissipated in paralyzed lassitude.

The self requires a rhythm of energy in order to effect the transaction among its structures; in the absence of rhythm, structures tend to remain discontinuous and, in their isolation, fade from consciousness. But rhythm is generated and trained only within certain symbolic structures—music, architecture, poetry, liturgy, cities. A culture that cuts its people off from the coherent rhythms of an integral cultural symbolism compels the people to rely wholly on the natural rhythms of the body and small communities that are generated out of this or that instinctual rhythm.

Thus the core offense of our culture is not moral—its mendacious exploitation of persons—for all cultures exploit large numbers of people. The true offense is its destruction of symbolic order, which is immoral in a new sense of the word.

THE FORMING OF THE GODS

The most essential part of process is the forming of the gods. The greatest of the metaphors are the names of the gods.

Gods are the decisive elements in the structures that make the world of a particular people. They are the manifestations of the essentials of that world, the embodiment of its structure, the origin of its energy, the quality and character of its pattern of relation. All those things done to place people in relation to the gods, thus into their most real world, constitute that people's religion, no matter if it masquerades under the name of politics, science or art.

The great gods are and continue to be. Insofar as we are inescapably part of our ancestry we are inescapably part of the gods they brought into being.

The gods may lose their names; among the gravest and most tragic of human dangers is the loss of the names of the gods. But the *power* of a god is never lost; without a name, and limits, the power of the god is an unconfined force that can destroy as well as create. We suffer now not from the absence of God but from the many gods nameless or falsely named, whose energies we do not understand and cannot control.

Religions name their gods differently and give them different histories. In human form the gods are protean. But all the gods have to be dealt with, for all the gods demand attention at the price of loosing terrible forces among those who condemn or deny them.

Have I dissolved Christianity into the reality of all the gods? Is Yahweh, the great Jehovah, the Lord Christ himself among the gods who are real, and yet, being among the gods, only as real as they? Yes, of course. Where else are the gods to come from except as they are recognized and given forms engendered by the human spirit? Are we to presume to speak accurately of the Lord of the Universe when we see only in the forms engendered out of our own experience of the world, build only with tools we ourselves have made?

Our hope and commitment, therefore, lie only in the conviction that the forms engendered in our encounters with the concreteness of life can be iconic to all that is beyond our naming and so beyond our knowing.

THE DEVELOPING PROCESS OF RELIGION

Symbolic structure shapes all that men do, including their techniques. Certain objects or images assume a singular importance. They, in their structural and rhythmic relations to each other, serve as the manifestation of being, itself. Both meaning and life itself depend on those structures. That is a people's religion.

A religion may not be understood by describing its creeds, dogmas, rituals even the "world-view" that inheres in these things. It is understood—known, apprehended—only by knowing, being grasped by, the structure and energies that are embodied in myth, ritual, art, architecture.

But men do not live only in the structure and energies of their religion. They live in the particularities and practicalities of the earth. They develop techniques for the accomplishment of purpose. Technique has its own logic and its own consequences.

Technique is initially at the service of religion as the symbolic structure. Then men discover that the hunt is just as successful without the painting, the crop as fertile without the orgy in the field, the bridge as usable without propitiating the spirit of the water. Then technique begins to dominate and finally to destroy the symbolic structure.

With mastery of techniques, men develop their myth, ritual, art and architecture. The components become separated. Ritual becomes drama and dance. Myth becomes drama and history. Technique shapes architecture, and architectural thinking makes possible new techniques. Technique and language generate science.

The symbolic structures, pressing against the great languages, emerge in some cultures into systematic verbal speech. Philosophy and theology in that case are embodiments of the paradigm. As all symbolic structures, they are to be understood primarily as systems of formal relations, as elements in a larger system, not as descriptive assertions.

The remorseless logic, interacting with the circumstances of a particular situation, produces a new imaginative structure, including (in our culture) an assertive propositional system. The proponents of the new system genuinely feel that the system is now the key to the secret of things and therefore authoritative; the common mode of speech of such new theologians is imperative. Yet what it does is designate where the man is within the particularities of the symbolic situation. There is, of course, always the chance that it is "true", but we can't know that. Any conclusion of the logic embodying the geometric and dramatic particularities of a situation is not defineable as true and therefore authoritative; it is always and only an act of commitment.

Philosophy and theology become, later, a reflection on the process and finally a reflection on their own instruments.

Theology is not religion, or the definition of religion or the authority of religion. It is one of the embodiments of religion. It is the self-consciousness of religion. When its concern becomes its own techniques, it is exhausted.

MORALITY

The fundamental problem of morality is the problem of the will. If I know the good, can I do it? *Will* I do it? If I am commanded to do the good, can I obey? *Will* I obey?

Popular moral theory, the moral theory that underlies political action, the judicial system, penology, takes for granted what much professional theory assumes:

1. The difference between right and wrong, good and bad, can be known.
2. Since morality can be known, it *is* known, and is to be identified with the opinions of the speaker's own party.
3. To know something is to be able to do it. Therefore failure to do it is a failure of will, punishable as a failure of will.
4. Since morality is an act of will based on knowing, its promulgation is essentially education or exhortation.

These assumptions depend basically on the Cartesian view of the universe. "Reality" is out there, *other* than me. I can be related to it only from outside by the act of knowing or the action of the will on it. In each case the will is dominant: *I* act on *it*.

But that is not the way I am related to the world; my self extends out into the world, it reverberates within my self. I am placed here in a structured and rhythmic order. To act *on* it is to place myself apart *from* it. Insofar as I treat things as the object of my will I make them something other than my self and cut them off from me. Therefore I interrupt the flow, the process that is the self's actions.

Morality is not initially an act of will. Morality is the placement of the person in harmonious and integral relation with his world. Morality is the making of dramatic patterns within which a human life can be enacted.

Therefore morality is not primarily in the care of dialecticians; it lies first of all in the design of the spatial setting, the establishment of the rhythmic order, the generation of dramatic patterns.

The source of morality is not dialectics but myth.

The decay of morality is not a failure of the will but a disintegration of the myth.

The generative metaphor is more crucial to morality than is law.

Therefore, the true immoralists are those who distort the spatial order, destroy the rhythms, deny the drama, by which a people sustain their moral acts.

PROCESS AND WILL

The discontinuities of our humanity compel choices—and choices require will. But choices are never wholly free; they emerge from the wholeness of process. The act of choice itself emerges, conditioned, from history and from nature. It is an act of an organism, structured, timed, responding. The possibilities of choice are never infinite, but are a part of the wholeness of process. Things to choose from emerge from nature and from history. The end to which choice is directed is never wholly clear; it emerges from the wholeness of the situation as an element conditioned to it.

If human life were ever whole, no choice would be required. The natural harmony of the organism would fulfill experience. But our humanity, our hope for a moral personality, is in our choices. Thus our only hope of fulfillment lies in the ensurance that we will never be fulfilled.

Therefore, the work of the will in the moral life is:

1. The construction or, better, the engendering, of those structured processes, those dramatic orders, which make it possible for a people to enact their lives according to who they are.
2. Casuistry: the application of the governing image of order to their verbalized statement of general principle, and the application of general principles to particular cases.
3. Innovation:
   a. the modification of existing casuistical principles to accommodate new insight.
   b. the engendering of a new metaphor which enables a new moral order. Thus Abbot Suger and his master builder ordered light in space and created a new image of divinity (which we crudely call the Gothic style). Abraham Lincoln became a metaphor to shape the American imagination and, therefore, American politics.

The work of the moral life is engendering structures that can shelter process. But a structure suspends process. Therefore, the work of the moral life is to engender processes that transform structures. But process dissolves structure.

The creative balance between structure and process is a rare achievement, answerable to no formula, controllable by no dogma or institution.

The work of being human is never complete. It always fails. It can never be abandoned.

The principle of rhythm is integral to the forming and the study of personality. There are persons who are, in their acts and personalities, jerky, incoherent. The acts may be separably defensible, but they emerge from no coherent whole.

Despair emerges from the idolatry of structure. Hope emerges from the life of ordered process.

Metaphoric Transformation:

An Essay on the Physiology of the Imagination

An appropriate attitude toward the past is not a matter to determine by easy assertion of principle; the place we come from, the road we used to arrive here, are valuable according to our feelings about the here we have arrived at. Our temptation is to repudiate the means we have used to become what we now are. The danger is that in repudiating our own past we will not simply be kicking aside a ladder we climbed up by but destroying the foundations of the house.

This is certainly the case with the dualisms that are so much the procedure and inheritance of "the modern mind." To get where we are now it was necessary to analyze out, to isolate, certain of the fundamental human activities. "Thinking" was understood and developed as a thing in itself, somehow related to but somehow other than matter, the body. The body has been minutely examined, dissected, analyzed in all possible aspects. But what the two have to do with each other we still don't really know.

Primarily our response to the problem, while varied, agrees on accepting its terms. There are those who reduce mind to physical processes. There are those who try to liberate mind (or spirit or person) as much as possible from body. There are those who try ingenious experiments with formulations that permit relating the two to each other in one way or another. There are those who try to abolish the problem by reducing it to a matter of nomenclature.

The only way out is forward, not back. We cannot pretend that our dualisms never existed; we must use them, not try to deny or overcome them, for they are part of the fabric of our feeling and understanding.

We can go through and beyond mind-body dualism by the very things dualism has taught us. We now know enough about the body to know that it is not "mere" matter. Matter itself is something other than "mere." Similarly, with the sense that matter is not necessarily either evil or limiting, it is no longer so fearful to think of the mind as an act of the body.

Nevertheless, the hold of ancient prejudices is tenacious. There is a nervous air about most of our discussions, as though we feel we may be doing something disreputable. As a consequence the ideas never really escape from the seminar room or symposium. They have had no effect on the general imagination. They have had no effect on education, which continues to be conducted as though the person were mind and mind were an operational memory. We have made no progress at all in fitting what we begin to know into common life.

The result has been to deliver the searchers, the eager or despairing young or the discouraged middle-aged to the two perennial extremes: materialism as power or profit, or mysticism as transcendence of the tyrannous self (what painful self-hatred is built into the constant call for transcendence of the "ego consciousness"!)

The way out, if there is such a thing, is not through this or that scientific theory; I am deeply mistrustful of attempts of reflective writers without professional competence to seize on a current scientific theory as the foundation for a very unscientific edifice of interpretations. In contradiction to the trustfulness of "science teaches us," there is no unanimity among scientists, no agreement, except on the conclusion that we simply do not know enough at this stage to say what happens even in simple acts of perception.

This does not mean that those of us concerned with an understanding of our place in the world must simply mark time until the scientists have made up their minds. Rather a combination of agreed upon physiological analysis and accurate description of our own experience enable us to say as much as we need to say at this time.

It is, by now, a cliche to say we suffer from the subject-object dichotomy, a surfeit of inside and outside, this and that, here and there, now and then. To live *only* in such a world is to make discontinuity the ruling principle of experience, to deliver the self to an instrumental relation to the world; things as instruments of the self, the self as an instrument of things. In such a mode of relation, power is the final determiner, power as control or as profit. Power as control is the ambition of the engineer and the intellectual; power as profit is the ambition of the businessman; the politician tends to both ambitions.

The counter movement is to condemn the subject-object dichotomy out of hand and seek to transcend it in the oneness of all things. As far as I am aware the people who take this way make little effort to demonstrate why the subject-object dichotomy is bad, or even that it is. Rather its evil is taken as given.

The question is not to be resolved by simply juxtaposing contradictory religious commitments, which is all we get, at the moment, from the opposition of culture and counterculture. The question is, what actually takes place in our transaction with the world?

The first principle, and one I think we can take as agreed on as achieved, is that matter is ultimately reducible to energy, as energy itself has mass. In perhaps more humanistic terms, energy is not something matter *does*, it is what matter *is*.

But our humanistic problem is that only a few people know such things deeply; a larger number know them superficially, but they play almost no part in our thinking about ourselves. We persist in thinking of ourselves as a coherence of substances in relation to other substantial units; the senses are considered avenues of communication carrying information to the brain to be appropriately processed. This is the image which the analytical intelligence has brought us to.

The trouble is, this is manifestly untrue. The simplest statement of its untruth is the experience of sensory deprivation. If the body were a self-sufficient unit, processing information from the outside world, then it could continue to function at its own decision when deprived of information. In fact, experiments with sensory deprivation demonstrate that the perceptual apparatus rapidly goes out of control. Clearly the senses "are" what they are only in their relation to their occasions. "A local vortex in the sea of energy, man is a visible emblem of the steady-state theory of creation," is the lovely description of John White.[16]

There is considerable temptation to the rhetoric of sound, not sense, at this point (and I shall come back later to the kind of rhetoric White promptly falls into). The temptation is enhanced by the fact that perception is not understood even by physiologists or physiological psychologists. In such a situation it is a grave temptation to select this or that disputed opinion and assert it as the proven basis for further argument. I have tried to select those conclusions from experimental demonstrations and professional argument that seem both to have professional authority and to account for the world as I think we experience it.

The task of interpretation and use of scientific evidence is both simplified and made more intelligible once we realize how metaphoric scientific reasoning actually is.[17] It is not essential at this moment to determine the source of the only root metaphors by which we order our experience. At the moment I need only the metaphor that orders our understanding of our relation to the world around us. In this case the controlling image, despite all that has been learned, is still thoroughly nineteenth century. The image can be described as either the telegraph or the freight train. The telegraph messages are sent out. The freight train carries materials into the factory where they are processed appropriately and sent out again. Thus we understand perception as the passive reception of information along the separate lines of the senses, the processing of the information by the brain (behaviorism), or the mind (rationalism), and the issuing of appropriate instructions along the nerves to the muscles of action.

Nothing of this picture survives present research and thought. We have no dominant metaphor to replace it as yet, which is why the assorted information and ideas remain a matter of special knowledge only, rather than having any real place in the general work of the mind. But there are things that can be said.

First, there is no point in the process of our transaction with the world where its several elements can be meaningfully analyzed out and treated as a separate line, either horizontally or vertically. It is a total process from beginning to end and the beginning and end are related, not along a line, certainly not as cause and effect, but as different elements in a field.

Thus, Zener and Graffron can speak of the different "phases" of the process:[18]

Phase 1. The world of object-events subdivided as:
       surface visible
       surface nonvisible and
       surface and interior
Phase 2: The medium world
       The means of transmission of the object-event to organisms.
Phase 3: Receptor processes
       Transformation process: including apparatus.
       Excitation process: action on receptor cells.
Phase 4: The central process (Phase 4 is the location of the effect of experience.)
       a. Afferent
       c. Central
       e. Efferent

Phase 5: The effector process.
Phase 6: The medium world
        Phase 2 in reverse.
Phase 7: The world of object events.

If this outline is too technically schematic, it can be more fully described as follows:

Phase (1). There is a world of objects, events and objects as events. These object-events are divisible into the visible surface (those parts of the object that act directly on our senses) the invisible surface (which we extrapolate from the visible) and the interior (which we only know by a variety of indirect devices).

Phase (2). All that lies between the object-event and the ends of our senses. This would include the airy space that transmits the waves of light and sound and all events that shape the waves that enlarge the medium world or modify it in some way.

Phase (3) is the receptor process, which is now understood as including more than the work of the sense organs. The transformation stage of Phase 3 includes all technological devices that alter and focus signals (telescopes, television, etc.) as well as the relevant neurological systems. Signals then excite the receptor cells in the excitation process.

Phase (4) is the central process, carrying signals to the center and the resulting signals out; but not in the image of the telegraph or the freight train: the afferent system is not a series of parallel tracks but a series of interacting systems which act according to their own inherent structures *and* according to the adaptations built into them by memory as well as by the shape of the incoming signal. Similarly with the later processes. But the later processes are not in line with the earlier, for they interact with the whole. The effector process changes the receptor process, alters the instruments of the central process. The whole is a single, rhythmically pulsating, or dissonantly contradictory, act.[19]

It is crucial to my argument to add here that Phase 2 and 3 are the peculiar locus of culture, with corresponding influence on Phase 4. The "medium world" is partly, and first of all natural, then shaped, controlled, extended by culture. The signals that constitute the object-event for the organism are thus given form by the interaction of nature and culture, and act on the receptor system. Equally, the receptor process, particularly in the transformation stage, is shaped by its prior experience and maintained by its memory. The effector process is equally rooted in culture, acting within procedures made possible by culture.

Such a scheme, for all its usefulness, can be misleading if it is interpreted using the old mechanical images. Zener and Gaffron do not use it this way. (They speak for example of "the energies of the medium world").[20] The whole process is continuous and active.

Each phase has its characteristic structure as a given, but the whole process is a transaction in which energies modify the relation of the structures. This is true of the action of the nervous system itself. So far from being made up of isolated lines of communication carrying separate items of sensory data to particular regions of the brain, the senses are active and interrelated and interacting *systems*.[21] They probe into the experienced world, actively cooperating. They combine in integrated activity. They interact on each other, both in direct stimulus and according to past conditioning.

Although we are not able to say *how* the process works, it is reasonably safe to say that we are dealing with the rhythmic transaction of energy, acting in patterns rather than reflexes.[22] The attempt to locate specific areas of control in the brain has not been successful; up to the point of massive brain damage, it is evident that areas traditionally thought to be control centers can be ablated, yet the function be taken over by the whole activity of the brain. It is possible that the activity of the brain is like a hologram, which is a kind of three-dimensional projected photograph. The film that is projected can be torn in two or more pieces, yet, when any fragment is projected, what is seen is not a piece of the picture, but the whole picture somewhat less clearly, and so on down to small fragments of the film.[23]

Matter, the old "substance," is now known to be energy, but matter is also not separable from this process. The physicist Max Born has said:

> Matter as given by our senses appears as a secondary phenomenon, created by the interaction of our sense organs with processes whose nature can be discovered only indirectly, through theoretical interpretations of experimentally observed relationships; in other words, through a mental effort. To designate the result of this operation by the old word "matter" seems to be wrong.[24]

Thus our experience of the world is, quite literally, an involvement in rhythmic pulsations. Some of this rhythm does not seem so; objects appear to have their characteristic solidity. But the impact of the world on our senses is in the rhythm of light and sound, of air and heat, of lived organic experience.

Our bodies are themselves structures of rhythmic pulsation. The grosser rhythms are evident to us but, evident or not, the finer ones are there, cells firing in their varied rhythms all the time, changing the rhythm under excitation. Whyte suggests that memory depends on the modification, by the electrical pulsations of the nerves, of the pulsating protein fabric of the cortex.[25] However that may be, the process now has to be seen as total, as more musical than mechanical, where change in one instrument can alter the timbre of the whole.[26]

Once again we, ourselves, are back in the world, participating in an intelligible natural process. But the argument is not complete. This account puts us back into the world as organisms—but not distinctively as persons. It accounts for our *nature* but not our *history*, our participation but not our personality.

The fact that analysis has tended to stop here justifies two distinct but related acts of the spirit characteristic of our day. I have described a physiological justification of all natural mysticism. I have also described a process that lies at the root of Arthur Koestler's fears about the human future and his strange prescription. More of that later. [p. 117]

There is every reason to think that the process here described is characteristic of all organisms, and if the time scale is large enough, of the inorganic order as well.[27] Life is the delicately modulated, endlessly pulsating, rhythmic transaction of all beings with each other and the whole.

That man can live within this rhythmic whole is obvious. How he feels about it is also obvious; a good part of human history is given over to the attempt of people to unite themselves with nature or to detach themselves from it. What is not so obvious is that he should feel about it at all.

There is no evidence that other organisms feel in this way. They do feel. Animals show a wide range of supposedly human emotions—fear, trust, desire, satisfaction. They have memory, the power to reason, the capacity to form societies. What they do not have, so far as we can tell, is the awareness of these things.

At some point in human evolution, the creature who was to become man became conscious, aware that he was something other than the things he lived with.

What form this awareness took initially we can never know—a word, a tool, a weapon, a reverential act. Since all of these are quickly and inevitably involved in self-awareness, it is not unlikely that all happened to one or another person.

We do not need to be concerned about the history of this moment. The psychology of the film *2001* seems to be quite sound, and therefore the epistemology. The ape-man was playing with a bone, as any animal with an opposable thumb could do. He began pounding with it, again a "natural" act. But the instrument shaped the response by way of the hand and the body. As no animal could, this man—no longer ape-man—could grasp the bone as metaphor. It was a club and therefore weapon. This is not a metaphor but technique only. The weapon could create victory

and therefore control. Control is power. Power is the means of social organization: this inventive genius became the leader of his
tribe; thus organized, this tribe expelled the other, creating a political hierarchy of dominance and subordination. The bone became the metaphor, transforming human feeling into purposeful
power.

Probably the crucial thing is that this awareness "took form".
To be self-aware is to see the other as an other; whatever the emotional consequences, this is already a form; self and not self establish here-there, this-that, this side-that side, inside-outside. The
emotion or feeling consequent on this awareness of duality was
awesome in its results, for all human culture emerged from it.
There would be desire of some kind—to return to the felt unity, to
escape from it, to dominate and use it—but whatever the desire,
desire creates purpose.

Thus there emerge forms of response and instruments of purpose. The first act, however elementary, disturbs the natural relation and alters the natural rhythms. This alteration demands to be
fitted into the sense of meaning and purpose, thus requiring new
forms. New forms generate new rhythms which syncopate across
the given natural rhythms. This new harmony of discordance requires resolution. And so, with extraordinary rapidity, the cultural
forms appear.

Thus the symbolic transformation begins, for every purposeful
form is not simply a tool but a metaphor, a transformation of
thing into meaning and purpose, the condensation of meaning and
purpose into a thing.

A vital part of this process is clear, however imaginary its stages
may be in the description: this was not something that happened
to a fully evolved human. It was an ingredient of that evolution.

Clifford Geertz says:

> ". . . not only was cultural accumulation under way before organic
> development ceased, but such accumulation very likely played an ac-
> tive role in shaping the final stages of that development.[28]

"... the human brain is thoroughly dependent upon cultural resources for its very operation; and those resources are, consequently, not adjuncts to but constituents of mental activity."[29]

Man is not a creature who has a history; he is his history, for his history makes him, even somatically. Man is not a person who does or makes these things; he is what he does and makes. Culture is not something added to his selfhood; it is a quality and a dimension of his selfhood.

There is one vital aspect of this process that must be emphasized, lest the process appear too logical and determined. Logical it is, but not determined. The initial stage, the formation of the human self in its awareness, compels a choice. If man becomes human by an awareness of his self as in nature, but, as aware, something other than nature, the first response must be decision. Nature, the organic rhythms, are desirable: man must seek to return to them or harmonize with them; or they are undesirable and realization of the self must lie in escape from them. Whatever the decision, the choice, there is an immediate cluster of decisions consequent on it: how do I accomplish what is now my purpose? The very asking of the question creates a sense of "I" or at least, "we" and the establishment of personhood. The resolution of the question requires understanding, technique, act, making.

Whether it is conceivable that the process could have happened in this way is not the point. Rather choices were made and things done in their natural fashion; certainly not in the fashion of an imagined process cast in academic prose. The pedantic description can be a paradigm of a process that was creative, intellectual and rational. People did not "think it out" like modern academics, nor could they have described it; but it involved the human mind, creative human action, as seriously as the more articulated model of the modern intellectual. There was equal occasion for human genius; their Miltons were inglorious only in that we don't know them, and they certainly weren't mute, for individuals suddenly, or groups in the slow maturation of time, created forms—places, things, rituals, narratives, institutions—that could gather the inchoateness of immediate experience and transform diversity into a whole that both completed purpose and generated persons.

The analytical intelligence has taught us what we know of these things, but there is, inevitably, a vice consequent on its virtues, which is the temptation to think that reality itself is divided as the analytic intelligence divided it in the act of understanding. Thus, "a person" is understood as contained within a particular physiological structure because, in our analytic history, a different technique has been needed to account for what is within the skin and what is outside the skin.

Analytical techniques are still useful if they don't dominate the understanding. But understanding now requires us to accept the fact that process is as real as objects, that relations are as "substantial" as substance, that rhythm is as closely experienced as the ordering of muscles. In short, physiology must be understood as being far more inclusive in its reference than the word usually suggests, and the limited elements of the traditional reference will be rightly understood only when they are related to the more inclusive definition. For we now know that the workings of our bodily structures are not self-contained, but extend far out into environing space in rhythmic transaction with the world.

Our most grievous errors come in neglect of any part of this process, or, undue emphasis on any part of it (even though one or the other, or both, is almost certainly inevitable in human decision—which is what Christians are referring to by the odd term "original sin"). The process which is human selfhood cannot be understood except as an interaction of what inherited terminology compels us to call nature, culture and history.

Were we not so preoccupied with the authority of the reasoning intelligence we intellectuals would know what children and poets, farmers and sailors know, that we are a part of the natural order in constant interchange with it. The narratives we enact create emotional states that shape our apprehension of nature; the heat or cold of nature shapes emotions and thus alters the rhythms of our narrative. Vision is not something we have, to use; it is something we do, therefore something we are in the light-filled order of things. What we make of it and in it creates the meaning and purpose of the light; the light is the sustenance of our vision and a part of our selfhood.

This is the natural dimension of being human. But the process is never only natural. It is not a natural communion to which we can or cannot add culture, at our choice. The very body we use in our transactions with nature has been shaped in its evolution by the instruments and institutions of our culture. Thus our history is not dispensable, either as understanding or as present experience. We experience the world by what we have received from our history, and we will understand that experience only as we can apprehend that history.

We know history only through present culture. All we have of history is the deposit of its record; we do not know the event, only the memory, record or artifact of the event; all time is always now. Therefore it is not history that carries the final authority, but what we now do with it. The fatality of process is that each new creation within it alters the whole, so that the rhythms that gave rise to the original act, the structures that have been set into energy, are no longer what they were and hence no longer effect the same ends they once did. To seek to fix culture into permanent structure is to seek the rigidity of death, for culture is itself process.

Metaphoric transformation is at the heart of culture. It is one of the formative acts of human selfhood. History, nature and culture are in constant interaction and exchange, and the transaction is through the great metaphors; a true metaphor is a ganglion as much as the clusters of nerve cells that make up the ganglia of our nervous system.

Thus all our cultural creations are centers for the control and transmission of energy; all culture is metaphor, a means for the human transaction. This exchange cannot be charted; criticism can never be a schematic discipline. Before we undertake the critical apprehension of the thing in the particularity of its function we cannot know the nature or direction of the exchange. The error of Freud and Marx is not that their range of metaphors is too limited; we could forgive them that, for the rest of us are even more limited. Their crucial error is in fixing the direction of exchange, thus fastening a rigid structure on the complex flow of the metaphoric transaction. Both sex and the means of production are great metaphors of the self but only the hard cases of analysis can show us the direction of the flow or the complex interaction between sex, the means of production, and all the other terms of our transaction with our bodies, our world and our history.

Therefore, without necessarily altering the internal operation of the critical disciplines, we thoroughly transform our understanding of them and their ordering and almost certainly extend the operations within them. Art, for example, is not something external to the self to be treated simply as a delectation of the senses, or satisfaction of the academic intelligence. Art is a dimension of the self. Painting can be, variously and in combination, a placement of our selves in light and space, an establishment of both the order and rhythm of our dramatic narrative, the display, contemplative and pedagogical, of our vital order. Architecture is one mode of setting out and controlling the human rhythms that we set in motion to place us in or take us out of natural rhythms; poetry is another ordering of rhythms; music is perhaps the most powerful of our rhythms, and we would do well to set out for our understanding the transaction between our natural rhythms and the rhythms of our music, for our bodies, the physiology of our imagination, are shaped in such events.

The great critical disciplines (known and too narrowly defined as philosophy and theology) are not to be understood as descriptions, and cannot, therefore, be given either primacy or authority. They are a particular way of making manifest the structures and processes of our transactions. They bear the heavy weight of our humanity because they are one of the ways of giving shape to the huge and terrifying energies inherent in our most important language. However indispensable they may be, they do not even have primacy in the determination of language, for poetry is the major instrument for controlling words to human purposes. But the critical disciplines are a vital part of our humanity, if only we depose them from their ancient seat of authority.

Thus our humanity is in the wholeness of our transaction with our total self and the total self is defined as the whole transaction between body, nature and culture (as history and as present construction). Metaphoric transaction becomes the controlled exchange between structure and energy to human purpose.

It becomes, therefore, far less useful to draw sharp distinctions between physiology and history, nature and culture. To do so is not "wrong", for each of these has its characteristic structures and processes which cannot rightly be identified with another. But equally, no one of these can be isolated from another. It is hyperbole to say that culture is an aspect of physiology, for the physiology of the body does not exist apart from its functioning extensions in the forms of culture.

THE PROCESS OF METAPHOR

With the groundwork laid, it should be possible to go further with an account of metaphor. It is not possible to go as far as it would be desirable and, ultimately, necessary to go, for we simply don't know enough yet. But at least principles can be described with some hope of accuracy.

Our ignorance is greatest about *context-as-physiology*, the integral involvement of our somatic selves with our setting. In part "physiology" in this context is a figure of speech, rhetorical exaggeration to counter-balance Cartesian dualism. But in part it is true metaphor, providing management for a wide range of experience and explanation. "Physiology" could be understood as those aspects of our total experience within our skin. It would be possible to acknowledge that I cannot exist without the rhythmic interaction with my world and, at the same time, recognize that there is a physiology which is constant to me whether I am in New York or Bombay.

Yet "I" am not the same in New York as Bombay, and the longer I stay in Bombay the less "I" become what I was in New York. Our selves may have a somatic core but it is not a matter of mind using body to act objectively on the environment. Rather there is a rhythmic flow from center to circumference and back, a total act in which each modifies the whole.

Being in culture all the time, we have a hard time imagining what it might have been like to be human without culture. It may be that being human required culture or that the first act of culture created the specifically human. In any case we cannot now accept the notion of "natural" man; Tarzan, the wolf boy, etc., are fictions; humans require culture. Thus the rhythmic flow of interactions is never left untouched or unshaped. It is already shaped by circumstance and by the natural structures; being human is inseparable from the metaphoric act that shapes and transforms the flow.

We cannot know the beginning. It could have been a peaceful tool, a language act, a devotional or ritual act. For this argument it doesn't matter. What does matter is that an object or act organized part of experience according to the time's principles of meaning and purpose.

However set in motion, the process inexorably compels further metaphors. A tool can create purpose by establishing possibility. The purpose achieved alters the situation and thus disturbs the rhythms of interaction. The disturbance creates a need which can be met only by an object or act—a metaphor—that, inserted into the flow, controls it.

Such a scheme, which seems very simple with the earliest tool or weapon of the ape-man, is still essentially the same with the far more complex tools, systems, institutions of advanced societies. The metaphors become more complex in both nature and function but they share a fundamental trait: they are not embellishments, made optionally and therefore dispensable. They are the fundamental means of thought, for the metaphoric act is the only way of controlling the flow of interaction to meaning and purpose.

What cannot be brought within any scheme is the types of metaphors. A little observation suggests that very nearly anything can function metaphorically. The obsessions of the fetishist may be just as tragic but they no longer seem quite so bizzare when understood as metaphor. There is a destructive desperation about, say, a shoe fetish, but the victim does not "love" shoes; the shoe has become a metaphor for a person and the means for organizing the energies—now out of control—of sexual attraction.

There are not, in other words, metaphors that work like the words in a dictionary. Rather the interaction of person and experience under the condition of particular structures and a particular history establish the occasion for human creativity or eccentricity. Metaphors are what they do.

For a more significant example, I will term the city a major human metaphor. The origin of cities is a subject of professional dispute. They may have begun as means for organizing groups of people, or for defense. But, having begun as a tool (therefore a metaphor of purpose) they become forms that, by their presence in the flow, organize experience in a different way. They become images of cosmic order and, simultaneously or because of the cosmic implications, images of the body.

But the process doesn't stop there. Having as an image of cosmic order, set out the image of relations, the physical form of the city is transformed into a working metaphor of the relational structure, with comparable consequences for all those experiences that are shaped by these metaphors. The shape of a city becomes a metaphor to control the order of the body. The processes of the body become a metaphor for the energies and thus the effective structure of the city.

Rhythmic transaction becomes polyphonic, a voice here transforming another there. Thus metaphor is never a thing but a process. The structure of the metaphor decisively shapes the event (the bone was a club, not a plow), but metaphors are part of a pulsating web of transformation, intricately woven of natural forms and processes as well as the objects, systems, institutions, modes of thought, that are the man-made metaphors.

It remains now to comment on the question of why I should feel a need to use a term with an already accepted meaning. "Metaphor" is a word with a more limited and generally accepted reference than I am giving it here. Is there really a need to extend its reference as I am doing?

The derivation of "metaphor" is, in crude literalism, "to carry change." As a figure of speech, a metaphor is as effective as it sets out, in its specificity, qualities of other things. It serves us by helping us to grapple with other things, to account for and enhance our experience of them. Thus, in the etymological redundancy of title, a metaphor is by function a transformation. If a metaphor in this ordinary literary sense were understood as a limited and special case of true metaphor (and a functioning part of a metaphoric structure) it might cease being an embellishment and begin to function more actively as an act of thought. Therefore, the limited meaning needs for its own usefulness to be incorporated into the larger.

THE PATHOLOGY OF METAPHOR

This account of the processes of the self is stated (perhaps inevitably) in somewhat idealistic terms, the organism functioning in rhythmic harmony with its context. Unhappily history and society are records of the failure of this harmony as well as its occasional successes. If the theory is to qualify for acceptance it must make disharmony as intelligible as harmony, and help in the explanation and the solution of some of the problems that face us.

Some of the implications for therapy are perfectly obvious, at least in principle. If the self is defined in terms of its involvement with the whole process, then disorder in one part of the process cannot necessarily be resolved by attention only to that part. To do so leads to a situation which often unhappily appears in penology and psychoanalysis, as well as in medicine: the symptom is ameliorated but the situation is basically unchanged, for the trouble was engendered by a disorder somewhere else in the system. Clearly then, any therapy is a part, the corrective part, of a process that includes the study of the entire human process in all its three dimensions—nature, history and culture. The best that can be said for division of the study as represented by the structure of the university, is that it got us to the point of understanding this process, but it has outlived its usefulness.

There is another aspect of disharmony that is peculiarly evident in our own day. It is one thing to envision disorder in a process that is intact and therefore repairable. It is something else to contemplate the results of the death of essential parts of the process.

There is little point in making moral judgments on this death for it is inevitable; the great metaphors, the symbolic structures reveal more about reality than they are ever capable of controlling. The process requires new and creative metaphors, but when the creative imagination fails—or, more optimistically put, between creative occasions—it is as though parts of an organism have died, leaving the rest in isolation.

This is the situation of our own day. In part, we live with the consequences of our own metaphors. In denial of the most elementary physiological process we decided sometime back that our guiding principle of relations would be discontinuity, the independence and self-sufficiency of each organ of the whole. Thus, art was isolated from all humane purpose because art existed only for the sake of art. Art was cut off from its ancient function in the organism with catastrophic consequences for the whole. People were left with part of their organism without fulfillment. Art was cut off from purpose. Artists continue to make moral or political assertions about the importance of their own work and the responsibility of society to support them, but nobody listens, for they are no more than an amputated limb, twitching.

Everywhere the great languages, the sources of metaphoric act, are similarly isolated from the organism. With no truly humane function, languages can only contemplate or play games with their own procedures: politics becomes the occasion for technical skills without purpose, philosophy is an infinitely refined reflection on its own language, engineers build dams nobody needs because that is what engineers do, theologians continue debates that nobody cares about.

But these are functions, operations, structures, that were engendered in the human imagination because the organism needs them to survive. What, then, of the organism that is deprived of its own outer functions?

The first consequence of such deprivation is the failure through starvation of essential functions of the organism. Physiological processes may continue to operate but the characteristically human parts have died, or gone flabby and inert. This is acedia, that failure of the spirit deeper than sloth. All symbolic act is abandoned, for none has meaning; all act is reduced to a minimum for no act outside those necessary for survival has any moral purpose over any other. There are no meaningful roles to play, so there is no mode of clothing to make evident place and function; the fat women in shorts and halters and curlers, the old men shuffling along Florida beaches in baggy shorts and baggy raddled flesh are all victims of acedia. It is not simply that they have no function in a commercial society and so look like debris, which is what they are. They have no role in a metaphoric structure, they are not images of purpose or even of end, they participate in no ritual, nor mark a rhythmic movement. They are not the occasion for care. In short, they lack nearly everything that enables a person to find completeness. So they are driven back on the simplest physiological functions, indifferent to all else. The structures of human communication have been destroyed, so people indifferently watch others being destroyed.

Perhaps, in more people, the energies characteristic of process spin out of control when there are no metaphors to give them shape and purpose. This generates all sorts of phenomena. One, for example, is Lifton's "protean man," madly changing allegiance because he must have structure but without any reason to choose one structure over another. There is the compulsion to perpetual movement and change. And there is rage, most destructive of all.

Analytical intelligence requires a kind of simple moralism; if the body is simply an instrument for the rational will, then by taking thought and making a decision people will behave properly. If they do not, then this failure is prima facie evidence of a failure of intelligent choice, which is amenable to education or conditioning, or it is evidence of a failure of moral will which is amenable to the discipline of punishment in school or prison.

But the energies of the self, the energies which are variously called physical or psychic, the energies which range out from the flesh through the great metaphors to things, these energies are true energies, no more to be controlled by the will than electricity. In a humane existence they find their shaping in the structures of culture, and their function through the lines of the metaphoric transformations. When the metaphors fail and the structures collapse, then the energies die out or drain away in acedia or they flash out unpredictably, striking at random as lightning does.

As yet, we know too little of these things to speak confidently. The theory presented here presupposes that, at the beginning of the formation of the self, there is an act of decisive choice which means that the responsible will is an ingredient of the self and so subject to judgment and discipline; morality is an ingredient of the self.

But choice presupposes something to choose. There must be the possibility of responsible act, materials for the construction of the self, linked metaphors for the shaping of energies. This is the moral function of culture, the corporate act by which the completeness of the self becomes a possibility. The construction of culture is the occasion for the exercise of the will. The engendering of metaphors is the creative moral act. In the absence of such a possibility of individual moral choice, moral or legal judgment is simply tyranny.

Arthur Koestler has addressed himself to this problem but, in my judgment, an incomplete analysis has led him to an altogether erroneous, if revealing, solution.

With great care, in *The Ghost in the Machine*, he has analyzed the interaction of physiology and culture. In my too-simplified summary: he presupposes three essentially concentric brains folded around the brain stem—the archicortex and meso cortex (forming the limbic system), corresponding roughly to the reptilian and lower mammalian stage in evolution, the neocortex corresponding to the higher mammalian stage.[30] The "mistake" in the design of the brain is that "evolution superimposed a new superior structure on an old one, with partly overlapping functions, and without providing the new with a clear-cut, hierarchic control over the old."[31] The limbic cortex is dangerous because it is not only the source of emotion but of a kind of thought which is without language, so essentially without morality and so out of the control of the neocortex.

From this "mistake" there proceeds the destructive forms of cruelty and fanaticism that are uniquely human and, according to Koestler, inevitable, because their source is physiological. This is a fascinating return to the doctrine of original sin in a wholly secular form. Here sin has nothing to do with the will, everything to do with anatomy. Solutions must, then, be similarly concrete; Koestler's solution is to alter, by chemical means, the processes of the brain to improve coordination between the areas of the brain and establish rational control of the limbic systems.

This proposal is not so active a possibility that it need concern us at length, but it does reveal what can happen when a serious and humane intelligence gets hung up on a partial analysis. I see two fundamental errors in Koestler's position.

In the first place, his physiology may be inaccurate. There almost certainly is a far more intimate relation among the levels of the brain than he allows for. Research on the control of the body by the "mind," from yoga to laboratory, seems to prove conclusively that the supposedly autonomous systems are far more accessible to deliberate control than their name suggests.[32] More to the point is the definition of the brain's functioning.

In rejecting the doctrine of levels, Livingstone asserts:

" . . . consciousness, emotional experience, and motivation are not exclusively dependent upon classical sensory and motor projection systems, nor upon the neocortical mantle itself. Indeed they seem to be more dependent upon projection systems belonging to the phylogenetically older, transactional parts of the brain stem and limbic systems."[33]

In other words, the brain is not to be identified only with its physiological structures but with its transactional relations. The structures (and, obviously, the transaction) can be negatively affected by surgery, electricity or drugs. There may be pathological conditions corrigible by these means. But to assert that man is by physiology pathological is to overlook the full nature of the human process, which is a functional whole, held together in a physiology that includes anatomical physiology and what I call cultural or imaginative physiology. Koestler errs in his analysis by attending only to the first and thus chronicling the destructive force of energies frustrated or wrongly directed.

Thus resolution is put right back where it belongs, into the common enterprise of a living culture. The enterprise of culture is not simply expressive or indulgent. It is essentially moral, for its primary task is the generation of objects and acts that make possible the wholeness of the person. If the self is contracted back into its neurological system, it may well be that the dissonances built into that system will become destructive and have to be controlled by artificial means. The disparate energies, provided with no channel of controlled manifestation, cancel each other. But it is the precise function of culture to provide shapes within which the energies— *all* of the energies—of the organism can be harmoniously enacted. Metaphor as transformation can give concreteness to purpose and to meaning and thus harmonize the diverse energies of experience.

When these energies are in destructive conflict, as they clearly are now, the prescription should not be a pill that would make us into androids, but a new metaphor that would enable us to be human.

There is another aspect of our own culture that is closely related to Koestler's analysis, but which interprets the evidence differently. These are the nature mysticisms that increasingly attract those who do not feel at home in the present culture, particularly the young.

Koestler accepts the analysis of man as a self-contained organism, ignores the physiological function of culture and prescribes accordingly. The new nature mystics rightly identify the analysis as an ingredient of the modern problem and they commendably see the person as far more of a process, intimately transacting with others and with nature. But far from seeing culture as a dimension of the self, they tend to repudiate it altogether, or to use it simply as a handy, available instrument. Thus they identify the self and its rhythmic transaction with natural rhythms. The result is inevitable. All the emphasis is placed on the rhythms and too little on the differentiation within the rhythm. The consequence is a rapid movement toward things like "cosmic consciousness," "world soul" and all the self-contradictory clichés of mysticism.

At the end of the passage I quoted earlier, [p. 105] John White says, "Who am I? I am the universe; I am Universal Mind."[34]

He isn't. That kind of thing may be some consolation to those who aren't content with their own self, or who find that self incomplete or find an appropriate expression of the self in making such statements. But his assertion runs against the fact that Universal Mind does not write books. Only Ego does, and a considerable assertion of Ego it is, too.

If Koestler overlooks the fruitful *possibilities* inherent in the self's involvement in culture, the new nature mystics ignore its *actuality*. We are, inescapably, a part of culture.

There is a place for mysticism in an organic culture, as a discipline of the self in a particular mode. In a disintegrating culture it may provide some solace or shelter for a few, but it is quite irrelevant to the larger task. For most it is a meaningless escape, a dispersion of energy or a form of acedia.

For the differentiations exist. My body is not whole except as it is in harmony with the natural rhythms, but the rhythms of my flesh are not just those of nature; they are those of humanity, a culture and myself. To abdicate from the responsibility for culture is to abdicate from a part of my self. I am placed in the world but it is I who is placed in the world. I cannot evade either.

A culture that has not provided me with the means to the completion of my self is a culture that has betrayed me. But to rail against "culture" for that betrayal is, among the articulate, to hide behind the anthropomorphizing of a process into a noun. "Culture" is what all the "Is" have or have not done; it is not of itself a moral person. If the beginning of humanity is in the choice of purpose, all culture is always the making manifest of that choice. If we fail, or when we fail, the failure is corporate. It is not to be overcome by the cynicism of black humor, the preciousness of the avant-garde, the purposeless indulgent in eroticism or power, or by sinking into the sloth of contemplation or the Florida beaches. It will be overcome by generation of the objects and the acts, the narratives and the spaces, the embodied rhythms and the energized forms, the manners and the style that indicate that, for a moment, we have made for ourselves a means for our own completion.

Thus culture and all its workings is not entertainment or indulgence; it is the very substance of ourselves. The making of it is not optional but an act of being alive.

PART FOUR

Structure and Process
in Theology

INTERLUDE: MEDITATIONS ON THE VERB "TO BE"

Goethe's complaint against Newton was that Newton's physics lacked reverence. Dealing with this circumstance has certain complications:

1. On every point that is testable, Newton was right and Goethe was wrong.
2. Newton himself did not lack reverence but avidly sought the worship and service of God.
3. Newton found no place for reverence as a hypothesis in his system, however much he intended his physics to be an account of the glory of God.
4. Newton's physics was an inescapable, unavoidable stage on the way to a physics that overcomes it.

By what authority, to what purpose do we define water in terms of a state that can exist, if at all, only in the laboratory?

It may be essential to recover Goethe's and Blake's critique of Newton; it does not follow that Goethe and Blake were any more right than Newton was.

There are things we now *know* that make it impossible to continue with the traditional modes of thought. We cannot always distinguish between what is truly and newly known and what is a part of a new symbol system—in any case a false and useless distinction. A new ordering of the mind, the sensibility, cannot be patched into the old garment of thought. Thought itself needs to be redone.

We have lost the sense of substantial things which can be accounted for by an outside observer. The verb *to be* is now function and relation, not substance. We cannot rescue the old metaphysics of substance by recourse to a capitalized verbal noun, "Being". We can replace ourselves in the order and energy of things only as we can truly think of being as ordered action.

A basic postulate of all analysis is that it is never true, never can be true. A major oppression of modern life is precisely the conviction that what emerges from analysis is somehow true or real. The results of an analysis are a tool which has or participates truth and reality only in its use. Analysis is not the making of idols but a mode of self-consciousness.

Neither nostalgia nor mysticism can save us, only living in the world as it is.

THE GENERATING ASSERTION

Theology is not description or representation or legislation; theology is enactment.

Any language into which the transformative experience of the sacred emerges is theology.

If a theology, a theological statement in any human language, has authority, that authority must rest on the same basis as the authority of all symbolic acts; the ability of a particular symbolic structure to contain the integrating rhythms of a culture within the immediacy of the experience of a particular historical situation, in fidelity to a complete human purpose.

Except as it be born again, no theology has access to the Kingdom of God.

The controlling condition for doing theology is not intelligence but love.

ORIGIN OF THEOLOGY

Rightly defined and understood, theology is not optional, incidental, or derivative. It is, finally, the setting forth of human purpose and the generation of structures for the achieving of that purpose.

There are numerous examples of "natural" or "secular" men (even in primitive societies which were once thought to be universally religious) who simply accept things as they are. To them the word "theo"-logy is irrelevant. To most people, and all cultures, "theology" is not optional; their energies are directed, in diverse ways, to one or another of these purposes, which is their theology.

"All cultures" because the concentration of structured energies for a common purpose is the definition of a true culture. Except for small homogenous groups, when theology is dead the culture disintegrates.

Originally the languages into which the enabling symbolic act emerges are simple, because techniques are simple, experiences few; there is no reason to think these primal symbolic structures are either more or less in relation to "reality" than the structures that come later. They do have the authority that rests with the act that shapes all that follows.

Nevertheless, there is no religion that is not a manifestation of humanity in its fundamental symbolic operation: telics, geometrics and dramatics; and, therefore, in some form revelatory of the ultimate order of things.

The *theos*, the gods or God, is the symbol and the metaphoric act which is the condensed, concentrated energies and purpose of a people.

This is not a doctrine of cultural relativism. The argument is thoroughly falsified so long as it is formulated in terms of relativism and absolutism. All gods, including Yahweh and God, are engendered from the human imagination. All gods are symbolic structures and the concentration of energies for the ordering of human experience. There are no exceptions that make it possible to say, "My god is a revelation; all the other gods are human constructs."

No god is ever an absolute; an "absolute" god too easily becomes a weapon. Only the absolute is absolute and, being absolute, is beyond categories, beyond speech, beyond language, beyond even this language for there is no language with which to talk sensibly even about the inaccessibility of the inaccessible.

A god who could be proven would be no god. God cannot be put into a sentence. Can the holy of holies be the subject of a verb?

Yet the language of the visionary is as culture bound as English or German. Ecstatic and wordless vision of the ultimate mystery at the heart of things is a language, no better, no worse, as holy, as blasphemous, as the habit-bound mumbling of the creed. There is no aristocracy in the life of the spirit, only wholeness. Any language is neglected at peril of the soul.

THE PRESENT WORK OF THEOLOGY

1. The traditional work of theology—the embodiment of the faith in systems of propositions—is exhausted. This is not a reason for recrimination or repudiation. Modern physics could not have done its work had it not been for the work of the Newtonians. Theological reality would not be possible without classical, "Newtonian" theology.
2. Most theological work now being done that is known to me is Newtonian rather than Einsteinian.
3. Newtonian physics, Euclidian geometry, and verbal theology continue to be necessary for all sorts of operational work. Verbal theology, however ingenious, can never again regain its ancient primacy and authority. Nor can a church survive, built on the propositional images of order. We are emerging into a consciousness, a sensibility, a structure of order for which there is no precedent and no immediate guide, except as we grasp the process.

Theology rightly emerges from experience, not argument.

The experience of our day is that of history and science—the past experience of man, the present experience of the earth.

The unique gift of the present age is the understanding of the process of our involvement with ourselves and the earth.

Thus, to understand the theology of the time is not to make an anthology of arguments but to analyze the structure.

Differently defined the work is, then, the absorption of past structures in their comprehensiveness and the absorption of the inner structure of the natural order.

The present task of theology is the recovery of the symbolic structures of other times and places so we can have some sense of who we are and where we came from and how we have, in different modes, been involved in being human.

THE END AND THE BEGINNING OF THEOLOGY

Theology, as enactment, is not proof but commitment.

Theology, as traditionally defined, has a function. But that function is as servant to theology. Traditional theology died because it forgot its function as servant to wholeness and took on a responsibility it could not fulfill. It was one language, pretending to wholeness or sufficiency. It was a servant, pretending to lordship. It was not necessary, in revolt, to kill it, for it died of its own presumption.

Theology, then, begins with a total commitment of the self to its purpose, a commitment so complete as to compel an engendering, in all the languages of the self, of those structures and directed energies that make the holy purpose a transformative power in the life of the community.

The commitment of the self is total; if it is an error, the self will finally dissolve, for the source of its continued life is gone. Theology is not, then, an intellectual exercise. It is an absolute commitment to that which alone can receive absolute commitment. If life flows from it then the commitment was made to whomever we blaspheme by naming "god" and assigning pronouns like "whomever". If death flows from the commitment it was an idol.

THEOLOGY AS COMMITMENT

Completeness of the commitment requires a completeness of the languages. The physiology of the self extends it into its relations with other selves and things; the languages are the nerves and blood vessels that sustain the body and sustain each other. A single nerve, an artery dissected from the body will shrivel and die. Life is only in wholeness. Theology is the whole structure and vitality of human language or it is sounding brass and a clanging cymbal.

The wholeness of theological speech does not require each person to be a Renaissance man. There are only two languages held in common by all persons: the infinite web of relations with other persons and the care of some portion of the earth. Any theology that declines responsibility for these offends against the whole. Beyond that, each person, in his group, works in care and service for the whole, for the nurturing of one language. The wholeness is in the community.

THEOLOGY AS ENACTMENT

Thus, theology in its propositional form has the same validation as theology in its musical or architectural form: it is a response to and contains the structure and rhythms of the forming experience. It is to be known, therefore, by knowing its organizing principles, its structure and processes, its controlling direction and figure, the emphasis and purpose of its logic, the order of human relations in its dramatics. Its descriptive propositions are the material it works with, as an architect works with the weight and texture of stone. The propositions inform and enliven the constructive imagination as Ictinus, the architect, dreamed his dream of order in the Pentelic marble of the Parthenon, and Robert of Luzarches dreamed in the limestone and the glass of northern France. But the essential human act is in the organizing structure.

Yet there is a logic of development as powerful as the forming logic of structure.

All art forms generate their successors. Gothic art began as a mode of making the sacred order of things present. It developed as a reflection on the possibilities of this creative vision. Gradually it became an essay on the technical possibilities of Gothic architecture. Gothic architecture as a technical exercise became an expressive authority that shaped the souls of those who used it.

Theology emerges from ritual as its manifestation in a propositional structure. Theology, rightly considered, is liturgical, not legislative.

Ritual is the somatic embodiment of the experience of the holy. Much of the contemporary return to ritual is falsified because it emerges from argument.

True theology is an enactment of the primary vision under the conditions of immediacy. But, as are all arts, theology becomes a reflection on its own processes. Displaced from its geometrics and dramatics, its sustaining authority becomes ordinary logic.

Argument has a homiletic function. Argument considered authoritative is always dualistic; it is dialectic. Therefore argument (as in most contemporary theology, "radical" or traditional) may begin with propositions that were once embodiments of the originating symbolic act and, by unknowingly subjecting them to a logical process foreign to the original act, compel them to purposes outside their nature.

Men do not live by reason or pleasure but by the structure of their images.

TWO DEFINITIONS

1. A tentative definition of religion: Religion is the organization of a people's geometrics and dramatics, their structures and their energies, toward a determined purpose which is understood as completing and fulfilling the person in the community.

   Notes on the definition of religion:

   1. It is deliberately dry and schematic. A definition is like a floor plan or a diagram; it should not attempt to include the spaciousness or the vitality of the thing itself.
   2. It deliberately insists on wholeness and purpose, thus including both more and less than definitions often include.
   3. There is no such thing as "religion" but only various particular religions which are to be described and apprehended as particular ways of organizing structure and energy toward purpose.

2. A tentative definition of theology: Theology is the systematic statement, in an appropriate language, of those aspects of a religion which are accessible to that language. It is a manifestation of the religion, and its function is reflection and exposition.

   A. Notes on the definition of theology:

   1. The theology of a religion is incomplete so long as it is understood as only one of the reflective languages. Thus Christian theology has suffered a near fatal drainage of its vitality because it has been confined to its verbal language and has not taken into account Giotto and Bach.

   2. *All* religions have a theology. It is fashionable to assert that many religions (e.g., Hinduism) do not. This is true only if its characteristic language in Christendom (verbal propositions) is taken as normative for the definition. All religions have a systematic exposition in some language. They differ only in the languages chosen. Disposition of

the appointed tasks among the languages and the extent of authority granted to such reflection is crucial to the understanding of theology.

3. In the fullness of being human, reflection (and its corollary, exposition) are essential acts. Those who would abandon theology for some simple gospel or "natural" act simply accept some other theology or defeat religion.

4. Verbal propositions are an authentic human language, and thereby an appropriate language for the enactment of theology.

THE ISSUES OF THEOLOGY

The issues, then, emerge from the analysis:

1. What manner of organism is it that functions as human beings clearly do function?
2. What are the functions of this organism that enable us to speak meaningfully of the things we refer to with such words as "psyche", "mind", "spirit", "soul", and how do these "things" function?
3. What are the extensions of this organism into its world that compels us to define the person in terms of the containing world?

These are the anthropological issues which are propaedeutic to any serious intellectual enterprise, for it is by their means alone that we can define not only who it is we are studying but what we are studying with. Only subsequently is it possible to approach the more immediately "theological" issues.

Anthropological issues are determined analytically by the categories, geometrics and dramatics, with all the elements of them already listed. Anthropological issues become theological in the category of telics, for it is within the category of primordial logic that purpose is defined. When that purpose is within man it is anthropological; when it is "outside" man it is theological.

4. What is the purpose of the person in his world? How is that purpose determined? How is it judged and validated? (This is the teleological and axiological function of theology.)
5. What structures and processes are required, under the conditions of a given moment, to preserve the sense of the purpose? (This is the constructive function of theology.)
6. What physical and intellectual habits of thought and action are required to prevent the processes of this or that field of human activity from becoming autonomous and thus denying the purpose? (This is the critical and disciplinary functions of theology.)

The traditional theological issues are determined within the particular religions (which use ways of organizing structures and energies to a particular purpose) and are contained within these generally defined issues.

These are still too close to the traditional issues. If it is true that we are our languages, *all* our languages, then there is no way to separate a full theology from the issues of all the languages. Thus the issues of theology are not simply those that concern propositional thought but those of the ordering of space, of time, of matter, above all, of rhythm.

Architecture is an exercise in dogmatics.

Bach was one of the major Christian theologians.

What shape should Christianity take to be presented to the Indians?

What is an orthodox rhythm?

THE PRINCIPLES OF THEOLOGICAL WORK

Theology, therefore, is comprehensive or it is nothing. To be truly human, human life must be complete. Theology, now, must be complete in order to be humane.

To be complete, theology must be enacted in all the humane languages. Each language has a function not replaceable by another, nor does one language have authority over another working in its proper sphere.

Equally, each language is responsible to each of the others, to be disciplined and restrained by it, to receive its insights, its structured energies as engendering material.

If the governing condition of theology's engendering is love, that love is not just the love of God but the love of God's gifts. Among those gifts are the languages themselves. A condition of theological creativity is an entranced respect for language in all its potential and its particularities. Only as the inner life, the engendering logic, of the language is evoked can it fulfill its theological purpose, which is to serve as a chalice for the holy.

Love as sentiment is no substitute for competence. Or rather, love in a language, love for a language is manifest only by competence. Competence is not simply a technical condition, it is a sacred trust, if the language is to be a sacramental.

And yet, neither wholeness nor love nor competence determines the final character of a theology. That is shaped by the primordial logic that directs all human work toward purpose. That purpose determines what a religion does and, therefore, how religion emerges into the structures and energies of the human languages. The determination of purpose is, finally and initially, the generative act of theology.

HUMAN PURPOSE AND THE MEASURE OF THE CHURCH

The Church is not something other than true humanity; it is the community of all those who have been reborn; it is the community of all those who have become fully human.

Therefore, there can be no quantitative measure of the work of the Church, no objective test. The work of the Church is being done when true community is engendered. Where true community is not being engendered, all else—wealth, power, display, numbers, influence, institutions, philanthropy, doctrine—are, again, as sounding brass and a clanging cymbal.

Institutions, doctrines, liturgies, are the necessary languages and tools of the Church. They are the formative structures, the transformative metaphors that we think with. To seek a truth outside the conditions of humanity is to deprive us of essential elements of our humanity. But when they become their own reason for being they become destructive of humanity, because they then deny rather than create community.

Equally, the Church can neither be apart from culture nor identified with it. The Church is rightly the soul of a culture, the cohesion of its elements that constitutes its essential structure. But that structure is manifest, transformatively, in many forms that have no direct relation to the Church as such and, therefore, take on a kind of distinct existence. Yet this process, too, is subject to the remorseless logic of human change. Community of purpose emerges through the structures of the situation, generating all those structured processes that we call culture. These quite naturally take on their own life, generating an energetic dialogue that creates new structures. Gradually a cultural weariness sets in. Evidence becomes too complex, the strain is too great for the intellectual and emotional resources available, procedures become fixed, institutions become static. Since communication is part of process, institutions become detached from each other and from the soul that engendered them. Since the soul of a culture, as in a person, is in relation, it disperses as though it had been sucked out of the heart. With no fertile principle to engender process, the Church becomes identified with its institutions, which now, inevitably, are the institutions of culture. Unable to provide either creative energy or prophetic criticism the Church collapses into impotence, basing its existence only on its ability to serve the purposes of the dominant political and economic interests.

This is too deterministic—human beings remorselessly imprisoned in the logic of historical development. There is a logic, and it is remorseless in its working, particularly for those who set an isolated will against the logic of fear, self-interest, deception, that make up the political orders. But structures are rarely rigid, human beings are cranky and unpredictable, and Christianity has resources for its own transformation that are unequaled in any set of human ideas. There are ways back into the fertile metaphors of the Church and then ways forward into the fructifying union with the forms of present existence. The act of love that generates community in the present requires the loving faith that gives new life to the community of the past and creates faithful hope which is the loving community proceeding into the future.

The End of the Declarative and Imperative Modes in Theology

An Essay on The Failure of Modern Gnosticism

We can learn more about the fundamental convictions of a theologian by examining his verbs than by looking only at his subject and object.

As every writer does, theologians use many kinds of verbs, and the examination of the modes of all of them would be useful. I have in mind now a particular kind; the fundamental working verbs that set out the implicit assertions and assumptions underlying the overt assertions that are the occasion for the writing. It is not quite true to say that the medium "is" the message, but there is no separation between form and content, and form is revelatory of the most important content.

Gathering evidence for these assertions turned out to be almost ridiculously easy; opening any book on theology immediately provides examples. Two useful examples are recent classic theologians, Karl Barth and Rudolph Bultmann.

Barth's writings are characterized by a lordly and confident "is". The imperative occurs as the verb "must" but always the imperative depends on the declarative; we *must* do thus and so because the order of things and the will of God *is* thus and so. The result is a certain security and majestic calm. Man may, by the assertions of the text, be a grubby and unpleasant creature but this would not be known from the style; there, God's in his heaven and all's right with the world.

Bultmann's verb usage covers a wide range. His sentences are generally declarative, as scholarly prose must be, but their tone is set by the tense and agitated imperative, "is incredible", "would be senseless", "no man can", "no alternative", "we are bound". These samples were chosen from a single page selected at ramdon.[35]

This style does not characterize simply the authoritarian theologians of our past. One paper by Thomas Altizer, 19 pages long, contains at least 40 "musts". If all other imperative forms are included, it is clear that the overwhelmingly dominant mode is imperative.[36]

There are a number of ways to take hold of this phenomenon. The expressive effect is strangely uneasy, agitated. There is a curious lack of confidence (if it's all that certain, why be so repetitive?) or an equally curious overconfidence (the truth is clear and all people out there must conform to it). In either case the tone is strained, tense.

Imperatives are imperial; by definition and necessity, there is an authority behind them. What, then, is the authority for these imperatives?

At this point the implied dichotomy between Barth on the one hand, and Bultmann and Altizer on the other, fades. Expressively, they are altogether different, but stylistically they are not. Barth is confident in a way that enables him simply to state the truth. Bultmann and Altizer are either less confident of their assertions or less confident of the reader's ability to accept the assertions. But in each case authority is imperious; the declarative mode, after all, assumes that the subject under discussion can be known, and the consequences of that knowing "must" be accepted. Neo-orthodoxy *asserts* that certain relations (man-God) are unstructured— but neo-orthodoxy is certainly not unstructured. What Barth's form asserts about man has very little to do with what Barth's argument asserts about man; he is very much in the same boat with the logician's ancient friend, the Cretan who says all Cretans are liars. It is not altogether convincing to construct a system that asserts that everything man constructs is corrupt.

Paradoxes of this kind have been known to others, nor would it be sensible to base our argument on the limitations of language, without acknowledging that the current obsession of philosophers is precisely the authority of language to make meaningful statements. The problem is precisely the one that paralyzes any discipline that begins to define its work as the examination of its own implements: the problem of infinite regress.

I have a book of aesthetics that spends three pages in a close examination of the statement "The sky is cloudy." The angels are beginning to dance on the point of the pin, but neither the argument about angels nor about cloudy skies is without purpose. But the sentence "The sky is cloudy" is being tightly examined by sentences which equally require tight examination by sentences which equally require. . . .

Any procedure involved in such infinite regress can be accounted for in one of three ways. It may be completely tautological, after the famous explanation "Opium produces sleep because of its sleep-inducing properties." I prefer to think more highly of these theologians than that.

Or their procedure is truly caught in infinite regress, in which case the only appropriate human response would be despair. In fact, this seems quite clearly to characterize much of the work done by younger theologians, who seem, by and large, to have lost all faith in their professional work having any real purpose and so continue to do it simply because it is the only thing they are trained to do.[37]

There is a third possibility—that the enterprise was misconceived in the first place.

To develop that argument I must try to indicate what I judge to be the authority behind the imperatives of Barth, Bultmann, Altizer and, so far as I can tell, all theological writing, including this one:

1. In some way, in some degree, man is set over against the reality of the world; he can "see" it, both literally, and in the revealing figurative use of that word.
2. He is able by his senses to acquire information about that world that is both adequate (there is enough of it to provide the materials for reasonable conclusions about the nature of things) and accurate (what is known is truly known).
3. He is able, by the action of the reasoning intellect operating according to principles of logic, to put together this information and to draw conclusions from it that put its essential attributes and relations into the form of verbal propositions.
4. These propositions are true, they are worthy of belief and commitment, as standing for the essential reality of things.

This account, as it stands, clearly represents intellectual history as dependent on some form of the empiricist tradition, which may appear as oversimplification. I am not, myself, much impressed with the distinction between empiricism (or nominalism, realism in its modern sense, or even phenomenology) and idealism. There are vital operational differences and very clear differences of proportion and emphasis between points (2) and (3) of the outline but these need not affect this argument; Plato and Aristotle are not really so fundamentally different when they are placed against, say, Lao-Tze.

Now the question of authority becomes a little clearer: it is placed somewhere along this continuum. Again the empiricist and the idealist will place authority at a different point, but to those of us who do not work according to this scheme, they are all riding the same train.

Traditionally, theologians would not accept this scheme as in any way defining their authority which, in line with their name, ultimately derives from God. But obviously there is no internal reliability to such an assertion. It simply adds another assumption or two to the initial scheme. For example, it adds the assumption that the whole process was created by God and the propositional conclusions are statements about God or about God's order. Or it adds the assumption that God, whatever his relation to the order of things, is something altogether apart from the order of things ("wholly other"). But this, too, must be known, either by direct illumination and communication or by communication through authoritative acts or documents.

Theological assertions are not testable by means other than those used for the testing of any other assertion; the ancient claim to authority is founded otherwise on a purely circular argument. Thus, if the theologian finds authority in the will of God, that will can be known only by some means, such as an authoritative scripture. But scripture thereby simply becomes the occasion for the process schematized above; it is taken in through the senses, acts on the intelligence and issues in statement or act. Another theologian might be less singleminded and extend the range of authoritative acts, making, for example, empirical or historical experience a far more important part of the process. But that does not alter the fact that it all goes through the reasoning intelligence of the theologian.

Therefore the differences between the declarative and imperative modes are expressionistic differences of great importance in understanding the specifics of a particular historical situation; they are of no considerable importance epistemologically. The authoritative assumption is the same: it is theological logic.

"Evidence" can be presumed available to all alike. It is the procedures by which it is handled and the assertions that are the product of the procedures which are decisive, and those procedures are governed by logical reason.

It is time now to look at the third term I featured in my essay title—gnosticism.

Gnosticism has a reasonably clear definition and historical provenance. Every serious student of contemporary culture is aware that gnosticism in something like its original form is appearing again. But it is not the theology of ancient gnosticism that concerns me at the moment. It is the gnosticism that promises salvation by a "knowing", a knowing that is achieved by discipline, that is a mystery available to the discipline of an elite.

Again, it is essential to draw the line between the significant parts of the theological statement. Another excursus is essential to avoid confusion, a confusion which is endemic to all critical activity.

Criticism has dealt at length with the problem of "form" and "content," variously asserting the relation between the two. But the debate has bogged down in the failure to make a vital distinction within the primary distinction.

"Content" has been made synonymous with "subject matter." There is, quite clearly, a difference between subject matter and form so, by transfer, it becomes an intellectual habit to think that subject matter is separable from form. In the criticism of theology, subject matter (a term from the arts) has its exact equivalent in the assertions of the argument (and, finally, the system) as distinct from the form in which it is cast.

But content and subject matter are not the same thing. Subject matter is a part of the *material*, that which is ordered by form. Subject matter is extraordinarily powerful. It can, by its action in the imagination, profoundly modify the form just as, in the work of art, the actual material of the work in its own quality both limits and generates images of order in the imagination of the artist.

There was a time, earlier in the century, when artists and critics thought that form could be abstracted from history, from content, from material, and made the primary concern of the arts. It didn't work because the pressures on form are too great. It didn't work because it goes against the character of all creativity.

The subject may, variously, be the purpose of the work or simply its occasion. The subject may ostensibly be one thing which actually conceals and expresses something else (the basis for all Freudian and Marxist criticism). The same subject may be very different things at different times and with different men. (A Madonna by Cimabue is Queen of Heaven, a Madonna by Fra Lippo Lippi is a lovely Florentine girl).

The material, including the subject, is shaped by the hand, the eye, the mind of the artist into a living form. The content is everything that the form stands for, everything that is communicated by the form, including the interpretation of the subject. The subject varies considerably both in character and importance in different stylistic moments. Nevertheless, it is always present, asserting itself insistently within the life of forms.

Thus there is no form without a content, for content is what happens because of the form. Equally, there is no content without a form, for much of what it "is", is the form.[38]

There are times when analogies from one discipline are useful in another. But this time I do not deal in analogies. The paradigm I am describing was first clarified in art criticism, but in no sense is it confined to the arts.

Thus the exact functional equivalent of subject matter is the argument and its contained assertions. It is given form in the structure and generative energies of the systematic ordering of the text, its proportion, rhythms, spacing, texture, etc., and in the use of the language which is the final material of the embodiment of the argument.

The content, then, is the whole: the argument, the assertions, shaped into a particular rhythmic structure, manifest in the particularities of the chosen idiom.

It happens that each art, including theology, places its emphasis at different places. Musical texture is normally of central concern to the composer, who will take great care to specify the instrumentation. But, in *The Art of The Fugue*, Bach was apparently interested only in the pure tonal relations and indifferent to texture so he did not specify the instrumentation. Even so, *The Art of The Fugue*, is a very different piece when played by a harpsichord than when played by an organ.

It happens that most theologians are not much concerned with verbal texture. Thus their argument can be played in German or in English with less loss than a poem by Goethe suffers in translation. But there is loss and there is change, for the matter and the formal possibilities of English are quite different from German.

There is a danger here of falling into the trap of language determinism; it is not true that we can think only those thoughts that our language permits us to think or that our language controls our view of the world. The human organism is much too complicated for that to be true. This suggests another distinction: that between content and meaning. Obviously the desire of the maker is that the work should mean its content, that the reader or spectator should receive the content as it was intended. But, finally, content belongs to the work and meaning to the reader. Content is what the form makes manifest. Meaning is what happens in the spectator or reader or hearer because of the work. Thus, conceivably, the same meaning can happen through a considerable range of forms.

But if attention is directed the other way, to the creator and his intended meaning, then the form becomes decisive. His "meaning" (the content of the work) is the fusion of material and subject into the particularities of the form. The decisive choices are made by him and decisive choices issue from the depths of personality, bringing up far more than the person himself ever knows; a theological work is a making manifest of the reality of the person as much as a work of art is.

Thus the divergencies of personality and of commitment are

made manifest in the form. What is asserted in the argument may be contradicted by the form.

This excursus was essential to make clear that it is not frivolous to speak of contemporary theologians as gnostics. Very few serious contemporary theologians would affirm a gnostic theology. But there is an ordering of assumptions manifest in the form that can, with risk, be referred to as gnostic.

The account of verb usage I offered at the beginning of this paper is certainly not a full, formal analysis. But in any written work, verbs are very important indeed. They set the rhythm and direction, they are the links in relation and therefore establish the tonality. And they decisively set out assumptions about authority, whatever may be said about authority in the argument.

It is not necessary to get involved in the debate over "God-talk" or all the assertions and debates over the possibility of saying anything meaningful about God. All these assertions and systems are internal to this gnosticism and represent no more than the system's validation of itself. Hence they are convincing only to those who are willing to accept their logic. It is futile, further, to argue against them, for the argument can be conducted only on the terms of the systems themselves, which is to surrender the case at the beginning.

It should probably be said that all arguments are ultimately of this kind depending on agreement about admissible evidence and the logical tools for handling that evidence. But it must also be said that certain kinds of argument have a wider range of discernible evidence, and the argument can therefore be subjected to at least a minimum of scientific method: a check by repetition. Arguments about God are entirely within the system, subject to no check whatsoever. They are mysteries to be indulged as ceremonies of initiation. They are, in short, not a knowledge but a gnosis.

It is not to be argued but stated: a god who can be known is not God. It is an elementary definition of God that he is not commensurate with human categories or achievable through human acts.

Yet the declarative and the imperative assume the authority of the logic that produced them. In earlier times the situation was worse: the logical assertions so clearly participated in the divine being that refusal to accept them was the same as an offense against God himself and punishable accordingly.

This argument may account for one of the most bizarre aspects of religious psychology—the compulsion of human beings to defend omnipotence. This is psychopathology. I judge it to be a consequence of the undemonstrable character of logic. All conflict should cease in the presence of the omnipotent and omniscient. The fact that intolerance and persecution are the natural accompaniment to the gnostic claim is perhaps a symptom of the strain and tension that inheres in a claim based on logic rather than evidence.

Thus, the gnostic claim did not insure the presence of the divine but the ruin of the church. Since suffering and not the peace of God seemed the inevitable consequence of the theological assertion, the conscience and the sensibility of men simply rejected the whole quarrel and turned elsewhere.[39] The church had to become dispensable because of its very ferocity. Therefore, the lordly confidence of the declarative modes and the arrogant presumption of the imperative sound not only strangely out of date but uneasily reminiscent of a day well gone.

Yet the question should not be left in this political arena. Quite early it was the judgment of the Church that gnosticism was false to Christianity, so the church ought to be able to accommodate itself to the failure of more recent gnosticism. If the claims to the knowledge of God sound as strange in the mouth of the theologians as they do in the presumptions of the evangelical preachers the necessary result is not to assume that there is no God, nor that God has died. Nor is it necessary nor even particularly profitable to scratch around in the debris trying to salvage some fragments of the theological furniture. A tamed and chastened theology might even have a useful purpose to serve.

The implications of the argument suggest a fashionable position which I do not intend to adhere to either: that words, logic, reason, rationality, the objective consciousness have failed and therefore must be rejected. Such a position is even more a betrayal of the nature of things. To talk at all we use words. Words are several things, among which is their function of objectifying our experience of the world. Words are ordered into patterns determined by their own function and reference and by the intention of their user. They, of necessity, submit to grammar and to logic. Responsible humanity requires a responsible logic.

But logic is a guardian of language, not the commander of the holiness of God. Logic is partial insurance that the acts and images of our speech should be respectful of the structure of language and the physiology that is doing the thinking. Logic is not the vicar of Christ. The ability to use logic does not confer on its user the authority of God.

Thus the authority of logic derives from the authority of language; language does not derive its authority from logic.

Therefore, it is not possible to develop an argument logically and then claim, declaratively or imperatively, that the conclusion carries the authority of truth.

The case turns, therefore, on the question of language and the capacity of language to embody truth or to give access to reality. It is not an unnoticed problem, but it is probably fair to say that not very much progress has been made toward its resolution. A good part of the difficulty in resolving the problem originates in a failure to conduct the debate according to an elementary distinction.

We persist in treating our language as though its components refer to things. It is, perhaps natural that we do so; we ask for a newspaper, we receive a newspaper, not a loaf of bread. It is natural that we should assume that "newspaper" applies to newspapers. But this is not the case. The word is function within a context, a complex of signals that represents a desire and a decision on our part, a response and a decision on the part of the seller. Thus Coleridge was perfectly correct when he said,

> . . . it is the fundamental mistake of grammarians and writers on the philosophy of grammar and language, to suppose that words and their syntaxis are the immediate representatives of *things* or that they correspond to *things*. Words correspond to thoughts, and the legitimate order and connection of words, to the *laws* of thinking and to the acts and affections of the thinker's mind. . .[40]

Even asking for the newspaper is a complicated interaction of persons, not a manipulation of counters which are equivalent to objects.

Whatever "God" is, the word does not refer to God but to an event (acts and affections) in our own minds.

The conventional view holds language apart from the uses made of it. Scholars develop skills in handling certain kinds of evidence and in finding what they consider the language equivalent of that evidence and the relations that exist among the items of that evidence. Thus, the language statement carries with it the authority of reality and with no sense of undue pride the scholar makes his declarative or imperative statement. He, after all, is only the servant or the agent of the inner mystery.

But this is not the way language works. Language is not attached to things but to our apprehension of things. The ordering of language is according to our understanding of our own apprehensions in fruitful intercourse with the structure and logic of language itself.

Thus the authority of any theological statement is not in God but in ourselves.

We apprehend the world in the structures and processes of our bodies. These apprehensions interact with our language—all our languages, including speech, gesture, moral act and all the disciplined languages of our art and scholarship. Given our limitation as persons only a few languages are available to each one of us but, equally, each of us has an appropriate language in which what we are becomes manifest. But what is manifest is ourselves and the unknowable God only as he chooses to make of us priests or prophets.

To make of theology a declarative or an imperative is to claim an authority that no man can rightly claim. It is to assume the posture of an adept and claim to be an initiate of the hidden mysteries.

It is neither accidental nor incidental that the history of theology should have been a history of intolerance and persecution, for intolerance and its offspring, persecution, are built into the theological claim.

The proper claim of theology is not "This is true," but "This is what has happened to me."

I have heard the claim made that a man does not have to be a Christian believer to be a Christian theologian. Scholarly theological journals, aping the false god of "scholarly objectivity", read as though they were written by such men. But theology is the outward and visible sign of an inward and spiritual grace.

This in no way diminishes the rigor or the importance of traditional theological discipline. The builder who makes his faith manifest in a structure is not emancipated by his devotion from responsibility to the principles of structural logic. If he builds badly, the building collapses and kills people. So the theologian bears a delegated responsibility to a necessary language; his failure is an injury to the whole.

Theology is not a command but an act of love.

Theology is properly a liturgy in the etymological sense of the word. The "liturgy" of an ancient Greek was a public service—outfitting a ship, production of a drama—performed for the state by a wealthy man. Theology is the public service performed for the faithful community by those entrusted with the languages of the mind.

Theology is a liturgy in the more usual modern sense, a public ceremonial setting forth, for the corporate participation, the wholeness of the common faith.

Wholeness is a large word; it is not in the attainment of one language. Theology in its inherited sense suffered and caused suffering because it aspired to an unattainable completeness as well as an unattainable accuracy. Theology is complete only as it is enacted in all modes of symbolic speech and act.

Theology—or theologies—is not a statement of eternal truth. It is the setting forth of the faith of this group, at this time, in this place, in the contingencies and particularities of a historical position. As men we can never know the eternal or aspire to the truth of the eternal. The eternal comes to us only in the remorseless and concrete particularities of our lives. Christian theology is not Christian by virtue of logical propositions. It is Christian by virtue of its mediation of the Christ through the immediacies of concrete experience. Christian theology is radically incarnational or it is as sounding brass and a clanging cymbal.

We learn from our predecessors. By participating in their written theologies we participate in their intellectual faith. We put ourselves to school to them and learn how faith is bodied forth in common speech. But we are not they, nor do we live in their world or speak their language. The only people who can do our theologies is ourselves, our selves, our souls and bodies, wholly dedicated.

Thus the authority of theology is never in itself but in its use to a service beyond its own decisions. It is offered as liturgy and sacrifice. If it is received and used as a sacrament and is a channel of grace, then it is for this space of time, beyond the assertion of the theologian, at a choice that is not his own, true.

Therefore, the theologian can surrender his imperial declaratives, surrender his claim to the defense of omnipotence and his presumption of sharing in the authority of omnipotence. The role of theology is servant, not master.

There is a program and a definition of the work here, both of which may be clear from what has been said.

The work of the theologian is not, in substance, different from what it has been. The point of origin, the claim and the direction of the work differ and this difference reflects back on the tone of the substance.

The point of origin is awareness of the role of theology as neither description nor authority but enactment. Thus the preparation of the theologian is not in the first place professional but is his life in faith.

Then to make the enactment faithful he must know his chosen language. If he is to make his language a chalice for the holy, he must hold it in its completeness and integrity, its immediacy, its eccentricity. He who would be a theologian in words is not speaking the language of the gods, but the common speech of men which can be used sacramentally only if it is accepted in its human depth and range, but then coaxed into obedience to the heavenly vision.

The theologian in any language must saturate himself in the reference of that language—which is the common life as it was shaped by the immediacies of the language. Only as the common life of man emerges into the language can theology take up that common life in liturgical devotion.

The theologian must saturate himself in the other theological languages, so he may carry into his own a sense of the whole of which his work is a part. Only so can he be saved from the presumption to completeness or sufficiency, and therefore authority.

The theologian trains himself by immersion in the work of those who manifested their fidelity in his chosen language as it appeared in the concreteness of their day. Only so does he learn his craft and art.

Having thus trained himself, he holds the common life in the reliquary of his language and presents it as his bounden duty and service.

The event is in the hands of God.

PART FIVE

Trinitarian Christianity

I. A Meditation on the Christ

INCARNATION AND RESURRECTION: AN ARGUMENT

For a century, for a long time earlier, the search has gone on for the Jesus of history and for the way to harmonize the Jesus of history with the Christ of faith, for the explanation that can give intelligibility to faith in a metaphysics of substance.

If the real is only tangible substance, if tangibility is the measure of the real, what is the reality of that which is not tangible?

Why is it so difficult to learn the lesson of Thomas?

We can know only what we have; history does not "exist". Only the artifacts of history exist, the detritus out of which we make history in our image of order. All time is always now. Faith cannot wait on scholarship any more than it can wait on argument, both of which are discipline and limit, no more.

Whatever happened *then* we cannot know; a stenographic or journalist's account, a film would come to us only through, shaped by, the structures of our own energies and so would be a part of us. Thus the record we have is authoritative and determinative. The ultimate order of the human soul, the logos which held all existence into being from the beginning, was given body by this man. The logos was present from the beginning, not as a mystery, a ghost, but as the principle of life itself. It was incarnate in this man as revelation and as method. It was incarnate in substance because substance is the matter of the real but incarnate as symbolic structure because only symbolic structure determines human reality out of endless and meaningless flow.

Because only symbolic structures are real, the only vehicle for the resurrection is symbolic structures. Therefore, the Christ is wholly present to us in the structures of mortal existence.

The only true church is the Christ risen into the true word and true sacrament and the living history of the church, proceeding from the man who made them present among the humble and the poor. The Christ is the final shaping of the body of the imagination, the metaphor holding the energies of our structure into the new body by which we live in and beyond the world.

CHRISTIAN APOLOGETICS

The doctrine of the Trinity is not a description of God. As a doctrine it is indefensibly illogical. Who can know or grasp or explain or describe the mystery of God? The very formula *doctrine of the Trinity* is a blasphemy, for it literally pro-fanes the holiness of the only symbol that can put us into the source of our life.

The Trinity can only be lived, not understood or explained.

Christianity is trinitarian or else it is only one of the many religions that men have used to order their lives.

It was the great dream of Joachim de Fiore that the Father, the Son and the Spirit manifest themselves successively and that his was the age of the Spirit which would bring time to an end. We are no longer so confident about dating the end of time, but we may be better located in time to talk about the Spirit.

If we can think only those things our languages permit us to think, then the Holy Spirit—and therefore the Holy Trinity—has been known to many in their flesh and in their acts but to few in their "minds" and their verbal intelligence. The life of fulfilling love, which is to say the language of fulfilling love, has been available; but those who use the verbal languages, burdened with a metaphysics of substance, have had too little opportunity to speak of the Spirit. They speak about the Spirit; by grace, what they say about the Spirit may be sacramental with the Spirit. But there is no way a metaphysics of substance can speak of Spirit. For Spirit is not a substance, but a relation, he who is the bearer of love. In a metaphysics of substance—or in the language of a metaphysics of substance—Spirit can only be talked of as a thing, or as the affirmation of a mystical and undefined abstraction, and neither of these is the Spirit.

The forms of the verb *to be* are affirmations of structured process, not passive and inert substances. "Is" cannot rightly mean "have a separable physical existence". "Is" means "being in relation with".

Thus the doctrines of the Holy Trinity (of which this is one) are not descriptions of the indescribable. They are attempts to map the holy order of things.

The Holy Trinity is not a substance or even three substances. It—or they—is the way itself into the final mystery of being.

THE MEASURE OF THE TRINITY

The measure of the Trinity (the measure, not the reality), is the model of reality that is the definition of purpose. There is some structure of relation that is the final ordering of all energies; dramatics and geometrics cohere according to the logic that leaves us to choose only from dualism, monotheistic unity, polytheistic multiplicity or anarchy. Where the Trinity is absent—as purpose, as model, as enspiriting guide—the order is unbalanced. For without the Holy Trinity, the all is absorbed into the one; or the one dissolves into the all; or the irreconcilable conflict is built into the experience of things and the primordial duality governs all experience.

Only in the Trinity, can the one and the all cohere without loss. Only in the Trinity does duality emerge into multiplicity without loss of unity.

Without the Trinity, dramatics can be defined and absorbed into telics and geometrics; history is absorbed into structure. Telics and geometrics without dramatics is metaphysics, the presumption to describe or enforce the ultimate order of things.

Dramatics and telics without geometrics becomes existentialism, the attempt to order the self in reality by the unlocated and isolated act.

Dramatics without telics and geometrics is only undefined and purposeless energy.

Geometrics without telics and dramatics is sterile and purposeless statics.

It is of note that Christendom is almost never trinitarian. It is usually imperialistically monotheistic, often polytheistic, almost always dualistic. No one has yet succeeded in making the Trinity the model for an institution.

In the Trinity, drama is given place and structure, yet neither place nor system are themselves holy. In the Trinity, place and systematic structure do not control the affairs of men but inform the living drama of the single person's relation to the others.

The Incarnation is the demonstration that the fullness of being is inseparable from the fullness of this earth, and that the purpose of being is not exhausted in this earth. Were Jesus only a god we would have no more than another monotheism. Were Jesus only a man, we would have no hope except in another polytheism.

THE TRINITARIAN RELATION

The relation of the Trinity is love that permits the one, the individual, to be and yet maintain the whole from which the one can draw its life. Since man's condition is duality, he might grasp the telics and the geometrics of the Trinity but not the dramatics and, in the name of the Trinity, reassert an imperialistic unity. Therefore, true love is defined by its openness to sacrifice on the model of love that was sacrificed.

Or man might grasp the telics and the dramatics of the Trinity but not the geometrics and, in the name of the Trinity, define human purpose as the sacrifice of the self in a larger order. Therefore, true love is conditioned by its willingness to sacrifice, but is defined by its openness to the love that generates the abundant life.

The condition of the Trinity is exchange.

The manifestation of the Trinity is relation.

To live in Christ is not simply to live in and for the other, which is only ethical monotheism. To live in Christ is also to let the other live in me. The one must become many, as the many can only live in the one. Love that is not sacrificial is not love in the Trinity, but love that is only sacrificial is not in the Trinity either.

THE ORDER AND THE PROCESS OF
THE CHRISTIAN LIFE

A *model* is a notional system that serves a notional purpose. By its means we understand who we are. But, as we use it so, a model is not the way to become who we are, for a model is by definition something outside our self.

Yet all our acts, including our models, are, by definition, our selves reaching out into the environing world. The model emerges within the interchange of our selves and our circumstances; the model shapes the self by shaping the apprehension of the self's circumstances.

A model is metaphor and, therefore, a ganglion, a structure, an act of transformation. The Trinity as model may be an academic thing, made for the purposes of understanding. But the power of the Trinity cannot be contained in a model, for the model becomes a part of the acting body, transforming.

Thus there emerges the meaning of *participation*, to be "in" Christ, to have Christ "in" us.

The Christian life derives wholly from the participation in the Christ. Therefore the crucial question for the Christian is: How do I participate in Christ? It is a statement that sounds good as a ritual chant, but does it truly mean anything? So fine an intelligence as Paul Tillich could say, "The symbol participates in the reality it symbolizes." It sounds impressive. It is certainly true. But there is nothing we can do with it unless we know how it is true.

For the Christian, Christ *is* the transformative metaphor. The trinitarian order is fixed in the logic of things but impossible to achieve by logic. The trinitarian order is achieved only by participation.

Participation in Christ is to take in—eat—the transforming metaphor, the act and order that reshapes the very being of a person.

THE ICONS OF CHRIST

The pietistic sects say that Christ is in the Bible and so reading the Bible is participating in Christ. The Catholics say Christ is in the sacraments, or in the institutional life. The moralistic sects find him in obedience to the moral law. The liberals find him in social action. To detach one of these from the whole is to turn it into magic, whether it is the Bibleolatry of the fundamentalist sect or the social conscience of the liberal, for magic is the use of the sacred act or object to achieve a desired result. Within the whole and as a function of the common life, each is a vital part.

The Bible is the authoritative Word, for it is the structure, chosen in the common life, that has the metaphoric power, the transforming energy. The argument over Biblical authority, over its errors and contradictions, over demythologizing, are quite beside the point, except in the old metaphysics of substance. Christ is not a thing, either to be boxed up in a Biblical box or boxed up in a demythologized liberal box. The Bible is neither kind of box. It is a function and a relation. It is one of the great transforming metaphors of the Christ.

So, too, do the sacraments truly contain Christ. The communicant truly receives Christ in the wholeness of the service, the totality of the service. Again the debates over the Presence originate in a metaphysics of substance; in the metaphysics of function and process they are without point. Christ is truly "in" the sacrament, but only in the whole act which requires the cleansing action of confession, the physicality of the elements, the intention.

Therefore to partake of the sacrament falsely is truly to partake of damnation—death—because to do it falsely breaks wholeness, relation, falsifies intention and turns the act into magic. It is not damnation in the sense that a judicial punishment is designated in compensation for an act. It is damnation because it destroys the relation that sustains the community. Therefore the person, separated from the community, recoils on himself, and the isolated self cannot sustain life.

Similarly, the moral life turns the relation outward. Here, too, charity can be done falsely with the same fatal effect. Done for my salvation it can destroy me, for my salvation is in the custody of my neighbor. Done for the other it becomes our common salvation, for the Christ is thereby truly—literally—in the relation thereby established.

Christ is never in the isolated act, the isolated thing, the isolated word. Christ is only in the relation, the Word.

CHRISTIAN METAPHYSICS

As long as metaphysics of substance rules our imagination, there is no intelligible account of the Christ. For whatever that deceitful word "is" means, it can apply to a relation, an energy, as well as to a substance. And energy as well as substance can have a personality.

The Spirit, the Trinity, "is" the relation, and life is only in the Spirit. Therefore, the sin against the Spirit is truly unforgivable, because the sin against the Spirit is truly death and therefore truly damnation. Forgiveness and resurrection are in the life of the Spirit only, for the Spirit only is life.

Therefore the crucial aspect of the Christian life is not the Crucifixion—sacrificial love—for sacrificial love is the common lot of man. The definition of the Christian life is rebirth into abundance of life. It is not of the essence of the child to be sacrificed but to rejoice in the abundance of being.

Yet the Christian is always open to sacrifice, as Christ was open to sacrifice. In our free will we have made the kind of world in which goodness and joy can appear only at the cost of sacrifice. The Crucifixion is not a price required by God; it is the price we exact for our right to sin.

Therefore Christians hold the conditions of life joyfully, because they must hold them lightly; life is with them but they are not purpose. In obedience to the Spirit, this life is joyful, for it is the gift of the Creator.

It is also subject to sacrifice because we required the wage of our sin or make a world in which sacrifice must happen. Sacrifice is a price often paid, the willingness to sacrifice is a condition of who we are. It is the nature of the Spirit to be the abundance of life and therefore his nature to be with those who affirm the abundance of life in their gracious willingness to depart from it.

THE VIRTUES

Three great virtues are the central virtues, because they define our life in time:

Faith is the virtue of the past
Love is the virtue of the present
Hope is the virtue of the future

Love is the greatest virtue because it is the means whereby time is translated into space. It is the decisive virtue of our present life because it defines our relation with each other and with the earth. Without love we are—literally—nothing. But love cannot be love without root or purpose. The root of love is faith, the participation in that which has happened, that which has been made. The nature of love is our present life. The purpose of love is hope, that which will be done and made in the future.

Faith without love and hope is superstition, the vain worship of idols.
Hope without love and faith is a vanity and a delusion.
Love without faith and hope is an empty, indulgent emotion.

The main emphasis of this book has been love, for love is the condition of the work to be done. Under the pressure of love we seek the community of faith that gives structure to the energies of love. But the account would be incomplete with no word of hope, for it is only hope that can sustain the wearying effort of the faithful work, the failure and falsehood that will be a part of it as of all things.

FAITH

The faith that redeems is not an affirmation of propositions, nor submission to institutional discipline nor participation in devotional or liturgical practices, which are training and nourishment only. The faith that redeems is an ordering of the structure and dramatics—the soul—of man into the open wholeness of the Trinity.

Eternal life is not a reward for good behavior or right belief, nor a possession of a selected elite. Eternal life is a consequence of the ordering of the soul, into the wholeness and holiness of the Trinity.

The resurrected body is not a material act, but a vital structure now so tuned, so organized, that it can enter into the fullness of being, rather than dispersing with the dissolution of the natural body which was, for a time, the occasion of its event.

Theology is not faith, but one of the instruments of faith. As a formal discipline, theology is valid only as a description and a discipline in formal thought of an ordering that happens elsewhere; theology is not legislative nor is it normative. Christian theology, Christian ethics and morals, the Christian life, is the placement of persons into relation with each other at rhythmic intervals and in a dramatic structure that makes possible their opening into the vital life of the Holy Trinity, the life of living love.

The tragedy of our time is that those in power are monists, those rebelling against power are polytheists or anarchists. The Church is monotheist and at the submissive service of monistic imperialism. Most of those who, in love, are rebelling against power, do so in the name of polytheism or anarchism and thus ultimately serve oppressive dualism. The great task of the Christian, outside Christendom, is to be open to the Holy Trinity, the integrity of the self in sacrificial love that is the only source of life.

THE MANIFESTATION OF THE HOLY TRINITY

The Holy Trinity is the abundance of being, the fructifying relation. In the world of our making, the Trinity is manifest in hiddenness, among the humble, among the few. The Spirit departs from those who violate the abundance of life and is manifest in the sacrificial suffering of those who are required to pay the price.

That the Holy Trinity is an impossible mystery for natural man is shown by the fact that Christianity (or Christendom) has been overwhelmingly monotheistic and polytheistic even when, hidden within it, the Spirit was making his redeeming way. Equally, in all the world's disorder, whenever the vision of trinitarian wholeness shapes life and relations, there the Trinity is manifest.

The primordial duality of man and woman can be resolved into multiplicity (polygamy or promiscuity) or unity (imperialism) or dualism (ascetic celibacy). A true marriage is duality resolved into a larger whole without loss of the individual. Wherever and whenever true marriage has existed, there is the Christ, in the living model of his only true church.

In its monotheism, Christianity has caused more human suffering than any other institution with the possible exception of Islam. Given the work of the Spirit and the nature of the world we have made, the presence of the Spirit is with those who suffer, not those who cause the suffering. Therefore, to be in the Spirit, we must take the suffering ones into our souls. They have paid the price we required; what they thereby receive is ours only as their fate and our own guilt become part of our structured energies and thus is taken into ourselves. We have crucified them and Christ in them. Christ is resurrected in us only as we can go down into the grave with them.

The task of the Trinity is the same for the faithful of all ages, from the first man to the last—openness to redemptive love under the condition of sacrificial love as the means of rebirth into abundance of life. The task of the Trinity is set before us in a particular form in each generation. Christ presents himself to us for our testing in that death, not in the heroic deeds we would have performed had we been present in the Garden, or the affirmation we would have made had we been present in the courtyard of the high priest.

SERVANT AND LORD

The Lordship of Christ has led Christians, against the express command of their Lord, to translate that lordship into the lordship of Christians. The idea of Christendom was born, the idea of a Christian society, a Christian nation.

But the imagery of the kingdom of God, the kingdom of which Christ is lord, is always of the small and hidden—the leaven in the loaf, the salt, the lost coin, things that are small and hidden, yet make all the difference.

There is no reason to hope for "the conversion of the world," nor, given the present state of our symbolic equipment, is there any reason to think that such a world would be particularly pleasant; the record of Christendom is not dominated by love and peace. The role of the Christian and the Christian church is to work as the leaven within a mass that is not notably Christian and, by working quietly and in hiddenness, transform it.

For one of the images is the mustard seed, which is small, is buried, dies in order to live, grows, and sustains the life and weight of many. The image of the mustard seed is not that of a conquering nation, but of organic life, growing naturally as the yeast slowly and at its own natural pace, makes paste into bread.

The force of the Christian is never to use force but to make, to create, in such a way that abundance of life is fulfilled and the Trinity made possible.

THE SOUL

Few things have done so much harm to religion and to the definition of the self as the principle of 'the immortal soul', the postulate of an indefinable, intangible, immaterial something, fixed or imprisoned in the body for a term but surviving the death of the body.

But the soul is not natural, not a necessary part of human existence. It is, rather, an achievement. It is not born with the body but engendered in it and by means of it.

The soul is the capacity for moral life, the organization, the structure of bodily energies, that transcends the natural and achieves the intentional. The soul is the bringing of the elements of the self into so strong a tension, sustained by the community, that it transcends the physical tensions of the body. It is the religious equivalent of the transformation of mass into ordered and patterned energy.

Thus we begin to sense the intent of many enigmatic New Testament sayings. Being *born again* is obvious; it is a precise statement of how the soul comes into being. "The kingdom of God is in the midst of you", "Where two or three are gathered together in my name, there I will be among them", "It is no longer I who live but Christ who lives in me." Again, these are precise statements of what takes place in the generation of souls. The resurrection of the body (which is the same as the gift of eternal life) becomes at least dimly intelligible; what is sustained by the faithful community is truly a body.

There is the possibility, too, of making sense again of traditional terminology. *Grace* is the awareness of ordered power which is felt as (because it "is") something other than the self. A saint is not a person whose behavior is entirely good. A saint is one whose soul is so fully ordered that there is an excess of energy flowing outward to others, seizing on the inchoateness of their unordered energies and dissolute structures and engendering in them a soul.

Similarly an icon can be the symbol as channel of grace but as idol it terminates process in an object and thus it is truly false. And so it must go with others.

It is for this reason that St. Anthony, revived by Charles Williams, spoke literally and not in pious exhortation; "Your life and death are with your neighbor."

THE FORMING OF THE SOUL

It is not the unique achievement of Christianity to generate true souls, but to define the process. All cultures, all religions engender souls. The Christians defined the process and shifted it to the center of human attention. It has been a long time since the Christian Church functioned in any distinctive way to engender souls; the sufferings of our day are as often or more often met by forces quite outside the church. But the Church's ancient task is yet there to be done.

Testing and discerning the spirits is a matter of discriminating among the calls to community, for false (and therefore deadly) community is offered in the guise of true community. The offered community may be in effect a call to submit or to dominate. But there is always the possibility that the false community has within it the potential for transformation into true community. The moral life is painfully, tragically difficult. It requires what only it can generate, the full sense of the other in the integrity of the self that enables the intention of the other to be felt acutely enough to generate appropriate acts.

Morality, then, is not a system of regulations issued from causal reason. Morality is the capacity for intentional act in the sustaining of community. Immorality is not simply breaking a law. It is the denial or violation of the community.

A danger: the presence of "intentionality" does not define the good; there is intentionality to evil as well as to good, a community of denial as well as a community of fulfillment. Great masses of people are Laodiceans, drifting off into nothingness. It is the community of evil intention that has generated all the powerful, obsessive imagery of the devil, hell, demons, evil spirits.

Another danger: it is not granted to any person to sit as judge on the state of another's soul or to predict its future fate. All other persons must be considered, always, as the potentiality of a soul. To assume the right to punish is to assume the right to break the only thing punishment can rightly do, which is to bring another self into community and engender from it a living soul. It is not willful or capricious that the Lord should reserve vengeance for himself. It is the necessary order of things, for vengeance in human hands is, by definition, the death of the soul that inflicts it. Life is only the trinitarian community; community cannot be forced, only engendered; the offer of community can be rejected, at the cost of the soul of the one who rejects it, but the offer must be sustained, against all cost of humiliation, all expectation of refusal, because to deny the offer is as fatal as to refuse it.

Every human relation, however modest and humble, every opportunity for caring and courtesy, is a chance to evoke, call up, the Christ or to cut him off. It is in these terms that the Christ is creator of all things, from the beginning.

FINITENESS, FAILURE AND SIN

This work, which purports to deal with a new Christian image of man—and an image of the Christian man—has said a little, but only a little, about human sin. This is deliberate. For:

Sin is an inescapable ingredient of human history; it is not definitive of human nature. He who would ignore the inevitability of sin will falsify the reality of human experience, but he who would found his image of man on sinfulness falsifies it as completely. Sin is a condition of being human and a consequence of the human condition; it is not a definition of the human.

Therefore, a definition of sin should follow, not precede, the definition of the human. No definition of sin can be constructed in the abstract but only by awareness of the human condition.

To the liberal imagination, there is no such thing as sin, only finiteness; and, therefore, error. To the fundamentalist imagination, sin and finiteness are parts of the same thing and equally characterized by human guilt. Error and guilt there are aplenty. What matters is to determine which is which. For it makes a difference in our decisions about the conduct of our affairs, and homiletic assertion won't help.

Sin and finiteness are inescapably linked. But they are not the same, and only error and suffering can follow confusing them, mistaking one for the other, reducing one to the other. Yet the assertion of them is not sufficient for intellectual use, and probably not very useful for devotions. That we are not God or gods is fairly obvious to most of us and hardly a problem or an answer to problems. The question is, what is the origin and the nature of our finiteness?

The most personal effect of duality is isolation. Separation is the descriptive word; what we experience is isolation, separation, difference, distinction. The world is the other.

The effort to bridge the gap of separation is the source of creativity, for the desire to bridge it is the motive for all our symbolic structures. It is our symbolic structures that define us as human.

But it is our condition that we are finite, and the symbolic structures do not work for the wholeness of things or for a very long time. Yet our symbolic structure is our personhood; if it fails we have no recourse but to fall into the terrifying abyss of the separation and our own meaninglessness. Thus fear prevents us from accepting our finiteness, and out of our limitations grows our sin.

A DEFINITION OF FINITENESS

Finiteness is part of the definition, the logic, of being human, for the human experience is built on a paradox, a contradiction. There is no escape from the contradiction, for being human is precisely what emerges from our attempt to cope with the impossible. We are created; natural, a part of nature; we are self-conscious and therefore something other than nature, separate from nature. Being human is neither alone. Being human is both. Simultaneously. Integrally. Which is impossible, for they are contradictory.

We contemplate the dread separation and out of pain and passion generate the symbolic structure that enables us to live within our condition. All of human greatness, human creativity, is in those structures. When they are newly generated, they work, they are a liberation.

But we perceive the world, think about the world, feel about the world only in the shapes and energies of our inherited culture. The presence in the world of the symbolic structures that we see with has altered the world that generated those structures originally. Thus by definition, by the logic of our condition, we are always out of phase with our world, always defeated.

However much we dream of the system, the discipline, the institution that might achieve the impossible dream and bring together the separated halves of our lives, the painful fatality of our logical condition always will defeat us. For a symbolic structure— our only means of intercourse with our world—is one thing as an achievement. It is something else as an inheritance.

Therefore, every symbolic structure that seeks to reconcile the two is doomed to failure.

When Paul said, "Who will deliver me from the body of this death?" he erred only in seeing this desperate paradox so exclusively in moral terms. The fatal paradox is inherent in our symbolic activity, the only means we have of becoming human.

A DEFINITION AND CLASSIFICATION OF SIN

The definition of a sin, a sinful act is not difficult; it is any act or attitude that blocks, denies, prevents, subverts, the trinitarian relation. But what is sin? Why are these acts "sin"–ful? Sin is a condition much deeper than the acts that manifest it.

The types of sin, or, at least, some of them:

1. *A limited structure is taken as a whole and actions are determined according to it.*

   Thus is the integrity of other people violated. No symbolic structure wholly overlaps another: to act without regard to the difference is to override another person by violating his symbolic world.

2. *To treat our personal symbolic structure as closed.*

   The reverse of (1). The denial of the other by refusing the integrity of his symbolic structure; the denial of the self by the denial of growth.

3. *To act in one structure, to think about and defend the act in another.*

   This is one root of falsehood. It is not possible for humans to live in one symbolic structure only, even in primitive and simple societies. Because any such structure is partial and finite we are compelled to live in several, which we so often do without integrity.

4. *To refuse to act, refuse to choose.*

   Awareness of finiteness and inevitable failure can paralyze the will.

5. *To flee from the dreadful task of being human to purposeless energy or dead abstraction.*

   These are the complementary sins of the physical and cerebral types. As gluttony or lust exhaust the spirit in the passions of the flesh, so does lust for the dominant abstraction. There is a rape of the body of the imagination as there is of the body of flesh.

6. *To make of one symbol, one metaphor, whether money, na-*
   tion, role, thing, idea, the key to a whole process of which it
   is rightly only a part.

   This is the root of all idolatry.

The primal duality, generating these several responses, hardens
into dualism which is the source of all forms of violence, fraud,
theft, anger and, finally, treason.

Thus we might account for the origin of the traditional sins and
even, perhaps, trace them to that state of the soul which is sin as
the engendering origin of sins, that rebellion against, that flight
from, the fatality of our own experience, denying what it is to be
human. But there is yet a deeper offense, a deeper sin that creates
all the others.

THE SIN AGAINST THE KINGDOM OF GOD

If our world is defined by our sustaining structures and our creative processes, if we act and know only in our symbolic structures and our imaginative process, then the choice to act in this way or that, the moral decision that shapes us as persons, has been made or nearly made by those who have engendered those structures, organized those processes, long before. Therefore an act, or a lazy refusal to act, that appears now to be trivial can shape structures to terrible consequences in the future. This is most often the failure to catch the essential rhythm of the common process in time, therefore to deny the wholeness of ourselves in our history, to offend against the wholeness of life and, by failing to fulfill it, to warp it.

If the denial of the trinitarian relation is the sin against the Holy Ghost, this is the sin against the Kingdom of God.

This is the sin of the slothful but also of the well-intentioned— to do a good now that is required of me but to falsify that which is to come. To have to act now, knowing that we can never know what we do to the sensibility of those who must work out their moral destiny in the world we have shaped for them. To act, knowing that the best of acts may defeat its own purpose. This is the tragedy, the deepest sin, of the human.

Yet it is only the fateful choice that creates the fully human. There is a remorseless economy in human affairs that balances small evil against small order; the precarious harmony of the primitive is matched by a limited order. The largest possibility creates the largest offense. The concentrated, malignant evil of our own day may be the condition for a greater achievement.

This is partly what is meant by the sins of the father are visited on the children. It is not so cruel as to mean that the children are punished for the sins of someone else, nor so jejeune as to mean that the children must suffer the consequences of the world the father made for them. Rather the father shapes the symbolic structures that determine the children's place in their world and partly makes them who they are.

There is a corollary and extension of this that is fully intended. *Sin* is a word hitherto applied chiefly to certain kinds of acts, not to others. But under this definition the willful corruption of language is a sin. Designing a city badly, or spoiling the design of a city is not simply an error of taste. It is a sin. For these things corrupt the means of our communication and thus block the achievement of community. Manipulating currency is sinful, not simply because it involves deceit and greed but because it adulterates a major symbolic language. A politician who lies is obviously guilty of lying. But his larger guilt lies in the corruption of politics, one of the means for making the Holy Trinity manifest.

The resurrected Christ and the body of the Trinity, the Holy Spirit are in the care of the only true Church.

JUDGMENT

From this definition of sin there should follow a whole penology. Society as society may, out of the general sinfulness, require punishment as protection. The Christian, as a weak, unwise man, remorselessly involved in society, may have no escape from his involvement with punishment, as with war. But the Christian as a Christian can never sit in judgment on another, or assume the right and power of punishment, for the only goal for the Christian is not retribution, but restoration.

It should be obvious that in the interchange of judgment, as in the interchange of love, there are two terms. One cannot act as though one's act affects only the other, for all act is part of the chiastic rhythm that flows outward and returns; the judgment is as much a judgment on the judge as it is on the judged. Judgment, like love, generates a relation. A relation is as much determinative for one participant as for the other.

It is possible for a person to reject the offered community, even to try to attack and subvert it; the forgiven one is as much participant in the act of forgiveness as the judge. It may, in the tragic economy of human affairs, be essential for a Christian community to make public confirmation of a person's rejection of the relation. But this can be done rightly only in humility and fear, in an agony of reluctance and regret.

Thus did Jesus say, "Judge not, that you be not judged. For with the judgment you pronounce you will be judged, and the measure you give will be the measure you get."

The restriction of language suggests a separation of the acts, obscuring the fact that the judgment we make is itself the act of judgment on ourselves. It is not something promised to us for the future, raising the possibility of escape. It happens in the act of judgment. It is well to take what Jesus says with complete seriousness, without assuming too quickly that what he meant was what we think he meant.

Thus pope or synod excommunicate at peril of their souls. Most excommunications are carried out vengefully, with gloating satisfaction, as though the omnipotent God has been defended from danger or insult.

The punishment of sin is death, not because a judge assigns that punishment to sin, but because sin is death. Sin is separation.

FORGIVENESS

Forgiveness of sins is life, because it is the nature of life to absorb and obliterate sin; as the body, so long as it is not killed by the cut, absorbs and obliterates a division made by the knife.

To err is human, because it is, inescapably, part of the human condition. To forgive is divine, not because in forgiveness we become as gods, but because the Holy Trinity is present to us in forgiveness. Truly, of his holy nature, present.

Christ bears our sins, not as Damon substituted himself for Pythias before a judge, if his friend did not return to bear the punishment himself. Christ bears our sins because in the presence of the Trinity, only in the presence of the Trinity, is the sin healed and obliterated, borne.

Christ was truly present to Damon and Pythias and, perhaps, through them, to the judge.

It is a nicely circular statement. Sin is obliterated only when the Trinity is present because the Trinity is present only where there is forgiveness of sin. The Trinity *is* (or "is") the forgiveness of sins.

Forgiveness of sins is, by definition, a corporate act, for it is in the community that the symbolic process of the common life is generated, and forgiveness is an ingredient of the trinitarian community.

RESTORATION

"Whatever you bind on earth will be bound in heaven and whatever you loose on earth will be loosed in heaven." In a symbolic world dominated by the sense of autonomous, willful personalities this has been understood as the authorization for judicial authority. It is, rather, a description of circumstance; what we do on earth restores community, thus sustaining life, or it destroys community, thus destroying life.

> After that he spoke no more, till we reached the house; then he stopped, and said to me in a strange and trembling voice, an offender must be punished, *mejuffrou*, I don't argue about that. But to punish and not restore, that is the greatest of all offenses . . . if a man takes unto himself God's right to punish, then he must also take upon himself God's promise to restore.
>
> Captain Jooste in Alan Paton's,
> *Too Late the Phalarope*

Judgment, punishment as such, is always dualistic, therefore always a sin against the Body, however necessary. The only trinitarian judgment is the judgment that heals and restores, for the Trinity is achievable only in the community of the forgiven and the forgiving.

To forgive is to love; forgiveness is not an act that can be separated from love. To love is to make the Lord present.

2. A Meditation on the Holocaust

The Holy Trinity has been manifested in our time among the Jews of the Holocaust, the shattered people of Vietnam, the poor, the hungry, the oppressed in every nation.

I bow to ask their pardon for the use of terminology they can only see as part of their oppression. Yet it is hard to say if they are worse profaned by the proud indifference of Christians or by those who would turn their holy suffering into scorn or hatred.

The Jews of the Holocaust suffered in all the emotions of the human—fear, despair, resignation, hatred, hope, love. They did not profane their going by melodrama, by futile gestures to nourish the pride of those who follow. The Jews of the Holocaust bore our evil and our sufferings, despised and rejected of all men and did not open their mouths. The Jews of the Holocaust have been gathered to the heart of grace, while Christendom sits in its inertness.

In recent years, disappointment often has been voiced with a gratuitous condenscension that presumes to excuse as it heaps scorn, at the silence and the obedient grief with which the vast majority of the Jewish victims accepted their doom. . . . The critics, one fears, feels humiliated by the record of the dead and are disappointed, as if they had been cheated of a merited right to trumpet forth equivalents of the Marseillaise in a riot of self-congratulatory memorial exercises. Death in the fury of battle they know as glorious, but meekness in the hour of death is curiously culpable, a sign of weakness, and it compromises in the eye of history. . . .

In the silence of the fulfillment of their vows, the martyrs teach, ever so gently amidst all the terror, the art of dying well . . . .

Their quiet manner in the face of death must have been accomplishments they worked out for themselves, not so much as a resolve as in that unspoken and perhaps unspeakable knowledge of the dignity of man that is acquired in the absorbing privacy of one's contemplation of death. The victims, aided by only the shreds of the life they once had led (or had been hoping to lead) as citizens of states participating in what we still call western civilization rediscovered in their loneliness and their suffering the foundations of this very civilization. As its breakdown was demonstrated to them in the hell that surrounded their agony, they reaffirmed its validity in the silence of their exodus to the gas chambers.

PHILLIP FEHL[41]

Phillip Fehl is an Austrian Jew who came to this country in the 1930s. I could not have written what I have written here, had he not written what he has written.

The Jews of the Holocaust looked for the coming of the Messiah and could not know that they themselves were the living presence of the Messiah.

We profane the Trinity if we turn the sufferings of the Holocaust into an instrument of oppression and hatred. We profane the Trinity as deeply if we are indifferent, if we pretend it did not happen. We receive the Messiah, the Christos, only as we receive into our souls the dignity of their suffering and all those who suffer our imperial unities.

3. A Meditation on the Construction of the Soul

AXIOM   If we are to see the other, we must first see into ourselves in order to be able to see ourselves in the other, who as himself can be known in the integrity of his self, only as we can find his self refracted in us.

PARADIGMS OF THE SOUL

Much of the difficulty in thought is caused by the difficulty of our words. Nouns, by and large, we can handle, along with pronouns, adjectives and conjunctions. It is verbs and prepositions that give us the trouble.

There is a double problem with verbs, occasioned by their division into one unique class of the forms of the verb *to be,* and all other verbs. The forms of the verb to be affirm something called existence. Other verbs are statements about action or conditions. All very straightforward until we try to decide what *existence* means, what character a thing must have in order to be said to exist. For this, then, affects the verb; verbs are actions by subjects which are presumed to exist. The condition of their existence affects the nature of their act.

Prepositions complicate existence and act; they state relations but in many cases they still suggest, and in all cases originate, in physical positions or directions. Thus prepositions still carry the potency of the things that are at the origin of all our words, even the most abstract; behind every preposition there is the sense of place or movement in space. Inheritance and philosophy join in fixing the image of things in our mind as the definition of being, the occasions of "to have existence." Things, in our imaginations, have concreteness, tangibility, substance. This is the strength of our poetry with its powerful concreteness, its evocation of the physicality of the earth.

But it is the ruin of theology. For theology is bound to the language of substance, yet equally bound to make affirmations about things that are not substances. Thus theology becomes imprisoned in its terminology.

What does it mean to say I am *in* Christ? Or Christ is *in* me? Or Christ died *for* me? The language of substance permits no true or reasonable answer to these questions. So the statements become devotional chants irrelevant to rational thought, and the explanation of them becomes an exercise in logical ingenuity.

New images of matter, the shift of definition from substance to process, makes possible the verbal affirmation and explanation of what has, heretofore, only been felt in devotion and liturgy.

Thus in a metaphysics and the attendant language of substance, the person is the sum total of his concreteness, an immediate coherence who is acted on and acts, who is here and not there, who is separated from other persons and other things, who, therefore, can be "saved" in his completeness, who is "in Christ". Such terminology loses all force because it makes no sense and, making no sense, eventually loses its authority in devotion.

But if the person is not a substance distinct from other substances but a particular coherence in a network of relation, then the same vocabulary not only takes on a different resonance but a different reference. It might even be possible to use it again with some sense of integrity and self-respect.

"I am myself plus my circumstances", says Ortega. There is a coherent center of my existence, an integral self, but it is in no way separable from its intricate interactions in the web of relation to other things and persons. The self itself is a structure of its own characteristic energies, but these are integrally a part of the infinite web of persons and things. So direct an experience as perception is not, as we have seen, a simple matter of transporting sensation along a line; it is an intricate interplay of the self and its world.

The person, therefore, is not a substance, a unit held in by the skin; the person is a particular center of an intricately interwoven, rhythmically pulsating web or field of relations.

This account not only affects one's sense of the self, it drastically alters one's sense of the self's will. The person-as-substance acts by willful decision, according to rational nature appraised according to known general principles. But the person as a part of a rhythmically interacting process acts by a significantly different process; there is a self that moves intelligibly within the process, but the will and the willful decision is only part of what happens. The self can decide the tonality of its participation in the whole, the extent and intensity of the participation. but it cannot alone determine the shape and direction of that participation. The analogy is to a member of an orchestra. He makes an initial decision about the instrument he will play. He can come to performances or stay away. He can play well or badly. He still has much freedom of willful decision. But, he does not alone decide the piece to be played. Once he has begun in the piece he has no choice about his role or the direction of the piece. And he certainly cannot play music that is not yet written.

Therefore it is literally true that the source of human action is neither law nor reason, but myth.

Myth is not a story invented after experience as primitive explanation. Myth is the score according to which human experience is played. Myth establishes the paradigms, the models for human action. Yet such figures of speech are misleading if they suggest the old image of a self willfully acting according to a chosen plan. Rather, as a part of the extended self they are truly part of the shape and process of the person.

In complex societies the self is involved in different myths, and can choose to some degree among them. But there is not a person apart from the shaped act of the myth, for the myth is a part of the person.

The Oedipus myth emerged as part of the creative act of persons in a particular culture interacting with their worlds. In its emergence it became a part of the persons engaged in the interaction, and thus created them. The "Oedipus complex" is an analytical instrument because we are part of a culture built into the Oedipus myth. We are, inevitably, the Oedipus myth. What use is the Oedipus complex as a diagnostic instrument in the Melanesian

Islands? The idea works for us because the myth is in us, teaching us, shaping our actions, being a part of ourselves.

Thus the discussion reverts back to its beginning and the difficulties of our verbs and prepositions. New Testament terminology was no innovation in the actualities of experience. It was a revolutionary innovation in language as an analysis of experience, so revolutionary that there was no image of the person, no modes of act or speech to cope with it. Christians stubbornly clung to their language even when it could be said they really didn't understand it. (And the sad thing is that, now when we are about to acquire the intellectual means for understanding the terminology, a failure of nerve has set in and many Christians are abandoning the terminology).

The process needs to be reviewed from the beginning, even while we know that it cannot be known in its early stages and only partly known in ourselves. It is necessary to lay it out this way because there is a development that must be known. It is not simply that we are part of our past, although that is certainly true. It is, rather, that by the incorporation of myth into the physiology of the person, we have developed into a fuller range of being human. It may be that, if we can ever understand how myth becomes a part of physiology, we can understand the possibility of a true evolution of the moral personality.

We might also understand more about the workings of the will. Too often the assumption has been that all moral conduct is possible at all times and that failure to live by advanced moral standards is proof of primitivism, weakness, or ignorance; all judgments of moral failure. Yet we can now see that all moral action is determined by the myths that are built into our culture and physiology—our selves. The narrative of the myth first becomes emplanted in the person and then becomes available as a new structure of personal relations and moral actions. Until the new paradigm is truly available, emplanted and not just told, then the act and relation which is its structured energy is not a possibility of human experience, except, clearly, for the creative person who first, by act or thought or making, sets in motion the process of engendering that produces the new mythical paradigm.

This process permits the possibility of moral development; it does not ensure its certainty. It is an evolution but, at human choice, it can be equally a regression. This process gives meaning and purpose to history; it is no justification for historicism.

The beginnings of moral evolution are lost. We have records only for a quite late stage in history. We can only assume that, as soon as human interactions became more than instinctual, certainly as soon as they involved more than technical cooperation, the shape of developing relations became precipitated in the ritualized narrative while the securing of the internal structure of the myth controlled or altered the narrative of human interaction. (Even to the people engaged in this process it presumably would be impossible to separate what is cause and what is effect in a continuous spiral process.)

At some point, presumably when the myth is adequate to the complexity of this people's experience and the people feel no special need to define their relations outside the limits set by the myth, the myth becomes basically stabilized in its essentials. There is no reason to think that there was ever a fixed schema, with a one-to-one correspondence between the myth and all conduct. Rather every culture has its characteristic sloth, indifference, infidelity, rebellion, as well as the modest creativity by individuals, particularly at time of crisis, which has great quality but no permanent effect on the shape of a culture's moral narrative. Equally there are alternate versions of the myth that accommodate it to a modest range of different acts or simply represent the free play of creativity, without altering the basic shape and action of the myth. This process makes possible storytelling, reflection, much of art and literature—in short, a great deal of what is really involved in being human.

Then came the unaccountable moments of true mythic creativity. We are now within the realm of history but, even so, the process is not always fully intelligible to us. There is not even a universal pattern (or universal agreement about a pattern), but that hardly matters for present purposes. What matters is that there is a transmutation of mythic structures into new and far more comprehensive forms. In some cases, it is a great poem that sets out and thereby shapes the people's narrative as did Homer's *Iliad*. Sometimes it is a great vision of sacred order, such as was shaped by the Hebrew prophets. Then, too, the great innovators—Buddha, Christ, Mohammed—set out the mythic paradigm in the dramatics of their own lives and the structure of their teaching.

In this sense both the fictive heroes (Oedipus) are "in" persons as much as the historical ones (Christ, Mohammed), for they set out the myth, the structured narrative by which life is lived. The preposition makes no sense so long as the person is understood as a moral intelligence directing a physiological unit. It becomes essential when the person is understood as process; then the myth is, quite literally, *in* the person, a vital part of his being.

Thus there is nothing particularly Christian about the sacred hero or sacred story being in the person; that is the way personality is organized. It is not quite so clear that it is equally possible in the other great myths to speak of the person as being "in" Buddha or "in" Oedipus, as Christians speak of being "in Christ".

Some aspects of these great formative myths are even more important than their different use of prepositions. The important thing is the shape of act and relation emplanted by the narrative. The characteristic Christian shape is, nevertheless, significantly affected by the implication of the preposition.

To have Christ "in" us can be rationalized, in the language of substance, as our behaving in accord with the attitudes of Christ; the statement asserts nothing about the "real". Christians have attempted to rationalize "being in Christ", but to even less effect in a metaphysics of substance.

But a metaphysics of process and relation permits intelligible use of the preposition in both directions and, at the same time, clarifies some of the more enigmatic sayings of Jesus. "Whenever two or three are gathered together in my name, there I will be among them"; "the Kingdom of God is within (in the midst) of you". These have either to be rationalized or to be left in some undefined "spiritual" sense. But in a metaphysics of process and relation the statements become literally true. Jesus had no hesitation in making such assertions of being, of existence. We now have a language for taking him seriously.

The whole structure and dynamics of relations defined by the Christian narrative (structure and dynamics are equivalent to "in my name"), *is* the presence of the Christ. It *is* the Holy Spirit, the Comforter, the Paraclete. There is nothing in New Testament language to link existence with tangibility or being with substance rather than relation. Being *is* the relation; to be in the relation is to be in Christ.

The question becomes, then, how to be in the relation. The question is crucial, for the New Testament makes clear that to be in Christ is to live, to be out of Christ is to die. Therefore, for the Christian the question of the great mythic models, the vital paradigms, is not an academic exercise.

There are, beyond doubt, many who have achieved this relation outside the Church, and so are in Christ truly, even if they have never heard of Christ. Such achievements require a rare moral strength of creativity. For most people it is necessary to set forth the vital paradigm in the generative myth, and in all the rituals, institutions, creeds, art works, that develop out of the generative myth and sustain the ordinary existence of ordinary people. These vital myths are not present for choice, cafeteria style, but are achievements (or gifts). They are torn out of the vital energies of the great, who are the explorers on the human pilgrimage. Therefore, it is necessary to look at the great paradigms of our own culture as they have been achieved.

Western culture has four such paradigms at the root of its formation of personality: "natural" man, the paradigm that emerges into fable, into popular song and saga from the conflicts and fulfillments of ordinary human passions; Oedipus and Orestes, the great tragic heroes; Abraham, the father of faith; the Christ.

It is not necessary to think that these paradigms are always, or even very often, consciously imitated. It is rather that they are built into our imagination as people, not as archetypal inheritance but as mythical paradigms around which are formed our drama, liturgy, manners, therapy and action.

For the source of human action is not moral law or reasoning from the basis of moral law. The source of human action is myth.

Myth is many things; as the source of moral action it is the model of human decisions and relations. Myth is a narrative that, among other things, sets forth the statement of the actuality and the possibility of human act.

Myth emerges from a deep and inchoate sense of what a human being is and how a human being behaves. Thus, given form, the image of person and act becomes pedagogical, and persons in society become what the myth says they are.

Moral law gives authority and specificity to the paradigmatic act. It is useful; it teaches and sustains. It is not the source of moral action. It is derivative from the myth.

The myth of natural man has three elements, which appear variously in historical acts:

1. Killing of the father by the son.
2. Killing of the son by the father.
3. The blood feud.

In each case, the defining mode of human relations is opposition, dualism. There is no reconciliation, only the victory of one over the other. Victory is achieved by the implacable law of sacrifice, which has no end. The blood feud ends only when one line is exterminated.

"Oh, pain grown into the race" Aeschylus described the fatality of the blood feud. The remorseless fatality of the law of the earth obsessed the mind of the Greek mythmakers and dramatists who brought to the myth their great creative intelligence.

The myth of Oedipus begins in infanticide and murder, comes to a climax in incest and the killing of the father, ends in the fratricide and the sacrifice of the daughter and the son. The myth of Orestes begins in infanticide and cannibalism, comes to a climax in the killing of the daughter, ends in matricide and insanity. It was the task of the great dramatists to resolve these fatalities to a moral purpose; it was a condition of their imagination that they could not deny what the myth was. The law and the logic of myth does not permit handling its structure lightly; to manipulate the structure of a myth is to imperil the health of a culture.

The blood feud is biological, built into nature. Persons can neither transcend it nor escape from it. To both Aeschylus and Sophocles, human tragedy is the problem of being human in the imprisonment of fate. Let us look first at the solution of Sophocles, then at Aeschylus', then at what they have in common.

The *Oedipus* plays of Sophocles can be presented as a trilogy covering the narrative of the tragedy from the offense of Oedipus to the death of Antigone. This is not the order of their thought, which began with the last stages of the story, the death of Antigons as the final victim of the pride of the house of Oedipus. *Oedipus Tyrannus* is the classic moment, the statement of high tragedy, complete in its dreadful grandeur. *Oedipus at Colonus* is, in the narrative, between the two, but its thought transcends everything else in the work of Sophocles. The highest reach of Greek faith is given in this play.

All imaginative structures suffer the infliction of interpretation that lessens them: only *Antigone* really shows human beings blindly pursuing the fatality of false convictions to a deadly end. Sophocles had too great a mind to build great drama on a conviction that man is ruled by fate. Rather the conviction of a rigid order in the substance of things leads moral agents to act under the compulsion of remorseless laws.

But in *Oedipus Tyrannus* the tragedy is not of act but discovery. In being what he is as a man, Oedipus discovers what he is in history. It is not fate which overthrew him; had he not been willing to kill an old man and marry a woman old enough to be his mother, he would not have wounded the order of things by patricide and incest. The offended order of sacrality exacts its remorseless price, but the price is not paid to fate. It is paid to the order of being human. Had he acted other than he did, Oedipus would have been other than what he was; the stately grandeur of the play is a reliquary for the greatness of the blind and bloody beggar, Oedipus, whom all men once called the Great. The play does not lament the victim of fate, but enshrines him who can be great above the remorseless order of things.

In *Oedipus at Colonus*, the greatness is lifted up in apotheosis. Oedipus is caught up into the company of the gods or received into the heart of earth; the mortal witness, Theseus, cannot see clearly into the consuming light to tell what happened. The suffering of Oedipus transcended the iron laws and he became one with the gods. The Theban came home to Athens and met his high destiny in the sacred grove of the Athenians.

Aeschylus deals directly with the remorseless fatality of the blood feud. Atreus kills the children of Thyestes and the house is cursed. Agamemnon kills Iphigenia; Clytemnestra kills Agamemnon; Orestes kills Clytemnestra; there is no one left in the family to pursue the guilty one, so the remorseless Furies claim their due.

There is no escape from this order of things. The conclusion of the *Eumenides* leaves Orestes almost incidental, the occasion, no more, the city now the hero, the city grasping the right to judgment, the city inheriting the right of punishment. Pain and death are remorselessly the order of things but they are caught up in the justice of the city; social structures now have a model, but the fullness of human personality does not.

There is, now, justice, to succeed the blind working of avenging will. There is also greatness, the city as the reliquary of the sacred act of judgment.

Under judgment, Oedipus became truly great, received among the gods, the sacred man. Under justice, Athens became truly great, the instrument of the gods among men, the sacred city. The order of things is fixed; men became human because there is that in them that affirms their greatness within the order of things.

Thus is fixed one of the great paradigms of order and act, moving beyond the fixed laws of remorseless enmity but leaving man fixed in the unalterable process of biological fate. Much could and did grow from these great myths. Oedipus, the transcendent hero, could fix in the symbolic structures of later people the myth of the hero, the myth of tragedy. The tragedy was rooted in biology and biological desire, as Sophocles knew, and as Freud made conceptual. Biology conditioned the tragedy; the hero goes above but never escapes biology.

Athens, the transcendent city, could fix in the imagination the myth of the state. And, because the city assumed the responsibility of judgment, there could develop the myth of decision and moral choice.

These myths—and others—became ingredients and working principles of Western man. But from them there could not develop the myth of Christ. Before there could be the Christ there had to be Abraham.

With Abraham the order of things was first transformed. Living in an order that required blood offerings to God, Abraham submitted, against all hope, in obedience to the vengeful will. Against all hope, the beloved son was given back to him, and only symbolic blood required.

And so the remorseless fatality was broken and Isaac lived. Yet Abraham was no longer the father of faith but the father of obedience. Free, he could only be a grandeur like that of the blind Oedipus. Such men are truly great. Before them, we can respond only as Kierkegaard has Johannes de Silentio say we respond, not with admiration or with pity, but with religious horror.

Kierkegaard gives us the expectations, the terrible, awful, three-days journey. He does not give us the way back. What could a man feel who had endured what Abraham had endured? How would he emerge from that dark night of the soul? It is not given to us lesser men to know such people. The pain of Abraham is a pain that can only make of a man an austere and remote figure. Not a tragic hero, no, for his resolution had not been tragic. But a hero; one who is beyond us.

If our sense of human glory and the majesty of human cities goes back to Oedipus and Athens, so our freedom goes back to Abraham. What Abraham's obedience did was enable us to see ourselves apart from the order of things. To see ourselves as selves apart from fixity into the fatality of sacred order.

Once freed, men could develop into persons of a kind not seen in Oedipus. Oedipus himself is finally caught up into the glory of the sacred order. Abraham walked home, in silence, in wonder. Oedipus was caught up, alone. Abraham walked home, with Isaac.

As sacrifice, Isaac, the beloved, was not a person. He was an old man's hope, an old woman's desire. But he was what he was in the order of human feeling, to be given back as a completion of the will of God. But, given back to Abraham, Isaac was free, a free gift of the grace of God and not the will of man. The shattered old man, irrevocably torn by three days in the knowledge of Hell, could only look with wonder. For Isaac is now something other than himself. Isaac has become a person.

Abraham is not a Christian; his is the purification of duality. Abraham fought his way out of the terrible dualism into an awareness of duality, of distinction that was an anticipation of the move that was to come. The selfawareness that is at the root of all that is human divides us from our world but also divides us from each other. So divided we are enemies, as Antigone was to Creon, or we submit to the holy gods as Oedipus was received as sacrifice and as Abraham would have given Isaac back to the holy order of things. Now, in obedience, Abraham received back his sacrifice. Nay, more, he received back the act of sacrifice itself and from then Isaac could step apart to be another.[42]

Into the world, the *Thou* was born, the I who is not myself but whom I know as a self other than myself, as an I who is not me but a coherence of existence that owes neither submission nor dominance to me.

The birth of the person required an acceptance of the other. The lost Eden, the destroyed unity, could now be felt in the tenuous, trembling, fragile bands that hold us to the other and make a world between us.

With the birth of the person is born true dialogue. The Socratic "dialogue" is not true dialogue but a cooperative search for the hidden reason of relation. What Abraham said to Isaac as they walked the three days back was the dialogue between two persons in the reliquary of wonder. For that which was dead was now alive and the sacrificing hand was clean.

It is no accident that the character of Abraham should be so complex, so heroic and so ordinarily human.

Orestes never truly comes alive. He is the one who enacts events which are larger than he is. At the end he vanishes and the stage is left to the gods and the holy city. Oedipus is intensely alive but grown beyond us. His motives at the beginning are ours, but what he becomes is beyond us, for he moves into the realm of the gods. The hero is not a person in dialogue.

But Abraham is the redemption of duality. He is greater than we, but his greatness is an extension of ourselves. Thus the fullness of Abraham is the fullness of human personality. Abraham is the model for transforming change. The Oedipus complex is biological, a pain grown in the race, to be known and accepted. The Abraham-Isaac relation was one thing and then, by pain, became something else, bridging the remorseless duality.

Out of this there grows Buber's beautiful dialogical model, the I and the Thou in communion. Abraham could set forth the image of dialogue. But Abraham could not know how to achieve it. For that, there had to be a new model, a new image, of sacrifice and the acceptance of sacrifice as the entry into a new order.

For there to have been a Christ there had first to be an Abraham. There is no way for our spirit to move from Oedipus to Christ. Abraham freed us from the remorselessness of nature into choice and therefore the fullness of personality. What Abraham began, Christ completed. Abraham purified and redeemed duality. Christ transformed duality into a new unity.

Yet the movement from Abraham to Christ is too great to make in a single step. There had to be a transition and that transition became mythically embodied in Job. Again, the mythical physiological significance of Job does not lie in his creedal argument (which humanistic critics have always found grievously inadequate), but in what he was and did.

The Job and his friends of the folk tale of the prose sections are the inert products of faithful obedience, without question and therefore without humanity. The Job of the poem is compelled by a spiritual anguish far greater than his physical suffering to ask questions no one else had ever asked, questions that struck at the heart of meaning.

There is no answer to Job's questions, then as now, but the asking of it made a new kind of man. The event that replaced an answer—when the awful, the remorseless omnipotent God spoke to Job—can never be an answer for the humanistic intelligence that finds its answers among the Greeks. But it created a new man who was prepared for the Christ.

These narratives are models; even those who do not "believe" them are parts of one or another model of the human place in the world. This is as it should be for only so is human experience ordered. But when a new model enters history only a few see it as truly new. For the rest it is too often simply an illustration of an older model. Thus the Christ has variously been the shaman of the nature cults, a hero, a Greek god, the imperial god or any other of the great symbolic models. More particularly he has been defined on the model of Abraham. But Christ is not Abraham.

Both theology and devotional practices concur in a method that helps produce this kind of result. They select from the wholeness of the Christ experience, the Christ model, a single principle that becomes determinative for the whole structure; thus the incarnation, or the resurrection as the source of hope, or the ethical commandments or the crucifixion become the object of devotion, the foundation stone or keystone of the system, the guide to action.

On the model of Abraham, the crucifixion is taken as the crucial principle of Christianity, and sacrificial love as its defining characteristic. And yet the express words of Jesus are that the crucial principle of his teaching is rebirth and the defining characteristic is the abundance of life. The crucifixion is a test and a price. Given the conditions of being human the test is inevitable and the price is necessary. But the evil quality in being human is the negative of creation; to make it or its consequences the definition of religion is to devote faith to death.

In the world men have made, children are too often born into suffering, live in hunger and pain, die in despair. Yet it is not the nature, or the essence, of a child to suffer but to rejoice in the abundance of being.

He who would deny the reality of suffering or deny that the source is in the evil heart of man is a liar and the truth is not in him. To do so would be to deny the crucifixion for the crucifixion is the consequence of our sin. But the crucifixion ought not to be understood as a mystical act, a price paid to an abstract judge. It is the cost of our own inclination, a measure of the world we have made in which goodness is known only as judgment and the price we demand for it is sacrifice.

Thus to be a Christian requires being absorbed into that sacrifice, to share that suffering. To be a Christian requires a true and genuine willingness to be crucified or to suffer whenever crucifixion or suffering is necessary, for this is the cost of being human. But crucifixion is nowhere required as a condition nor sacrifice made a definition of the Christian life. The leaders of the early Church forbade the search for martyrdom, which not only abets another man's sin (his murder of me) but denies my commitment to life.

In a burst of near sentimentality, Christ has been defined as "the man for others" and the Christian life defined as standing with the other where he is and in his condition.

Which is to overlook completely the recurring nature of the acts and the teachings of Jesus. That ministry centered to a most remarkable degree on himself. He would, indeed, go where the religious could not go, to consort with publicans and sinners, but to heal them he did not confirm them where they were or validate the world they thought they lived in. He drew them to himself.

Jesus dominated every scene he appears in. He could demolish pride and personality in a single slashing phrase. He could be insulting to the point of racism ("It is forbidden to take the children's food and give it to the dogs"). He could be harsh and intemperate, he could be profane and judgmental. He could also be gentle when gentleness was needed. In other words, he manifested the abundance of life and human possibility. The description denies him certain forms of sensuality to the point that the conscience of Christendom is mortified at the suggestion. But any man who permits a woman to kiss his feet and wipe them with her hair is no stranger to the sensual attentions of women nor was he indifferent to them.

The imitation of Christ, then, cannot be the imitation of Jesus, who was too great to be the model for our acts. The imitation of Christ is obedience to his principles and a participation in his models.

Thus we take seriously those strangely selfish injunctions like "you shall love your neighbor *as yourself.*" We are not instructed to love the neighbor instead of ourselves nor are we instructed to sacrifice ourselves for our neighbor. The sacrifice may be the price of our love as the sacrifice of Jesus was the price he paid for his love for us. But sacrifice is not the definition of our love.

Who can truly want another to be sacrificing himself for us? What oppression of relations is there in the incessant pressure of sacrifice! The comic figure of the "Jewish momma" is not a figure confined to the Jews nor any comedy to those who endure it. It is the death of the person, endured by too many women, to empty their lives into the lives of others.

All cultures have their examples of sacrificial love; many, perhaps most, have their imaginative models. To identify Christianity with sacrificial love is to empty it into religion-in-general.

To love others truly is to love them as I do myself and thus grant them the opportunity to be themselves which is to include their capacity to love me. My responsibility is, in part, to be what can be loved, as loving me is the fulfillment of those who are with me. If I willfully destroy myself, in the fire of martyrdom or in the willful martyring of my personality, there is no true self to be loved by the other.

Given the condition of ordinary life, those who would make of their lives a sacrifice are too often nuisances and busybodies or else they are self-indulgent. What good is it to me to think that my life or security is in pawn to another man's search for his own salvation? What kind of relation is it, to another person who is not a complete person?

So our ethics should become something other than the rules or iron principles of sacrifice. It becomes a way of making room for others to be themselves and live abundantly. It may—and often does—mean moving away to give them room. For if I love my neighbor as myself I cannot want to dominate him or shape his world or compel him to my will anymore than I can desert him to be alone and afraid.

Christian love is only between true selves; a concern for the other requires a concern for myself just as care of myself is as much an obligation to the other as the other's care of himself is part of my desire for the good that I would have come to him as much as I would have it come to me. Christian love is a selfish unselfishness, an unselfish selfishness.

Thus if he must sacrifice himself for me, I am increased and not lessened. Perhaps in pain, for his sacrifice may be required by my own blindness or stupidity or evil. Perhaps in the different pain that comes from knowing that his sacrifice is the price for the stupidity and evil of this world. But despite the pain, it increases rather than diminishes me, for I would know it is done, not as a good that purchases his salvation, but a gift of love for me.

I can no more use another as the instrument of my salvation than I can use another as a tool of my ambition. To be with each other in willingness to sacrifice is to turn the Christian life into competitiveness and deliver the holy community to our ancient dualisms. To love the other as myself is to enhance both and to make a new unity that had not existed before. Not only a new unity but a new kind of unity, a unity that requires and depends on the fulfillment of the parts. The individual is not swallowed up in the whole, nor can one dominate the other, nor can one rightly sacrifice himself or the other for his own good. Rather it is a unity that requires the fullness of life for both and, since each neighbor has another neighbor, enables the whole of creation to flower into one new unity which is the final vision of the kingdom of God.

Such is the vision that is the body of Christ and the unity of men that is the Holy Spirit. But the evil and perversity of men is such that we cut the bonds; with us, death enters into the world. With the blessing of the children and the raising of Lazarus, Christ showed us the way, but mostly we are used to teaching and immune to it. Only as he pays us the price we require of him by our sin, do we see the sin as death against the life he presented in his own resurrection.

This is not a moral teaching and example. Only Cartesian analysis could have thought it so. The isolation of thought from all other human action inevitably creates the sense of a moral will that has committed acts for which a punitive cost must be extracted to compensate for the sin or placate the judge. But human beings are not intelligences governed by a moral will operating a body-machine. Human beings are physical and psychic energies organized by symbolic structures. Symbolic structures are not used by people, they are a part of the self.

Thus, to say that it was necessary to have Abraham before Christ was possible is not to speak in mystic riddles. It is to speak of the process of becoming human. We live in and by means of our mythical models, and they are in us. It may well be that desire for the mother and hatred for the father is in origin biological. But it was the myth of Oedipus that fixed the structure of the myth into the explanatory intelligence and made therapy into the acceptance of the fatality of history. Oedipus is not an interesting myth but is flesh of our historical flesh.

Therefore, it was necessary, in order to have the kind of person Christ could "save", that Abraham release us from the remorseless fatality of historical forces. With Oedipus the highest reach of man is the tragic hero, the man who can assert who he is against the fatal laws that compel him to the measure of the order of things. The story of Abraham enters the symbolic structures to alter their shape and their rhythms; Abraham is a hero but no longer tragic. The biological order, built into the imaginations of men, is transformed. Now the order of persons can be changed, transformed by the grace of love, and the possibility shatters the fixed structure, makes possible separate persons.

But the freedom of man is not simply a freedom to possibility. It is a freedom to sin. Sin is not simply a theological phenomenon or a moral event (although it is both). It is a violation of the order of things. The order of things is no longer biological but relational; sin severs the relational system, a system that sustains life as surely as blood vessels are a relational system that sustains bodily life. To say that the wages of sin is death is no more to speak judicially than it would be to say that death is a punishment for cutting the aorta. Sin brings death for sin is death.

Therefore, goodness could be manifested among people only at the cost of death; the crucifixion was not a demonstration or a charade anymore than it was like paying a fine for us. The crucifixion is part of who we are and of the world we make in our fatal dualism. It is the price we require for the privilege of being what we are in the order of our natural history.

The suffering itself is of no moment and only the sentimentality of those who misread the crucifixion can make it important. Not only can disease cause more suffering; our sin causes, to our hideous pleasure, worse suffering. The decisive thing is that the crucifixion happened *to this man* and, in happening to him, revealed for those who would see, what it is like for all. Many do not see and their blood drains away through the wounds of their sin.

But there are those who receive it and when they do, it enters their very flesh. Again, this is not picturesque speech. The crucifixion shatters their symbolic structures and remakes them so that they are reborn.

Faith is not belief, for belief is only opinion. Faith is the life of the remade self. Faith can never be faith in the crucifixion or even in the crucified Christ, for to make that the object of faith is to focus our selves on the consequences of our own sin. Without acceptance of the crucifixion there is no faith, for it is only the crucifixion that reveals to us who we are. But who we are cannot be the object of our faith; all men sin, and sacrificial love is no monopoly of Christians. Rather faith is the life of the resurrection. It is not faith in the resurrection or even hope for the resurrected life. Faith is the life of the resurrection, for the death of the Christ carries the death of the old structures, the old man, and to live, then, is to live in Christ. Again, the preposition is meant literally; the resurrection of Christ remade the structures by which we ex-

perience the world and live in the world and to live in these structures, these vital metaphors, is to live in Christ.

When Paul spoke of the fruits of the spirit he meant what he
said. The reborn no longer live in the same world and, having giv-
en up the old, can receive it back in a different modality. It is true
to say that an unhappy Christian is a contradiction in terms. The
Christian is the one who has been received into the abundance of
life—not in hope, but now—and to live in the abundance of life is
to be happy.

That this ideal is attainable in this life is an illusion; it is both
unwise and intolerant not to know our own weakness and thereby
expect perfection. It would, indeed, be a cruelty to use the ideal
either as test or measure, for we are both weak and partial. But it
is the ideal, and as ideal it is definition.

Sacrificial love is both tragic and heroic but Christianity has
nothing to do (in its definition rather than its operation) with either the tragic or the heroic. To be Christian, Christian sacrifice
must first surrender or sacrifice, the idea of sacrifice, for in sacrifice I give up what is mine. To give up what is mine is a heroic act
and heroism engenders pride and pride in his own moral conduct
is precisely what a Christian should not have. That is why the
Christian must first die with Christ—accept Christ crucified—for
the true acceptance of the crucifixion is truly the death of the old
man, and that old symbolic structure that was truly a part of the
old man, and a rebirth, a remaking of the new, who is in the life
of abundant love.

In the hard uses of this corrupt life, sacrifice may be a condition
of love. The Christian may sacrifice as Christ sacrificed, as a price
and a ransom for all time, sacrifice even his life for the other. But
the Christian cannot seek it, or define himself by it or value it in
himself or for itself. Crucifixion, sacrifice, is always a cost, never a
prize. It may be a condition but it is never a purpose.

For crucifixion is, inalienably, death, and the Christian narrative does not end with death but with the resurrection. The life

surrendered is given back and the commandment was not "preach death" but "feed my sheep." The Christian narrative does not end with the grandeur of Oedipus or Athens or the glory of Jerusalem but with the restored earth and childlike wonder.

PART SIX

Care and the Kingdom of God: Essay Meditations

The Definition of Brokenness

Utopian vision has its use as model. But neither vision nor model can rightly be seen as a thing, out there, in front. Their use depends on their being functioning terms in the work of the imagination. Yet, if they are process and not simply image, their difficulties are as much a part of the process as they themselves are. And the difficulties that are a part of realizing this vision are appalling.

The briefest way of stating the difficulty is to say that the course of our development has brought us now to the point where, for our rescue, we must learn how to do consciously those things that require to be done unconsciously if they are to be done rightly. This is no more than a mundane way of restating the dreadful statement of Jesus, "He who finds his life shall lose it. He who loses his life for my sake shall find it." If, to move towards something we must first desire it; if in the desiring of it we move toward it with the intention of achieving it; then the act we make to achieve the desire invalidates the act and prevents the achievement of the desire.

It is not ordinarily discernible in the work of Jesus that he sought to destroy human hope in paradox. Paradox there is aplenty in his work but it is paradox with a humane function: heard rightly it breaks open the restricting mold of old thought.

It is a paradox that concerns more than ultimate issues, for it characterizes—infects—most of human conduct. The consciously reflective intellectual knows too well how intrusive deliberation can be in ordinary human affairs, for the intellectual is the most extreme type of the violation of naturalness by thought. Thus what he most wants he loses in the deliberate acts taken to achieve it and his envy is directed at the simple, inarticulate, intuitive types whose relation to the world is spontaneous and instinctive. But self-consciousness is not the prerogative of the sophisticated alone; the articulate intellectual may be more capable of putting his distress into words, but the inarticulate as well find the desired relation slipping away in the imprisonment of intentional desire.

It is inevitable that this be so in the divided consciousness, for it is of the nature of the division. Yet the division—which is self-consciousness—was essential to our humanity. It is only as we can analyze out from the whole, first our consciousness, then our modes of being related to the whole, that we could learn what the fullness of being human is like. At the same time the analysis itself, by the definitions of its own work, destroys the wholeness of our experienced reality.

Again, the dilemma and the paradox. We learn about wholeness by analysis, which is the breaking of wholeness. For our completion we need wholeness but, by definition of our humanity, we cannot achieve it. So fixed are these principles that we would offend our own hope if we thought there were any final escape from them. Being human is brokenness and from our brokenness springs all our offenses.

Our earliest ancestors, some of our more recent neighbors among the primitive (or pre-literate) people achieve a small wholeness at the cost of a considerable abridgement of possibility. It is probably that many of those who are nostalgic for the primitive harmony with nature would not really want to pay the price that would be required of them. Their very yearning denies wholeness, for any society is itself a whole of sorts and not to be used in bits and pieces.

Thus our search for wholeness is ultimately doomed to failure;

all is change. But our humanity is in the search and in the achievement, however partial, and it is the possibility of our own time to
generate a new kind of wholeness. To do so we cannot retreat to
the ancient, partial unities or enthrone any of our analyzed discontinuities. Rather we should seek to reincorporate our analyzed
units into organic wholeness without losing the integrity of what
we have learned. It is at this point that we are required to do those
things that are so difficult to do, to do consciously, self-conscious-
ly, those things that have heretofore had reality only when they
are done intuitively, instinctively.

Myth that is known to be myth becomes story, then entertainment. Can we hold our myths with their integrity as myths, while
knowing that they are the means for placing ourselves within that
which is on the other side of the myth?

Theology known to be a human construct becomes opinion,
then artifact, then museum piece. Is it possible to generate theology out of the fullness of experience, knowing that it is not "true"
but knowing, too, that it is an essential icon?

Ritual done in order to accomplish an intended purpose becomes a magic technique. Is it possible to generate ritual and a
mode of participation in ritual that will be both deliberate and a
rhythmic placement of ourselves in the order of things?

A woman is either a particular person or Woman, as the force
of fertility, to be used or worshipped or truncated into the Pro-
crustean bed of one of her roles. Is it possible to develop a mode of
sexuality that will let the man and the woman participate fully in
all her roles while making them an intensification of her personality?

Can a man be, for himself and for his woman, both a person, a
man, and Man?

Asceticism is too often a dualistic denial of the uses of this earth,
a technique for a selfish purification of the self. Can there be an
asceticism that is a service to the whole, a reminder that there are
the forces of discipline, of control, of disembodied abstractions?

Can there be an asceticism, a celibacy, that is truly love and not repression?

Sensuality is too often a dualistic denial of the integrity of the person or a monistic immersion of the self into the formless forces of the whole. Control of sensuality is too often cramped and mean, expression of sensuality too often selfish indulgence. Can there be a hot, passionate, vulgar sensuality that is truly a carrier of the holy?

Contemplation is too often private, a selfish indulgence as intense as sex. Can there be contemplation that is truly a flow into the other and a service to the whole?

Action is too often dualistic domination of the other. Can there be an action that is truly the making of care for the other?

This listing could be prolonged, but the principle should be clear. And another principle is clear; the pairing of problems, itself a dualism, is a rhetorical accent for one of the great methodological needs, the sense of the place of all our acts in the whole. To try to develop a new method of contemplation in isolation is to fall back immediately into the idolatry of technique. Contemplation is a function of the whole organism, the personal and the social organism. If it is not developed within the rhythmic tensions of the whole organism and particularly its distinctive counterpart, action, it will go sour and false. Sensuality without true respect to asceticism, asceticism without true respect for sensuality will become unrestricted and, therefore, destructive energy.

So there is work to be done separately, according to inclination and commitment. It is not only to be done for the whole, which could easily sound like a committee reporting back to the authority that set it up. It is done in, from, out of, because of, into the whole.

And so respect for the needs of our separateness is nourished in the existence of our relations. There is no life, only death, in the breaking or the absence of relation. The search for relation is not the search for mechanical links, but the rhythmic interchange, the flow by which our separate acts, our separate personalities nourish each other.

Rhythm is not a mystic reality. It is the living relation, the life of relation. Another name for rhythm is love.

Grace and Faith in the Time after Christendom

It is the genius, and the burden, of Christians that they should have developed a vocabulary to use to speak of their commitment which has served many languages in many cultural situations, which doesn't make very much rational sense in any of them and yet survives, perhaps because it doesn't make sense enough in the context of any single culture to go down with the death of that culture. Yet the words work within each, as principles emerging into the forms of the culture, as sources of energy for the processes of that culture.

Faith and *grace* are words of this kind. For Christianity to be intelligible they are necessary words. At various times in the history of Christendom they have been sources of great energy. But they are words defying permanent definition. The instinct of Christians has held tightly to them as essential, even when there has been no really intelligible definition of them; they seem to work as talisman, as amulet, as icon. But, even as icons, they require renewal, regeneration. The only advantage we bring to this task is the possibility of finding, in the language of relativity and process, a definition that is more in harmony with the thing itself.

Where does this advantage of ours come from? Wherein does it lie? It won't do to say that we understand better or know more.

The egotism of that understanding of our situation is no longer supportable. It is not the quantity or even the quality of what we know that matters, for we are neither wiser nor better than those who have gone before us. It is precisely what we know that makes the difference—or can make the difference if we let it.

The problem heretofore has been the entanglement of the discussion in what might be called *the fallacy* of *explanation*. The problem of explanation, in turn, rises out of a complex of factors, chiefly the various means by which we attempt to account for our world.

The chief points of our traditional view to keep in mind is the assumption that man is—or possesses—something wholly other than the world he lives in, that he has the capacity to know that world in its essentials, that given the will to do so he can act decisively on the world, that the failure to act decisively is either a failure of knowledge, which is ignorance, or failure of will, which is evil. From this complex of assumptions, there grows the fallacy of explanation.

The fallacy of explanation holds, first, that man has the capacity both to know and understand the world he attends to, and to set out that understanding authoritatively in one of the two accepted languages, verbal propositions and mathematical formulas. These explanations are considered authoritative to the extent that possession of them is equivalent to the possession of the thing itself.

The fallacy of explanation becomes, then, the logical foundation of Christendom. Explanation of this kind confers authority on those who possess it. Explanation becomes a thing, surrogate for the explained. To reject the explanation is to reject the thing. Therefore explanation not only confers authority, it requires authority, for rejection of the explanation is caused by ignorance, which is to be corrected, or evil, which is to be chastised.

The practice of explanation has joined with a great many other characteristics of our culture (it is based on the principle of causality) to make possible extraordinary achievements. In many ways, this book is an exercise in explanation. But the fallacy in explanation may be fatal to the idea of man. What, then, makes explanation into a fallacy?

Explanation becomes fallacy in any situation in which the explanation logically involves the observer, yet is treated as though the explainer is apart from the explanation. This is a well-known paradoxical situation in formal logic (e.g., The Cretan who says, All Cretans are liars) but it is hardly followed into systems of explanation. Thus the theologian who says that everything man does is corrupt rarely includes his own theological system in that account, yet there is no logical nor experiential reason why it should not be included.

Exactly the same reasoning can be, must be, applied to all the great systems, particularly the great modern systems that haunt our imaginations. A Freudian analysis of Freudianism, a Marxist analysis of Marxism would leave us considerably further ahead than we now are.

I would judge this to be true even of Ernst Cassirer. It should be evident to anyone who knows Cassirer's work that this book owes an enormous debt to him. It was Cassirer who proposed that man should not be defined as an *animal rationale* but as an *animal symbolicum*. Yet even Cassirer did not follow his own definition to its own proper conclusion. No doubt he knew perfectly well that, as a man, he was symbolic man, but he assumed that, as a philosopher, he could account for man's symbolic activity as an observer of it. It is this assumption that has left us with so full a range of explanations, so wide an amount of knowledge and technique that have developed out of our explanations, yet we are paralyzed in the midst of them, because we don't really any longer know what to do with them.

Yet such a description, which is said as accurately as I can, is itself a precise account of the problem. We think of our explanations as an instrument for doing something with, so we can only confess our failure when we don't know what to do with our explanations.

It might be well if we were willing to confess failure, for another response is humanly a good deal worse. Since our explanations are thought to be a true account of the thing itself, the presentation of the explanation is equivalent to the presentation of the thing itself, possession of the explanation is thought to be equivalent to possession of the thing itself. Therefore education is often defined primarily as the exposition of these explanations treated as discrete objects without regard to the symbolic structures of those who receive them. The explanation may be a genuine symbol in the processes of those who engendered it out of a true experience of the event itself. It may function metaphorically in the processes of those who are in harmony with, in tune with, the teacher. Yet, failing that tuning, no clarity or completeness of presentation can save the explanation from being received as an inert, uncomprehended object. The inability to make such a thing function is no true measure of intelligence, creativity, or human worth. Yet that inability is taken as a true and accurate measure and no teacher ever considers that *he* has failed when his student goes down in a welter of incomprehension.

Theologically, the fallacy of explanation functions in much the same way, often to more terrible effect. Explanation is equivalent to the thing itself. Therefore (in our culture) the religious life becomes a search for this mysterious thing. Those who possess the thing possess the authority that is within the thing. Those who reject it or will not receive it are deemed to have rejected the originating event and since, in religion, the event is holy, rejecting the explanation is deemed to be rejecting the holy one himself, an act that is judged to deserve the punishment inflicted by those who, by possessing the explanation, claim to possess the authority of that which the explanation explains.

It works the other way, also. Those who rebel against the claims of such orthodoxy basically accept the principle of explanation.

Thus, any plausible explanation is deemed to have authority, at least for the person making the explanation. There need be no particular connection with evidence. It is, rather, the internal satisfaction of the explanation. "It seems to me that . . ." is the simple, crass, form it takes in popular statement, but professional statement is not much more subtle.

The languages and prejudices of that strange creature "modern man" are made authoritative over the order of time and the cosmos. No one stops to prove why modern man should have such authority (or, for that matter, to say who he is; he generally is the class of persons to which the speaker belongs). No one makes any external evidence authoritative, for authority inheres in the explanation; if it satisfies the speaker then, of course, it carries authority. "God is dead" because that is an explanation that suits the experience of a group of persons. It is a proposition absolutely immune to either argument or evidence, which seems not to trouble its adherents at all. It is satisfying as explanation so it has all the authority of truth.

Under such an intellectual tyranny it was inevitable that there could be no truly operative definition of faith. Faith is an act or a relation that people could do or be or "have" without any pretense of explanation or even a false explanation. But ideas have consequences. Words have extraordinary formative power.

Under the general grant of authority to the act of explanation, explanations of faith replaced faith. Faith, therefore, subservient to the act of explanation, became identified with it. But explanation is received by an act of belief. So faith became identified with belief, with an act subject to the will and decision of the person.

This worked, and worked for a long time. It is possible to form the soul around verbal images, to construct a personal, and a social and political order around a set of beliefs that have no real connection with evidence or experience and thus create a world within which generations of people can enact the drama of their lives.

In the case of simple, primitive, secluded societies this state can continue to last for centuries.

But the pressure of the immediate and the particular (the "real") is remorseless. The immediacies of the world, the lust and lethargy of the flesh, the energies of personality, erode belief and gradually the protective structures weaken, until they suddenly collapse like a dam eroded by winter cold until it is swept away in the spring floods.

This is no more than the natural dialectic of human work. It would not trouble us basically if the principle of explanation did not exercise so compulsive an authority, even when all actual explanations have been emptied of content. Explanations have failed; but to be human is to have explanations; therefore we despair of being human or else we seize desperately on any explanation that seems to offer some hope of filling the void, flinging it aside when it too proves unsatisfying and seizing another.

Even if one of these explanations is "true," even if it conforms word for word to the most accurate statement that could be engendered from the deepest, most profound experience of the real, it still would not suffice. For, held as explanation, it functions as something other than what it was as engendered. A symbolic structure works, survives, only as achievement, never as gift or inheritance.

Explanation is not faith. Faith is not belief.

"We are ourselves both the instrument of discovery and the instrument of definition," says Charles Olson.[43]

Thus explanation has to be put back into faith, where it lives, and deposed from its authority.

How, then, do we explain faith?

The first step is to take seriously the logical difficulty that points in the direction of descriptive actuality; there is no reason to exempt the observer or his observation or his definition from the image or the definition of the real. Respect for this principle is likely to modify a good many definitions, which cannot be what they are if the definer is involved in them (for example, if man is by nature both finite and corrupt, his definitions partake of finiteness and corruption, which rather substantially alters the authority of the definition).

It is even more important that taking the principle seriously wholly alters the sense of the person making the definition. For we are the instrument of definition as well as the instrument of discovery and, as Olson says, "definition is as much a part of the act as sensation itself." And, in the words of Elizabeth Sewell, ". . . method constructs the mind at the same time as it constructs the constructions of the mind."[44]

Thus it is impossible any longer to think of "having" faith, whatever definition we make of faith. Not only is faith not a thing that can be had, the act of faith is not a person having something other than the having. It is, rather, a state or condition or a relation. It is to be, or to be in or to be within or whatever combination of words suggests the intricate structure of the self.

For faith is that intricate interplay of rhythmic structures, of ordered processes that make up the self in its world. In a coherent and integral personality, belief may be the outward statement of faith, the emergence of faith into certain kinds of statements. But there is no necessary connection between faith and belief; it is common to the point of being usual to find a person with a collection of incompatible and disorganized beliefs that have little to do with the reality of his faith, whatever it might be.

Nor is it either true or useful to say that every person has faith in the manner of defining religion as each person's "ultimate concern." Faith implies a coherence of organized process out of which the essential aspects of the person's acts might proceed. It is impossible to look into another person so deeply as to be able to say he lacks such coherence. But there are indeed those who appear to be a collection of incompatible patterns, picked up here and there and held loosely, in a jumble. There are those, also, who appear to be locked into one pattern, one idea or principle. They can be more terrible in their consequences, but there is no engendering coherence to their commitment, which is more nearly an abdication from the human.

It is possible, even probable, that nearly everyone has the potentiality for such coherence; Dante had only certain kinds of traitors dead before their bodies died and therefore put beyond hope. Out of such a principle develops the possibility of deathbed conversion. But it is still true that many people dribble out their lives in bits and disorganized pieces.

It does not follow that intelligence and learning are either an insurance of coherence or a bar against it.

Once so defined, faith can appear as that which is generated out of the cultural forms it generates. Therefore, even belief, explanation, takes its place as an instrument of faith, as a formal manifestation of faith, even a condition of faith. But never faith itself.

Words are of great power in every culture; explanatory, propositional words have great power in those cultures whose symbolic structures require them in addition to, or in place of, the great mythic statements. In such cultures, the formal statement in propositions is an unevadible responsibility. But adherence to the "correct" belief can only, at best, discipline the soul to faith. It cannot, it can never, be faith.

At a time when the weakness of words is most apparent, there is a strong temptation to reject words altogether. But there is no more reason for depriving propositional words of their symbolic function than there is to give them ultimate authority. Our culture has undoubtedly erred in the extremity of authority granted to explanation, definition and belief but all cultures, infatuated with the success of their particular language, give too great authority to that language and suffer the same desolation of spirit when, inevitably, the language collapses under the double weight of its own achievements and the expectations loaded on it. So, in that sense as in so many others, we are as all people have been, parts of the logic and limitations of a culture.

So we undertake our present task with the final knowledge that our beliefs have not made us different from other people, nor superior to them. We do not possess one fragment of the authority carried by that to which our beliefs point or, better (if we are faithful), that which is made manifest in our beliefs. If we are humbled by the knowledge of our own pretentious failure, we might be able to receive the work of other people, to our own great good. For the Holy Trinity is present to us only as we can receive the work of others as the manifestation of their selves which is the reflection of our selves and the insurance of community.

Yet it is decisive how we receive the work of others. It would be possible, in all respect, to receive them eclectically, as an anthology or a collection and thus, by being respectful, deprive them of their power and therefore, of their humanity. Great Hector did not flee under the walls of Troy, nor Simon suffer the sandy winds at the top of his column that we should display and enjoy them as quaint customs or specimens in the study of the history of religion. We should take them seriously or not at all.

The only way to take them seriously is to take them faithfully.

Faith is not belief but the coherent community. We live in faith only by the symbolic structures, the ordered energies, of our metaphors. There is no faith outside the forms of faith and the forms of faith are generated in the languages of culture.

But the languages of culture are not absolute and faith is not reducible to nor exhausted in the relativisms of culture. Faith engenders in the languages the forms that transform the languages. Faith is always subject to what Spengler called *pseudomorphosis* (a geological term meaning the forcing of one mineral into the form of another). It is hard to imagine an institution more antithetical to the spirit of St. Francis than the Franciscan order and the great basilica in Assisi. The hagiolatry in the basilica would have appalled Francis. That there is both blasphemy and hypocrisy in this profound misuse of a man's devoted work is quite true. But there were no other forms to embody the vision of Francis, and those forms have carried Francis as a chalice carries the consecrated wine.

Thus it is with all the faiths by which people have tried to make themselves human. In so far as this process is a condition of being human we, in our culture, are as all people have been, charged with the responsibility of engendering the forms of our faith.

Yet even so—if it can be said without pride—it is given to us to perform a new function in the human pilgrimage. For the first time the true historical consciousness has been born, and with history comes the possibility of recreating the world of the other.

The two great and unique achievements of our culture are history and science. It is by means of these that we can, if we are granted grace and will and courage, bring into human awareness as never before the world of things as other and the world of persons as other. This will not be if we take history and science as they are commonly defined, in the masculine mode, as raids on the unknown. History without true science, science without true history would remain, then, as instruments of conquest and authority. But history and science, the study of persons and the study of things, taken in the feminine mode, contemplative, engendering, might achieve trinitarian faith. For it is by their means that we can recover the world of the other.

This begins the definition of theology yet to come. But that theology is not the norm and the origin of faith. That will remain where it has always been, in the relation of persons, however humble or however great. The task to be defined here is the task of the literate and the learned as their appointed service to the community and an indispensable means to community. It does not carry special authority in the community except as part of any whole is indispensable to that whole. If there is authority within the whole it is in the immediacies of the Trinity to be found in the interaction of persons. Thus personal relations as sacrament is the engendering center of the Christian faith and there is no advantage at all to learning or greatness; the simple and the obscure can love as surely as the great. What is more, the learned and the great can know the Trinity in their own special work only as they know the Trinity in their own lives; they learn their profession as persons and derive their most important intellectual tools from what they are as persons. Theology is not a technical exercise to be managed by those not committed to it, for theology is—is only—making the engendering faith manifest in one of the humane languages.

The common task of the ordinary human is care for persons and for the things of the earth. The task of the Christian intellectual is the reception of that which has been done and made, for the instruction of the Church and for the determination of who we are. Thus history and science, redefined and made into coordinates of a single act, become the normative work of theology.

An essential condition for the proper doing of this work is what might be called, with some strain, the metaphysics of the argument: a "reality" is presupposed, although what we know is not reality but our knowing of reality, the structures and the processes engendered from our intercourse with reality. Thus our selves are constructed in rhythmic interchange with reality; what we know of reality is given form in the structures of our languages which are themselves part of ourselves and part of reality. And to know the knowing is to bring into relation with it the structures of our lived world.

Therefore, no experience of the real has authority, for all are engenderings within the forms of a particular culture and a particular self. The meanest grovelling before stick or stone and the most intricate structure of Christendom are alike in having emerged from the interaction of persons with reality, and neither can claim to be true.

Equally, all experiences of the real have authority for all are encounters of persons with reality. The meanest grovelling before
stick or stone and the most intricate structures of Christendom are
equally true for they are the engendered organizations of human
spirits.

This tolerance does not require abdication of judgment, even
when judgment is not, finally, separable from opinion. There are
symbolic structures that are engendered from themselves, owing
more to the logical development of their language than they do to
any encounter with reality. Most philosophy owes more to the un-
packing of its appointed language than it does to an experience of
reality; Heidegger's work, for example, could be called "Fantasia
and Fugue on the German Language." There is no narrative too
fantastic to be believed and made the skeleton of a theology, no
practice too bizzare to be the engendering ritual of a religion.

Yet language itself and what we do with our languages are parts
of reality. No narrative is so fantastic nor practice so bizzare as not
to have proceeded from the human; knowing our history and our
pathology is part of knowing the world we are now in.

Thus we reconstruct our past because the reconstruction of our
past, in love, is a reconstruction of ourselves. That all the symbolic
structures have authority liberates us from the deadly act of judgment. Whatever our opinions of them, we receive them as embodiments of the human and by taking them into ourselves we become more completely human.

In taking them into ourselves we do not, if it is done in the
awareness that is love, use them or seek their use but receive them
for what they are. Yet if we receive them in respect we learn from
them what they uniquely knew. The Zen sand garden is part of
the ritual of Zen Buddhism, not to be used as ornament in the garden of the local Presbyterian church in zealous ecumenicity. But
that contemplation which is awareness of the simultaneous flow
and suspension of rhythm is better learned at Ryoan-ji than anywhere else on earth. We do no respect to Zen or Ryoan-ji if we

claim a right to baptize it. But to absorb Ryoan-ji is to take into ourselves something that Christendom does not provide.

The Christian, once emancipated from Christendom, can do this to the enhancement of his theology and therefore his faith. Can the Zen Buddhist, in fidelity to his faith, equally absorb the rhythms of Amiens?

As my vocabulary has tried to suggest, the study of Christendom is, in the same way, a part of our study of history. "In the same way" because Christendom is in the same way our engendering in the languages of a culture of the relation between Christian people and reality. In so far as they are people their symbolic structures have no more truth than the meanest grovelling before stick or stone. In so far as they are Christian their symbolic structures make manifest the Christ to those whose sensibilities are so organized and tuned to receive these cultural forms.

The authority is only in Christ, not in those who claim to mediate Christ, not in Christendom. Christ is the way, the truth and the life, Christendom is not the way.

As we unfold to ourselves the integrity of symbolic structures, including our own, so we chronicle their decay and disintegration. All human structures, including Christendom, are doomed to destruction because, as human, they are partial. Every achievement creates institutions and practices that fail because the institutions and practices transform the situation that engendered them and they no longer fit what they once resolved.

We owe to ourselves an awareness of the collapse of other structures, because as we scratch through the debris of our own we are tempted to see only the great age of another and try to find in it a refuge from our own failure. The greatness of our own past seems only a logical and therefore villainous prelude to present offense and we look for relief to the fullest statement of those structures which are most distant from the decay of our own. In doing so we are false to the humanity of the culture we choose as model, and false to the possibility of our own. We cannot wear the garments of another culture as a costume and if we take over the habits of another culture we take as well the fatality within that leads as inevitably to the dissolution of their institutions as it does to ours.

Yet the word *fatality* is misleading; we are too tempted to ascribe to the blind workings of fate or the dictates of a remorseless history the event that is a consequence of our own character and situation. So we find in the responses of our own day a sense of despair, of futility, of cynical rage which may be an understandable human response but which has neither human dignity nor historical use. It is not likely that we will be able to generate any more permanent symbolic structure or social order than human beings ever have for we are not emancipated from the common condition of the human race. But we do have the possibility of achieving something that is not only distinctive to our own day and our own situation, which is no more than all people of integrity have always done; we have the possibility of achieving something genuinely new.

To do so we not only have to understand the process but know the particularities of our own past. We learn both process and possibility by knowing what other men have done, including our own predecessors. There is a special need to understand our own past and our own present, for that is who we are.

The Kingdom of God

I have tried, as best I can, to outline the preliminaries of this process; that may be all an academic can do. The first stage is to understand the process, and thereby know better who we are and how we live in our world. Historical study gives a better grasp of the process, an outline of possibilities as they have been seen and a sense of where we now are. The discipline that grows out of this may be all we can do, till the discipline itself teaches us more than we can know now.

Other problems block our understanding. They are problems only because we, or our language, make them so, for they are problems of definition. The problem here is the meaning of that classic term, *incarnation*.

The definition of the incarnation is implied in all that has gone before. But it must be made explicit if words like "faith" and the "kingdom of God" are to have purpose. For incarnation is the crucial principle of what must still be called a Christian "metaphysics," the order of being, the structure of what "is."

The linear, causal intelligence knows only discrete beings or a mystic All, detached and distinguishable substances or abstract forces. Incarnation was felt to be a critical principle of Christianity but the metaphysics of substance couldn't cope with it. In a world of discrete substances, of persons occupying a neutral space in a spiritless nature, God could enter only as an actor might come on the stage, as a *deus ex machina*, or as a messenger sent from somewhere else, or as an abstract spirit that, by its abstractness, could not be confined to one distinct substance but would pervade all things.

Out of this grew all the Christological controversies, the desperate ingenious attempt to fit into a language, principles of order and relation that didn't belong to that language. It is a symbolic ignorance approaching barbarism to condemn that attempt, as liberal humanists are used to doing. The early Christians had, in the language of their lives, a full grasp of principle of the incarnation. But they had no exact verbal language to express it in. Their attempt was admirable, courageous, brilliantly subtle. It is still revelatory of how we live and work with our languages. But the verbal language no longer has the same authority and use, so their formulas have no function for us.

The sense of an abstract, formless God, a principle rather than a person, leads to pantheism, a nature worship that some find sustaining. But many or most do not find it has ethical force. It lacks personality.

Because the image behind them is spatial, definitions generate a division between sacred and secular. The sacred is where God "is" or it is what leads "to" God. The secular is all that is left over.

Modern ingenuity has created a somewhat different evaluation, in which the secular is understood as a special case of the sacred, in which Jesus is a man with a very special function.

It is only when metaphysics shifts from substance to process that our understanding of the incarnation might approximate our experience of it. For then the word "is" has true reference to the insubstantial.

We are not substances placed *in* a world. We are particular concentrations of energy and relation integrally part *of* the world. Our world is not a neutral space containing willful substances. Our world is an intricate interlocking of wholes, within which willful personalities enact the rituals of their energies in inescapable interaction with the whole.

The incarnation does not happen as an actor walking on a stage or as gas filling a room or as an impersonal magnetic force. The incarnation is a particular ordering of relation.

Exactly what is being incarnated is not a question we can deal with, except as our insatiable curiosity compels us to try this or that formula (like the Christological formulation) that makes usable sense within the languages we actually have. There is, fortunately, no likelihood our languages ever can accurately set out the ultimate order of things. In a metaphysics of substance such a conviction can only create relativism or skepticism but no such fate is required of us. Only the absolute dominance of the fallacy of explanation could ever have made it possible to think our languages could contain the infinite or that their failure to do so was a proper cause of despair.

The Christian commitment is that God can be truly known, or that what is truly known is God. The condition is that what is *truly* known is God. There is no commitment that God is no more than what is known, or that knowing is to be identified with any one of the languages we are fated, as humans, to use; not the verbal, not the liturgical, not the ethical, not the devotional. But neither is it to be thought of in the fashion of the perpetual, "Not this, not this," for the language of mystical vision in the ecstatic quiet beyond the senses is itself a language; the incarnation denies us that retreat as well.

Yet neither is the knowledge of God to be separated from the languages. There is no structure without the forms which make it manifest, no form without a structure, so the knowing of God is never isolated from the languages, nor can it be identified with any one of them or with the sum of them.

The knowing of God is in the wholeness of things and our relation to them and to each other and in all the languages by which we generate that relation.

The promise is both clear and sure: "For where two or three are gathered in my name there am I in the midst of them." "The Kingdom of God is in the midst of you."

There is nothing in the promise to prevent us from using the Holy Name and the Kingdom as instruments of magic or weapons against our enemies or to ensure that they won't work as magic or as weapons, even though one of the workings is the damnation of those who would use them so. To use them in pride or possessiveness is to offend against the whole order of the sacred. The Christ, the Kingdom of God, is no object to be boxed up in the most "Christian" of boxes, but a mode of being related in the wholeness of things.

Thus the Kingdom of God is the redemption of things for it brings them into wholeness. The Kingdom of God is the redemption of languages for they are the means of wholeness. The Kingdom of God is the redemption of ourselves for it is the human that completes and transforms wholeness.

It is for these reasons that no one language can claim primacy or authority. To claim authority for a language is to set it above wholeness, outside the intricate harmony of the whole. It is for these reasons that the sum of the languages cannot claim authority, for to add them is to assume they are things to be added whereas they are elements in a harmony. It is for these reasons that the Kingdom of God is not something apart from or other than our languages, for we are our languages. Our world is the rhythmic interchange between our selves, each other, and the things of our context in the shapes of our languages; the incarnation is the enactment of the Christ in the world.

It is in the nature of our languages to require community, for no language can be a part of the whole unless ingredient to it is the work of the others. Any language developed in isolation from the others leads only to the destruction of itself and the death of the soul. We have had to attend to them separately for we could not know them humanly otherwise. But we have pursued them separately long enough, too long, dangerously long, and we see all around us the death of souls in the confusion of tongues.

Thus faith is not belief, but the life of love in the wholeness of being human, which is, finally, the Kingdom of God. The Lord is not in our languages so that we have control over the holy one. But the promise is sure; if our languages, all our languages, are truly used, which is in his name, then he will be among us. The mode of his being among us will not be such that we can point to it, or control it, or use it, or prove it or prove anything by it. For the mode of the presence is not in the determination of human forms but is an act of grace.

Yet, in grace, it is not separate from us or from our acts; faith is not inert passivity but a making and engendering of those things in which the Kingdom can happen.

Such assertions stir memories of old controversies; Pelagianism, free will vs. grace, faith and works, original sin. Such controversies were firmly caught in the interstices of living symbolic speech and only mythic illiteracy permits us to speak of them as irrelevant or of no consequence to ourselves. A false decision on those questions would, at that time, have thrown symbolic speech out of shape, with drastic consequences for the ordering of the self. Now the issues are the same, but the symbolic structures are vastly different. This does not mean a different answer to the question, a different solution to the problem, but changing the terms of the question in accord with our very different symbolic order.

We are caught in one of those paradoxes the Gospels abound in: "Seek ye the Kingdom of God; and all these things will be added unto you." So we set about the task of building the Kingdom or of making it possible. But also, "He who finds his life shall lose it and he who loses his life for my sake shall find it."

These are not offered as proof texts, a procedure that was useful only under a conviction of the authority of language that is no longer supportable. These texts are offered as descriptions of our working, a working that is understandable with our present understanding of symbolic process. In short, what the statements seem to say is that, when we choose as purpose even the purpose that we are enjoined on highest authority to choose, we are cutting it out of its contextual relations and thereby altering the whole, distorting the unity that is the final purpose. And by destroying the unity that is the source of life we destroy ourselves.

This is the paradoxical fatality of consciousness. We could escape from it by becoming either more or less than human, which, indeed, has been the purpose of so much of religious activity—to rise above the fatal imprisonment of the flesh or to sink back down into undifferentiated unity. The intent of this work is not to escape from the conditions of humanity, but to try to fulfill them. The Christian paradox is one of the fundamental conditions of human purpose.

And both terms of it are true. The resolution, therefore, is not the search for new ways of seeking that which would enable us to overcome the fatal duality of our search, as though we could by fiercer and more determined concentration evade the danger. Rather it is a matter of evolving new ways of being in the world which place the kingdom where it belongs, in the midst of us, among us, not out there to be made, to be won or conquered, to be reached at the end of the pilgrimage.

The fearful and arduous quest ends where it began; in its beginning.

The first step in this procedure is the sexualizing of the imagination. At this point, the eroticizing of the imagination is not at issue. That is or ought to be an essential act of our imagination, but it is not the concern of this moment. The sexualizing of the imagination is a matter of bringing into consciousness those modes of symbolic action that we define according to the sex that makes them manifest.

The issue at this point is not basically sexual. The issue is concerned, rather, with bringing into our symbolic process, the sense of engendering as a part of our humanity, that is as humane as "making," the sense of care as a valid human purpose. Engendering care is not identified with the work of either sex; it is a part of the work of the farmer and the artist as well as the mother. It can be abused by the mother, who can falsify the growth of the child, as well as the farmer, who can attack and exploit the soil, and the artist, who can try to compel the inner life of his material to false purposes.

Nevertheless our imaginations are controlled by the primary processes of organic life; engendering care is symbolically a woman's mode. It is abused, when it so often is, because its real nature is lost under the dominant masculine mode. The mother, then, defines her role, not as the nurture of a person to fulfill the self, but as the making of a plastic personality to the intention of someone else. Farming becomes an impersonal assault on the earth. The artist is excluded from important affairs because what he does is womanish. Thus we are not likely, in our culture, to recover the centrality of engendering care except as we can recover the sense of its sexuality, except as the womanly role becomes as central to our imagination as the manly.

In our culture, this will require great care, for the sentimental idolatry of motherhood has been a device for controlling women while removing them from all actual administrative authority and, therefore, all true and public symbolic authority. The womanly symbolism, therefore, works itself out uncontrollably in corrupting ways, the detached voyeurism of advertising and *Playboy*, the masculine chauvinism of pornography, and of the official image of persons in politics and popular imagery. How this problem should be handled, I cannot say. What is needed is mythological speech and my chosen language is academic argument, which might persuade the academically inclined but certainly not most people.

But it is, despite all difficulty, the necessary first step. It may be that increased respect for the work of the farmer, the artist, the teacher, the forester, all those charged with the nurture of other beings in their integrity, will help raise the womanly role to full consciousness. But in the nature of mythology and metaphor, the movement is more likely the other way. It is politically and socially necessary for the true emancipation of half the human race. It is symbolically necessary because our plight is basically symbolic and mythological; there are not the imaginative resources among men alone sufficient to this work, precisely because our mythological distortions prevent most men from having any deep sense of the womanly.

There is, obviously, an opposite danger—the return to a matri-dominant order. The dominance of women, or a feminine mode as dominant as the masculine has been, would be no more successful. The myth of forgotten matriarchy is part of a probing into ourselves, but it is not a prescription.

There is little archaeological evidence for there having been matriarchal societies in any full sense, although the archaeology of myth provides considerable evidence that can be read that way. Many myths and related customs seem to chronicle a transition from a matriarchal to a patriarchal culture, for those who see myth emerging from historic events. It is more probable that myth grows more actively from personality than from events; thus the mythological account reflects the transition—the rites of passage—for men, from childhood which is the world of women, to maturity, the world of men.

In this the myth is not only psychologically sound but suggests an ordering of engendering and making that needs to be recovered if our making is not to be the death of us. Engendering precedes making as men grow from the world of women to the world of men and back again.

The very bodies of men reflect this movement. Until puberty, often well into adolescence, the bodies of boys are not significantly different from those of girls. In old age, the body of a man is again much closer to that of old women. So, too, the care of children is entrusted to women until they pass to the training of men.

In our dilemma, the dominance of women would be of no use, but the temporal priority of the womanly role would be. Once this were achieved, the function could be dispersed more generally, for engendering care is the fundamental human role. The fundamental definition of the human is the use of all resources to allow the other to be what it, she, he, can be, to protect and to nourish the growth of the other.

From this caring there proceeds, in order, making. This ordering is the true condition of being human and should protect us against the temptation to exhaust the human in the act of caring. The abuse of making, the definition of both the human and the order of society as exhausted in making, has caused many people, naturally, to take refuge in the simplicities of elementary caring and to look for nurture to those simple societies that have rested primarily on caring. These acts, this search, are good as reminders; they are not sufficient for the ordering of society.

To assume that the human can be defined exclusively in the act of caring is to forget the primal dualism of the human condition. As soon as the world and all that is in it becomes the other, as soon as the self becomes self-conscious, there is, both inevitably and necessarily, the assertion of the self. This is as it should be; if there is no true self, how can there be love for the self by which to measure the love for the other? But, in the absence of making, enmity and not caring is the logical consequence of duality, for, once beyond the instinctive care of the parent (and that is not instinctive in all species), there is neither reason nor means to care for the other. Caring requires imaginative, symbolic structures which make caring a requirement and a fulfillment. Caring requires the means, the tools, the occasion in which caring can take place.

Once we were launched into consciousness, making became essential to caring.

It is not realistic (and therefore not humane) to refuse to admit that caring takes place under the conditions of power, for with the transformation of duality into dualism, power became one basic operating condition of human relation. Therefore, the proper control of power is a necessary aspect of caring; to define the human as caring in its most limited sense and make of politics the enemy of the human is, finally, to defeat the human.

Of all problems in the order of caring, this is the most difficult, for caring can be the tool of the oppressor as well as a means of oppression. Care can require resistance to the oppressor, even revolution if that is the only way to secure care for the oppressed. The oppressor (or the priestly instruments of the oppressor) will preach loving care to the oppressed in order to disarm them; the right to enjoin care must be earned by true caring and those who use it as a weapon use it to the damnation of their souls.

But caring can be used, too, as a weapon of pride, and the passion for revolutionary care grow less from true caring than from the use of care as a cover for a dualistic lust for domination. Oppressors are not always of evil intent; they may be caught in symbolic structures organized around hierarchical domination. Care for the oppressor may dissolve hierarchy more surely, if more slowly, than revolution.

There is no rest and no surety in the search for the truth of intent.

The range of care-full making goes further. The human is a complex thing. The conditions of human life have always been such that care had to be defined as care of the most immediate physical needs. But from the beginning and particularly under the conditions of our present luxury, the human involves a great deal more than immediate physical needs, so much more that a great many people have always been willing to sacrifice physical needs to those further, more complex, human requirements.

Therefore, the definition of care must include the whole complex ordering and energy of being human, and much of human making is directed to the care, the true and humane care, of the whole range of our symbolic speech.

Care that is confined to the physical can be as intrusive and as oppressive as that kind of oppression, masquerading as care, that would compel the other to the shape of my own symbolic order.

True care requires, then, not only closeness but moving away, the clearing of the space and the time that are essential to growth. How much space and time is needed, when to move away, when and how to return, are the intricate problems of caring. They are not problems to be resolved by calculation and argument but by a sense of timing and of interval which are taught in the mythical narrative, in the stories that are shaped by the myth, in liturgy and the drama that grows out of liturgy, in music and dance, in architecture and painting, in geometry.

Yet timing and interval are ingredient to the order of things; they themselves are the occasion for care, for the careful engendering that brings into being those things that develop timing and interval in fidelity to the material that embodies them. Thus is care rightly extended to the whole of human and natural life. Care is the purpose of making, as making is the shelter and means of care.

An aesthetic and an ethic emerges from this, or rather, a new ordering of knowledge that both blends and blurs aesthetics and ethics. All human making is done for its own sake, for it is a protection of the essential character of some part of the natural order, or the abstract principles that are of the structure of things. All making is properly humane when done for the holy purpose of care, that care which heals and sustains and builds. The dance not only has the inherent ethic of its inner discipline, it is an ethical act, in cherishing and developing a part of what it means to be human in the earth. Technology has the ethic of its use and its inner discipline, but it achieves its truth only in the realm of its respect for matter and for process that is the essence of the aesthetic.

So, too, is the definition of all study, all thought and education. They are acts done "for their own sake," else there is yielding to the eternal temptation to make knowledge subservient to power. But left solitary in their own ingrown purpose they are sterile, unfruitful. All study, all thought, all education, are for caring, for the care of some particular aspect of the structures of the earth, finally for the true care of people in their pilgrimage in the earth.

Thus, all thought, all learning, all education, are humane only as they are, truly, moral.

We should now be able to say more about the purpose of our lives, for "care" becomes mere sentimentality if it is separated from purpose. There is no inherent reason why caring should be the decisive purpose of being human. Domination is far clearer to many as the purpose of being human, and always has been, for domination is an inherent purpose of dualism. If dualism is turned inward rather than outward its mode of purpose is indifference to the other. Other purposes can equally lead to indifference. The test, the measure is consequence and commitment, not proof.

The test that we can offer in our own day is the double consequence of death and boredom. Out of dualism and the lust for domination there has come only death and destruction. Out of the dualism of competitive success there has come only boredom and despair.

The problem of war is too obvious to need further elucidation. The obsession with death has complex origins, not always related to this particular discussion, such as the dark dream of chaos and disorder. It is the myth of success that affects most people most deeply, short of the terrible destruction of war.

To define human purpose by success is to reduce most people to failure, boredom or despair. Competitive success presupposes winners and losers and, in a complex society, there are bound to be many more losers than winners. For the losers, life lacks savor and dignity, for the loser falls short of the measure of being human. The result can only be envy, despair, inertia, fantasy. What must unavoidably be done has no interest or savor or sense of fulfillment.

This is the life to which the majority of men and nearly all women are condemned.

But life has little more interest for the successful. Since success is its own purpose, once achieved it has nothing more to offer. If there is not the unceasing pressure of maintaining success there is the boredom of its achievement, for success is an empty thing in itself. The drive for success has produced great human good but it does not serve for complete human purpose.

It is understandable that the poor and unsuccessful should look back on war as the only time in their lives when they lived with any sense of the fullness of life. But the successful do so as well, for only their war experience directed their energies beyond themselves.

With true caring, the whole world comes alive. It is there, to be permitted to be, for the being of the other in its fullness is the fulfillment of me. Caring provides complete equality and democracy, for each of us is placed in the earth, in the structures of human making, and in the order of our relation with others. The measure is always the same for all, the fullness of care in the opportunity given to us. The rich and the powerful and those of high estate are judged according to their greater opportunity. They are not to be honored for their success or even their ornamental philanthropy, but according to the fullness of their care.

Care is the source of joy, for joy is the response to the fullness of being. Competitive success brings only pride, not joy. True care can never be boring, for the world is change and change that fulfills is the completion of care and therefore joy unceasing.

True care is truly womanly, the immersion in the fullness of being, the nurture that permits the other to grow. It is, therefore, the fulfillment of women and of the womanly in men. True care is truly manly for it requires protection and the sheltering condition of making. It is, therefore, the fulfillment of men and of the manly in women.

True care is the link between the world of nature and the world of the human. The world of nature is both setting and means for the human act. Therefore the world of nature requires care as a part of the care of the human. But the world of nature is also the other, requiring care, and the care of nature teaches the rhythm of care for it compels the rhythms of the maker to wait for the rhythms of growth. The care of nature is required and, being fulfilled, generates care.

True care is the link between the world of drama and the world of things, for drama is enacted in the world of things. True care is the link between the things that are given and the things that are made, the world of nature and the world of art, for true making, which is true art, is the careful fulfillment of the life of things.

True care is the link between the past and the present, the distant and the near and thereby generates true ecumenicity. At the structured center of every culture there is a caring from which its creativity proceeds. We do not abdicate the right to a judgment of purpose, if we affirm the order of caring. All cultures, all religions are based on a caring, and our care for their integrity can teach us their care. There can be a disagreement with their purpose, a condemnation of the abuse of their caring, but their caring becomes part of the human heritage. Purposes can be misdirected, arguments can be false, but true making is not wrong for it is, of its nature, a care for a part of humanity in the earth.

True care is measured by the care of the human, and all other caring is measured by that care. But care of the human is not only the care of the physical needs of persons but a care for all the structures and the processes by which our humanity is achieved.

Thus the trinitarian relation that is the fulfillment of the human is not simply a relation between persons, but a relation to the things that have been made and the things that grow in the earth. Or, in another statement of the same thing, the trinitarian relation includes the whole of creation, for there is no humanity apart from the orders of the earth and the symbolic structures with all their embodiments that people have made to place themselves in the earth.

Thus the purpose of the human is not competitive success but the achievement of that relation in which the Trinity can be manifest. By this means alone the Kingdom of God will come into being. The key to the Kingdom is engendering care.

This, too, is misleading imagery; the Kingdom is not, even metaphorically, a place to be entered by a key. It is a relation to be engendered. It is not out there, or beyond, or after this. It is here. It is now.

Every relation is a chance to create the structure in which the Trinity can be embodied. Every relation is a chance to evoke, to call the Christ or to cut him off. Every relation of engendering care since the beginning of time has been the reality of the Christ who has been the creator of all things from the beginning, for without him was not anything made that was made.

Yet to consider the Christ as a structure to be generated by our energies is to defeat the Christ, for the power of God is not accessible to human will. The promise is sure, that the Christ is among us in our engendering care. But the condition is equally sure, that the Lord is present in our caring only if we do not care in order to make the Lord present. To do that is to turn love into magic.

It is the fatality of the human that we will always treat the Christ magically. So long as we define the Christian life solely in terms of the moral will, there is no escape from this dilemma, for every act will be an act toward our condemnation. Our recourse, then, the hope we have for the reconstruction of the life of faith, is not to find new devices for exhortation, new arguments to convince the mind; it is to generate the structures in which community can come alive.

This, too, is not at the disposal of the intentional will but will emerge only from engendering care, which is love.

A Meditation on the Being of Love

You shall love the Lord your God with all your heart and with all your soul, and with all your mind. This is the first and great commandment. And a second is like it, You shall love your neighbor as yourself. On these commandments depend all the law and the prophets.

MATTHEW 22:37–40

It is part of the fatal limitation of the human that we can understand absolutes only in the language available to us, and no language is itself capable of containing an absolute in its absoluteness. The intent to obey an absolute command becomes, therefore, a disobedience.

It is also, and painfully, a frustration. Our Lord has placed at the center of his faith a double commandment on which all else depends, an absolute and unequivocal commandment, that we love absolutely. Our languages enable us to conceive of love only as an affection, an emotion, a feeling. Therefore, the commandment becomes impossible to understand. We can love with our "hearts," since the heart is the figure of that aspect of ourselves that feels. By extension we can love with our "soul." But how do we love with our minds? By definition, the mind is that aspect of ourselves that thinks, that has concepts, not affections. And, in our own day, the work of the mind is increasingly required to be objective, to be a disinterested instrument for dealing properly with objective information. To feel at all, much less to feel an affection like love, is considered an offense against the true work of the mind.

Further, the absolute command to love absolutely can mean only one thing in languages that define the world according to substances and the person according to will. It can mean only an increasingly intense act of will to feel the proper desire and affection for that which is other than the self. Unhappily, it is of the nature of feelings that they cannot be sustained or increased by increasing the stimulus. They become, shortly, numb, as the body shields itself against sensation.

Love, indeed, exists as a feeling, an affection, a passion, and to know it in that mode is to know the delights of being human. Yet to define love in terms of its action on the affections, to exhaust love in the emotions, is the romantic fallacy and to indulge it is to give over human joy to the ravaging of time. For the affections are stilled or distracted in the dailyness of human life, the ordinariness of human acts. Love retreats from high passion and beautiful feeling. The wife who looked so like an angel in her wedding gown, so like Aphrodite in the wedding bed, is another person in her illness, vomiting into the basin with her hair sticking to a sweaty forehead. The baby whose rosy purity is the cause of delighted pride, is another person wallowing peevishly in excremental soil.

Another person? That is the voice of the romantic love—and romantic love is no guide to the reality of persons. That requires an irrascible Christian such as Dean Swift:

> Thus finishing his grand Survey
> Disgusted Strephon stole away
> Repeating in his amorous Fits,
> Oh! Caelia, Caelia, Caelia shits.

The romantic vision cannot contend with this. Neither can any form of idealism or any religion that defines the human as spiritual. Yet this is the way human life is lived, and to reject it is to alienate us from ourselves. To define love in terms that reject the human is, finally, a condemnation to despair.

Yet is is equally romantic sentimentality to think that excrement can itself be loved simply because love *ought* to be larger than it is commonly defined. Excrement and vomit are what they are and, in less extreme examples, the ordinariness of life has its inevitable monotony and boredom. The feeling of love, the emotion, is compensation for squalor and the ordinary, investing the banal and the routine with a kind of glow. But this, too, falls victim to the passing of time.

Romantic love is not simply inadequate. It guarantees the defeat of the human. It displaces so much that is essential to the human, yet cannot of itself sustain the human.

We must, therefore, define love anew. In doing so we are not without resources; there are many people who know what love is but cannot say what it is or define it. But definitions are paradigms to which we shape our actions, metaphors that transform the things we do. Definitions as paradigms shape the images which are held before us as example. So a definition is required of us.

Yet we falsify love again if we define it as something, or as an act, that is other than ourselves, for we are ourselves the act of definition and love is definable only in the doing of it. For love is a relation within a structure that permits the engendering exchange, the generation of a whole which sustains the parts which make up the whole. Therefore to love truly is to generate the kind of self that is generated only by love; to love truly is to make those structures within which love takes place.

Love, therefore, is less shown in those feelings which are its expression and reward, than it is in that ordering of things which generates wholeness. The work of love is not a private matter apart from the whole order of life. It is coterminous with the true work of all making, of thought and politics, of art and of science.

Love is the substance of life. The meek will inherit the earth, not as a reward but because they are the ones left alive. We love or we die.

It is reported of Auden that he regretted the poem which concludes with the great line, "We must love each other or die." It is a pity that the poet should feel as he did. The line is not first rate poetry, but it is literally true. Love is as essential to human life as the circulation of the blood is to bodily life.

To be loving, then, is to sustain and to care, to open one's self to the truth of the other and to build those things that protect and nourish that truth.

The feeling of love, the deeply emotional yearning, the fulfilled desire, are ornament and enhancement, pleasure and reward. Without them, we would not only be immeasurably poorer, love itself would be reduced to calculation, which in affairs of persons, is inhumane. The feeling of love, the pleasure and the passion, is the civilizing of the beast in us.

Yet love is not in the feeling. It is in the caring, and the caring is not emotional but is sustaining the process of the human. True love is building, watching, sustaining. True love is being that which fulfills the other, making that which sustains the other.

Love is both the source and the purpose of being human. The true life of the human pilgrimage and, therefore, the true material in the study of history, is the development of love, the slow engendering of the structure of care, the dissolution of structures gone rigid in self-concern, the rebirth of new structures that make love again possible.

The resiliance of the human spirit often surpasses belief in its possibility. The natural affections of the soul often generate true love under conditions of appalling difficulty. But the terrible truth is that love can be killed in the destruction of those structures and instruments of relation that alone make it possible for love to come into being. And when that happens, the habits, laws, institutions that emerge from the death of love become the measure of our acts, even our theology. The treason of the Christian intellectual is nowhere more evident than in willing acceptance of present modes of dualism as authentic statements of the faith.

Thus the decision on matters of both private and public policy cannot be made, or ought not to be made on the basis only of the immediate, the sensible and the personally gratifying. A momentary advantage bought with the price of an institution, a style, a metaphor, a place that is indispensable to our loving is bought at too high a price. Yet we measure our acts and shape our policy by calculation of private advantage. To do so is finally the death of the human.

Love makes it possible for us to be larger than ourselves and thereby fulfill ourselves. But there is no true love if it is directed only toward ourselves, for the final structure of love is the order of a society that makes love possible.

Our offenses are varied but, finally, as they are offenses, they are single and our offenses become our sin. For sin is that which prevents love, as virtue is that which increases love.

The nature and the future of the human is to make and to sustain all that within which love can be enacted.

The pain of history is the offense against love and wholeness. The glory and the hope of history is the submerged but constant generation of the structures of love. The center of history, the proper center of our purposed energies, is the slow, steady development of a final community of the faithful made up of all those in all times, in all places, in all cultures, in all religions whose lives have made the Christ manifest in the holy and trinitarian ordering of their living process.

A Meditation on the Sacraments and the Sacramentals

For I through the law, died to the law, that I might live to God. I have been crucified with Christ; it is no longer I who live, but Christ who lives in me.

> Paul the Apostle, in the letter to the Galatians, 2:19–20

A definition by way of an assertion:

A sacrament is not a sign of anything, including inward or spiritual grace. It is a means for constructing the soul.

A PRELIMINARY MEDITATION

In truth, we do not know what Paul meant when he says "it is no longer I who live but Christ who lives in me." It might be better to say we cannot *explain* it; we may, in fact, know it by means other than our argumentative reason. But, unfortunately, our argumentative reason has gotten us to the point where we mostly think we must be able to explain things in order to use them and, therefore, we block our own access to so many things that cannot be explained precisely because we have defined ourselves, as persons, so dominantly in the mode of explanation. That is, we think of ourselves primarily as thinking, rational creatures even though we actually behave in so many ways other than thinking. If we are not, in fact, primarily thinking, rational creatures but have made ourselves dependent on thinking, on ideas, then we can extricate ourselves from that situation by using our powers of thinking to open up all those things that are more than, other than, rational thought.

So long as we were not so wholly dependent on the principle of rational thought, Paul's statement could, in ecstatic devotion, be received as an affirmation of union below conscious thought. Under present definitions of rationality and thought it can mean nothing at all. Our gravest temptation is to reject rationality, go back to a much earlier time and thus make the statement mean things it was never intended to mean.

Paul's statement is more inclusive than the problem of the sacrament; it would appear to go back to the beginning of the Christian life and describe the process of "conversion." But the sacrament is one of the means to carry forward what was begun in conversion and the sacramentals are all those things which fulfill and sustain the Christian life. Thus, to explain the statement is to explain the sacraments; to know what the sacramentals are is to come closer to understanding Paul's statement. If we can understand them both we might be able to know them better and participate in them more fully.

A SUMMARY AND RECAPITULATION

The origins of religion are forever lost to us. We can guess, even guess with some small hope of probability. But guesses are no more than that, useful to ourselves. The origins of religion go back beyond any evidence at all.

The oldest evidence is certain works of art which are profound in their consistency. They are representations of naked women, faceless, fat, and pregnant; representations of the great animals; both in caves, usually deep in the earth.

What these great works meant to their creators we can never know but, again, only guess. What we can do is try to experience them as deeply and seriously as we can, knowing that we can experience them only through sensibilities that are very different from those of the prehistoric people who made them. If we do so, we find, by general testimony, that we are in the presence of tremendous energy, the swarming abundance of the life of the animal, the soft abundance of the fertile body of the mother.

Beyond that we cannot say. We do not know what the figures meant to those who made them or how they were used. We know only that they were used ritually. They were probably used for the success of the hunt, and to ensure the fertility of the real herds and the real women. That is a distinction we make as observers; they (probably) saw no difference between the real and the painted animal except one could be eaten and the other could not. One is as real as the others.

But we do not need to go much beyond what we can know of these works for what we can know is God's own plenty. What we can know is that deep in the body of the earth there is the fruitfulness of the earth. In the darkness in the caves, the modern visitor can learn what must be known, that we too are part of the fruitful energies of the cave in the earth, that the power of the creatures of the earth and the fertility of the bodies of women are grounds and origin of our own work on the earth.

Among the more painful of the superstitions that beset us, is the conviction that we, coming so long after those who made such things, are by nature and education, immune from their power or the need for their power. The past is not distant from us, but deep within us. It would be sentimental to say we are the same as the people who painted the animals at Lascaux; too much has happened to us for that and the things that happen to us become part of ourselves. But we are different, not as creatures transformed, caterpillar into butterfly, tadpole into frog, but as a tree adds rings. The painters of the caves are within us, the painted animals and the carved women are parts of our very selves.

We will know our selves only as we can go back through those layers of ourselves, knowing each and its relation to all that went before it. We should not consider ourselves as human beings on a pilgrimage through time, perhaps learning something on the way, sending ourselves picture postcards to remind us of the interesting and instructive experiences we have had. Rather we bring essential parts of our journey with us. We bring our past with us as modifications of our body, because our culture began well before the evolution of our bodies was complete and so shaped who we are physically. We bring our past with us as modes of thought, for experiences such as those of the painted caves shape institutions, social structures, habits of thought and work, engender new forms that move steadily away from their origin but never out of touch with their origin.

As we sense ourselves so deeply involved with our past, so must we be equally involved with our bodies. Our bodies have, indeed, changed but they, too, bring their past with them. Genesis and Darwin agree on the ladder of ascent or descent—both spatial images of value, which should be replaced by the image of the tree growing out from the center.

We began in the sea, grew to reptiles to mammal to humanoid to human and the quality of each remains within us, only barely covered by the subsequent layers. There is the cold, pitiless subintelligent vitality of the reptile; the passionate energy of the beast using intelligence as a tool and a weapon without moral judgment; and finally intelligence at the service of moral decision. The tree image is almost literally present although not quite rendering the anatomical picture. The oldest "reptillian" brain is, in us, the brainstem at the top of the spinal column, controlling those bodily functions we conceal behind the terms "automatic" and "instinctive." Folded around this knob and nearly enclosing it is the bulk of the brain, the "mammalian" brain, or, rather *paleomammalian* brain. Enclosing this brain mass is its outer surface, the neocortex.

A lot is known about these brains and their functions. But a lot is not understood, particularly in their relation to each other. It is not for the layman to pass judgment on controversial technical problems. But there is evidence of a kind that the layman observes and experiences, that points to certain conclusions about the brain. A few examples:

1. All people, in varying degrees have the experience of rage, which may or may not be controlled by will or belief.
2. Old people whose cerebral cortex has cease to function, and the most pious people under anesthesia, will talk and behave with the grossest sexuality, entirely in conflict with principles of their responsible life.
3. In nations, judgment of morality and of greatness are entirely separate. In nations professing morality, the murderous tyrant is idealized as a hero, as Napoleon and Caesar have been.
4. The most reasonable and pious people have dreams of an appalling immorality. Even amateur analysis can easily uncover the powerful sexual and economic bases for much of our ordinary acts.

The conclusion: our lives are under the control of distinct bodily systems. They are hierarchically ordered; the cerebral cortex is both physically and figuratively "higher" than the brain stem and the limbic system. The higher levels can partially control the lower but that control can be weakened or destroyed, temporarily or permanently, by chemistry, by aging or by culture. The crocodile, the tiger, and Hitler are within us, integral parts of ourselves, ever waiting the opportunity to control the body.

I mention the names of symbolic forces, energies, power. Also within us are the pregnant female, the impregnating male, the rutting baboon, the whore, the pimp, the rapist, Aphrodite and Artemis, Kali and Parvati, Galahad and Lancelot.

How is power controlled to peace, lust to love?

Not alone. Morality is generated in community, developed in community, transmitted by community. No statement I could make goes more counter to contemporary conviction, which holds that the individual is both whole and all, that each individual has an absolute right to control his or her behavior from childhood on, without control by parent, teacher or any social force. Such a conviction can only be based on the belief that morality and reason are linked within the organism and need only to be left alone to develop fully. There is no evidence at all to sustain such a conviction, and all evidence is against it. "The kingdom of God is within you" said Jesus, meaning the collective you, the community, or "The kingdom of God is in the midst of you."

This conviction that the individual is both good and complete has been taken up by those who think of themselves as a liberated part of the newness of things. In its weakness, the church has acquiesced and surrendered its sacramental function. But it is not new at all; it is part of nineteenth century positivism which was an outgrowth of a primitive stage of science. Too simply put, this view is that of "the ghost in the machine," a spirit or mind which is somehow separate from the body, which receives information from the body, thinks about it, issues instructions to the body. Curious companions are found agreeing on this view of nature of man; they differ only concerning the purposes of the instructions given to the body. The purpose may be the indulgence of the body economically or sexually, the control of the body for some intellectual or spiritual or moral purpose. But, whatever the different purposes, the analysis is the same; the ascetic and the licentious agree, the bank president and the hippie are brothers underneath their stated purpose, because they act on the same image of the human.

Yet we are not at all related to the world in that way. It is now necessary to describe still a third hierarchical structure making up our way of being. The first of these in my account of them was the growth of the human psyche historically, the successive layers of the self's development. The second was the hierarchical ordering of the nervous system from the brain stem (and its attendant nervous system) to the cerebral cortex. The third is the system of relations between these two. The key word now is "pattern" or "paradigm" or "model."

At the lowest, most elementary level, the principle of the paradigm can be illustrated by the simplest form of the reflex arc: what we do when we touch something hot. If the conventional picture of thought were accurate, our nervous system would inform the brain that the hand was against something hot. The brain would then think about it, deciding that the contact was both painful and dangerous and therefore the hand should be moved away. That being the case, the brain would issue instructions to the hand—but by that time the damage is done. No, there is a pattern of response built into the nervous system. The heat sets the pattern into action and the hand is immediately snatched away. The word "instinct" is an evasion of the problem because it defines nothing; an instinct is simply a pattern of response in the nervous system.

There are a great many such patterns which we are born with or which early experience forms into our nervous system so thoroughly that they are beyond conscious control. There are others which are clearly learned but which are as deeply implanted; take, for example, simple perception.

Conventional understanding of the human process has bits of isolated information arriving at the brain which would then combine them into an identifiable whole. Were this true, simple perception would be exceedingly difficult, and preceiving complex objects impossible. Everything in our world is changing, nothing is fixed. A door, for example can be as small as a dollhouse door, as

large as a cathedral door. It can be many shapes, an infinite range
of color. It can be seen in an infinite range of light from the hot
blaze of the sun on the Cathedral of Seville, the soft gray of a
rainy afternoon in a village, the dark dusk. No organism could
ever experience enough doors to build up the definition of "door"
by accumulated experience. Rather we develop a paradigm in our
nervous system, which when stimulated by one of these endlessly
different doors, responds instantly with the sense and, if necessary,
the word, "door."

This is learned and is therefore cultural but it becomes a part of
the reflex apparatus. It goes further. We build up a paradigm,
woman and wife, man and husband. Such a paradigm has nothing
to do with inheritance but it begans to be formed in the womb (it
is not beside the present point that the earliest formative human
experience is the experience of the female). It is built up over the
years by experience of particular persons, by culture in the form
of stories, by the stories indirectly in that they form the persons
who form us. It is not just persons and stories. The experience
works its way into very nearly every aspect of culture from advertising to architecture, economics to liturgy. All then combine to
build up the picture.

Two people, so formed, get married. Their ability to reason out
the problems of marriage is a help but only a small help against
the extraordinary power of the paradigm. And this is precisely the
problem of marriage: *nobody*, no specific, cranky, concrete, particular person ever can fit the paradigm. Something has to change.
Either one person or the other voluntarily changes or is compelled
to change, or the paradigm changes, or there is no marriage.

This example clearly points two ways, only one of which needs
to be followed. We do not have *ideas* about what a woman is or
what a man is and, therefore, what a marriage is. Or, rather, we
do have ideas but they are only, at best, expressions of something
deeper. What controls us is the pattern, the paradigm, the image,
the model which is as surely fixed into our nervous system as the

reflex arc that causes us to snatch our hand away from a hot stove. It differs from the elementary reflex arc in that it is changeable, although with considerable difficulty. But it is a reflex arc of a kind, in that it determines behavior without conscious decision. It determines the conscious decisions which are themselves a mode of behavior. What we think of as our freedom to choose is remorselessly shaped by the paradigms that have formed in our nervous systems. In fact, such freedom as we have consists mainly of two things; the ability to classify (to decide which paradigm applies to a particular situation) and the ability to choose among the differing and contradictory paradigms that are contending in us. But classification and choice are not wholly free. They are shaped as cultural paradigms. Our freedom, then, must include the choice and the shaping of these paradigms.

So far from our culture being something outside our selves which we, as whole and complete beings, experience, our culture is a part of our selves as much as our nervous system is. We don't think *about* these images, as though they were ideas. We think *with* them, by means of them.

Another illustration will show how a culture can be controlled by abstract principles of relation and not simply images of persons.

American businessmen and politicians (who are mostly instruments of the businessmen) unceasingly claim their own place as Christians and extol the role of Christianity. Yet their dominant pattern of relation to the world is not Christian love but competition. Competition is a zero-sum game; what one wins another must lose. Thus, it is the very antithesis of Christian love, which would have two come together to generate something new. Yet no principle is more powerful in American life. It controls business, where it is defensible on the grounds of utility but it also controls other areas where it is inappropriate, such as foreign policy, and education, where it defeats the purpose of the enterprise, and the churches, where it contradicts the whole thing. Christianity is the religion of only a few Americans. Many more Americans, including most of the American churches, are controlled by the idea of competition, the compulsive need to be "No. 1," which is a principle of a far older, more primitive religion than Christianity.

These are two consequential examples but they are two of a large complex of images that control every range of our experience. The study of them is quite without end. They shape how we behave, how we are related to each other. They determine the purpose of our lives and how we know the physical world. This last may be the most dramatic illustration of all. The materialistic, postivistic conception of science would have it that science knows only hard and demonstrable facts and "discovers" the "laws" that govern those facts. Such an enterprise is opposed to all myth, religious and other fantasy and presupposes the image of man I described earlier. But Thomas Kuhn has demonstrated how an initial paradigm controls the development of a science. We see with understanding only what our paradigm permits us to see. Science stops when the paradigm is exhausted and we then see more than we can make sense of. It resumes with the development of a new paradigm.

Walter Ong called physics "a vast interior network of consciousness." And Albert Einstein said (with Leopold Infeld)

> Science is not just a collection of laws, a catalogue of unrelated facts. It is a creation of the human mind, with its freely invented ideas and concepts. Physical theories try to form a picture of reality and to establish its connection with the wide of sense impressions. Thus the only justification for our mental structures is whether and in what way our theories form such a link.[45]

If this is true of physics, how much more true is it of the rest of our life! The word *mental* ought not to mislead; *mental* does not mean the ghost in the machine, but a way of using our whole thinking body which is grounded in our physical bodies and includes the systems of our cultural bodies.

For these paradigms, these complex systems of paradigms, are not simply things we have as we have small change in our pockets or even, at a more important level, as we have clothing. They are more nearly something we *are*, for they shape our world, our feelings about our world, our actions and purposes within our world. They are an ingredient of ourselves.

A FINAL MEDITATION

Paul's statement "It is no longer I who lives but Christ who lives in me," now becomes intelligible. I cannot, of course, know what Paul thought he meant; I do know what the statement can mean to us, and, in the definition of the self I have described, it is literally true. The whole structure of images, the paradigms, that made up Paul's world had been shattered; the old man had died. Christ lived in him by the new ordering of the self in the world. It is, truly, the Christ, the power to shape feeling and action and purpose.

This controlling paradigm is not wholly within the individual. "The Kingdom of God is in the midst of you" refers precisely to the fact that the image of Christ is shared and most particularly from the fact that the Christ paradigm, the Christ model, is inseparable from the materials of culture. Paul did not die as a first century Hellenistic Jew to be reborn as some abstraction called a "Christian." He was reborn as a first Century Hellenistic Jewish Christian. So, receiving the Christ paradigm, living the Christ paradigm, is a communal act.

Being a Christian, then, is not holding to certain opinions, behaving in a certain way. Being a Christian is letting the old structure, the old paradigm die, and being reborn to the new being which is the Christ paradigm.

In this account of the self, taking either the hierarchical ordering or the outward development from the center, like a tree, this symbolic layer of the self is at the top or around the outside. It is not the whole, but it is the part that determines the true self. The lowest level of the innermost circle is shared by all living creatures. To go higher or toward the outside is to pass through those levels of the self that we share with the increasingly complex creatures. We finally arrive at the level of intelligence which is, first of all, the nonmoral intelligence of the animal, and finally achieves the human level by the paradigm of order and purpose that constitutes the highest or outermost layer. It is this outer layer that secures the uniqueness of the self. It is the truest self, so when it is broken and remade, it is truly a new self, even though the lower and inner levels or layers remain, in part, undisturbed.

It is possible now to define a sacrament. A sacrament is one of the things or acts appointed to the Church as communicating Christ to the worshippers in the sense of emplanting and renewing the image of Christ in the soul, the paradigm which is truly the real presence. A sacramental is one of those things, any of the things or acts that function the same way without having been appointed as always and everywhere central to the liturgy of the Church for all the faithful. There is no difference in purpose or effect between a sacrament and a sacramental.

This definition makes it possible to see the sacraments as other than magic and magic is the most grievous of all the temptations of the church. Because there has been no fully adequate understanding of the sacrament and because sacraments are obviously extraordinarily powerful things, it was nearly inevitable that many would think the power inheres in the thing itself. Consequently the sacramentals are thought to have miraculous power: the Bible heals or saves the life of the soldier, the cross controls demons, the Eucharistic elements do various miraculous things. Or alternatively the things or acts are deemed to have power even when they are wholly outside the life of the church. The Eucharistic elements are used in a black mass or services conducted surreptitiously and irregularly are deemed to control the work of the Holy One.

But Christ is in the community or nowhere. A misused sacrament is not profaned; it is nothing. Or, in another mode, a sacrament wrongly used becomes a sacrament in another religion. Paul also said that those who partake of the sacrament falsely, do so to their damnation. This does not mean that an arbitrary judge punishes a naughty child. It means that a Christian element or act has been fitted into another order of faith, made a different kind of self who cannot participate in the order of eternal life.

One of the great complications of this question is the relation of the form and material of the sacrament to that which is communicated by the sacrament. Is there any inherent relation or is the appointment merely arbitrary and convenient? A symbol, as Paul Tillich was fond of saying, participates in that which it symbolizes, while a sign is chosen arbitrarily as a pointer to something wholly outside itself.

A sacrament is not a casually selected sign. But neither is a sacrament a box containing a sacred power which can be distributed by the keeper of the keys. It is not a faucet dispensing the sacred power to anyone who turns it. It is one term in a relation, and the nature of a relation is determined by the terms being related as well as by the instrument of the relation. The elements of a sacrament, the ritual act in which the elements are used, have their own character, their own structure and rhythm which inescapably shape the sacramental relation. Equally, the use of the elements and the acts shapes the relation, making possible the false use of a sacrament. The sacrament conveys the energy, the power, and in conveying it, defines it. But the reception of it also defines it, and out of the false use of a sacramental proceeds a false religion. A sacrament performed surreptitiously is a valid sacrament all right; it is valid in a religion other than its founding community. If it is true of the sacraments appointed by the church for use in the community of the faithful, it is, obviously, even more true in the sacramentals which are, outside and beyond decision, part of human existence itself. In its appointed sacramentals, variously recognized among the churches, the Church has, in detail, accepted the sacramentality of human social and economic life. Of the seven appointed sacraments, six deal wholly with social and economic life and the seventh almost as much. Baptism sanctifies the entry into life, confirmation the entry into the sacred community, confirming the death of the old and the birth of the new. The Eucharist sustains the life of the sacred community with the fruits of the earth transformed by human labor. Marriage and ordination establish special offices within the sacred community, penance is the pedagogical and restorative punishment. Unction confirms the passage to a new mode of life.

Thus, in magnificent detail, the Church takes up human life into its ritual, shapes it, places it in the context of the sacred community. This Church has not yet learned how to use the last of the great human sacramentals, sex. In the sacramentals as presently constituted, human experience is understood almost wholly as social and economic; sex appears by implication only and grudgingly as a part of marriage.

In the economy of history this is as it must be; sex is a fearful power. Sex is and always will be a sacrament. But it is not, in itself, a Christian sacrament, a carrier of the image of Christ, the Christ paradigm. When the mind of the church has generated from its faithful life a metaphysics and an epistemology for the true reception of this great sacrament, then it can be received safely into wholeness.

Out of this there begins to emerge a definition of the role of the Church. It is not the primary role of the Church to soothe and comfort, to support the reigning orders, to advise on morals or to do, in fact, most of the things the Church spends its time actually doing. It is the function of the Church to communicate the Christ to people so he can be born in them and thereby make a soul for eternal life.

It is the function of the church to engender and form souls.

In actual practice, the church rightly uses all these things and many more besides. But they are the means, not the end, which is the engendering of Christ in the soul.

The Resurrection

A Meditation on the Final Mystery

Imprisoned in a metaphysics of substance, Christians attempted to imprison the omnipotence of the Holy One in their own expectations, their own categories. That Christ should rise from the dead was understood only as the liquifying of congealed blood, the animation of rigid muscles, footprints in the earth as the body walked from the tomb. But what could be done with such a body at the end of its appointed days?

The second coming, in a metaphysics of substance, was understood as a *deus ex machina*, the machine a cloud enthroning the triumphant Son of Man. The event was to be soon, then a little later, then at some ungraspable end of Time. Faith, wedded to an inadequate metaphysics, failed.

There is no way of knowing what took place at the Tomb. No eyewitness document would help, for the witness sees with the structures of a time-bound language which is read in the structured expectation of another culture. It is the metaphysics of substance that imposes an idolatry of historical "fact" and expects to find the solution to the ultimate in the reconstructions we call history.

History does not exist. There remains to us only the detritus of human making, the fragments of human artifacts which we then make into an idol of our own sense of order.

Perhaps the Holy One, omniscient and omnipotent, knows his own workings better than we do.

The Christ promised that he would come again. In the pride of knowledge and the apostasy from faith, we concluded that he didn't know what he was talking about. But he did come again.

In accordance with his promise he is present among us for our re-calling, if we are truly faithful.

Then Job answered the Lord, and said,
I know that thou canst do everything,
And that no thought can be withholden from thee.
Who is he that hideth counsel without knowledge?
Therefore have I uttered that I understood not.
Hear, I beseech thee, and I will speak:
I will demand of thee, and declare thou unto me.
I have heard of thee by the hearing of the ear;
But now mine eye seeth thee.
Wherefore I abhor myself, and repent
In dust and ashes.

After such knowledge, what forgiveness?

T. S. ELIOT

Now what is yet to come I do not know, except that they will go to some other country, far from us all. I trust they will find some peace there, even if he is to be for ever so silent and so grave. And I too, having lived this story in grief and passion, close it in some kind of peace, remembering God's mercy, who gave us all such friends.

Yet my grief can still come back to me, when I read of some tragic man who has broken the iron law. Was he two men, one brave and gentle, and one tormented? And has he friends, or will he suffer his whole life long? And was there one perhaps, who knew why he barred the door of his soul and should have hammered on it and cried out not ceasing?

And I grieve for him, and the house he has made to fall with him, not as with Samson the house of his enemies, but the house of his own flesh and blood. And I grieve for the nation which gave him birth, that left the trodden and the known for the vast and secret continent, and made there songs of *heimwee* and longing, and the iron laws. And now the Lord has turned our captivity, I pray we shall not walk arrogant, remembering Herod who an Angel of the Lord struck down, for that he made himself a god . . . .

Now all that I have written here is true, for I have seen the secret book, and all the things he wrote in prison; and my sister-in-law says it is true, though parts she would have written otherwise. And I wish she could have written it, for maybe of the power of her love that never sought itself, men would have turned to the holy task of pardon, that the body of the Lord might not be wounded twice, and virtue come of our offenses.

ALAN PATON

HETERODOXOLOGY

Life is poorly measured by its monuments and monsters;
the myriad meek inherit what the rest merely adorn.
Praise all, from whom God, blessing, flows.

JAMES WORLEY

Notes

Epigraph. Charles Olson, *Human Universe*, ed. Donald Allen (New York: Grove Press, 1967), p. 10.

1. Bruce Winstein, "Wanted: New Hypotheses In High Energy Physics," *University of Chicago Magazine* 69, No. 1 (Autumn 1976): 20.
2. Stephen Toulmin and June Goodfield, *The Architecture of Matter* (New York: Harper & Row, 1962), p. 375.
3. Erwin Schrödinger, *What is Life?* (Garden City, N.Y: Doubleday, Anchor Books, 1956), pp. 70–73.
4. John Platt, *Perception and Change* (Ann Arbor: University of Michigan Press, 1970), p. 40.
5. José Ortega y Gasset, *The Modern Theme* (New York: Harper & Row, Torchbooks, 1961), p. 138.
6. Thomas Kuhn, *The Structure of Scientific Revolution* (Chicago: University of Chicago Press, Phoenix Books, 1964).
7. Benjamin Lee Whorf, *Language, Thought and Reality* (Cambridge: M.I.T. Press, 1956).
S. *Ibid.*, p. 134
9. John Cassel, lectures delivered at The University of North Carolina School of Medicine.
10. José Ortega y Gasset, *Meditations on Quixote* (New York: W.W. Norton Co., 1963), p. 33.
11. J.C. Carothers, "Culture, Psychiatry and the Written Word," *Psychiatry* (November 1959); quoted by Marshall McLuhan in *The Gutenberg Galaxy* (New York: New American Library, 1969), p. 27.
12. Carl Friedrich von Weizsacker, *The History of Nature* (Chicago: University of Chicago Press, 1952).
13. Herman Broch, Introduction to Rachel Bespaloff, *On the Iliad* (New York: Harper & Row, Torchbooks, 1962) pp. 18–19.
14. von Weizsacker, *The History of Nature*, p. 189–90.
15. Rollo May, "Contributions of Existential Psychotherapy," in *Existence* ed. Rollo May, Ernest Angel and Henri Ellenberger (New York: Simon and Schuster, 1967), p. 59.

16. John White, ed. Introduction, *The Highest State of Consciousness* (New York: Doubleday, Anchor Books, 1972), p. xvii.

17. Colin, M. Turbayne, *The Myth of Metaphor* (Columbia, S.C., University of South Carolina Press, 1970).

18. Even specialists cannot command all the relevant literature in this area, and I am no specialist. I have consulted more material than there is any point in listing here. What I have to say is based most heavily on *Psychology: A Study of a Science,* ed. Sigmund Kock (New York: McGraw-Hill Book Co., 1962), vol. 4, *Biologically Oriented Fields: Their Place in Psychology and in Biological Science,* especially the essays, "How Man Looks at His Own Brain: An Adventure Shared by Psychology and Neurophysiology," pp. 51–99, by Robert B. Livingston, and "Perceptual Experience: An Analysis of Its Relations to the External World through Internal Processing." pp. 515–618 by Karl Zener and Mercedes Gaffron; James J. Gibson, *The Senses Considered as Perceptual Systems* (Boston: Houghton Mifflin Co., 1966).

19. L.L. Whyte, "A Scientific View of the 'Creative Energy' of Man," *Eranos-Jahrbuch* 1952 (Zurich: Rhein Verlag, 1953), reprinted in *Aesthetics Today,* ed. Morris Phillipson (Cleveland: World Publishing Co., Meridian Books, 1961), pp. 349–374.

20. Zener and Gaffron, "Perceptual Experience," p. 526. See note 18 above.

21. Gibson, *Senses Considered as Perceptual Systems.* See note 18 above.

22. Zener and Gaffron agree with Livingston on this important principle. (Livingston, "How Man Looks at His Brain," p. 68. See note 18 above.) "Incoming sensory signals streaming upward influence successive groups of neurons which are more or less directly associated with both sensory and motor functions. Sensory impulses also contribute, all along the neuraxis, to neurons that cannot be identified as being either sensory or motor, e.g., to neurons of the spinal and veticular formations and diffusely projecting forebrain systems, limbic lobe, associations areas of the cortex and cerebellum. These important sectors participate in complex transactions going between their own intrinsic ("spontaneous") activities and activities taking place along both the sensory and motor compartments. Such transactions may be initiated by incoming sensory signals, but they are demonstrably affected in accordance with previous experience. Such transactions find their only outward expression through behavior. But in their intracentral trajectories they have served to unify the organism into a functionally integrated whole . . . the distortions of capacities resulting from ablation is less an expression of *what the missing part did* than it is an expression of *what the remainder of the nervous system can do in the absence of that part.* . . . The idea of *interaction,* as between linear cause-effect sequences, is inadequate. Instead what occurs may be better described by the term *trans-action.* (Livingston, p. 70).

23. Nigel Calder, *The Mind of Man* (New York: Viking Press, 1970), pp. 128–130.

24. Quoted in Livingston "How Man Looks at His Brain," p. 90.

25. Whyte, "Scientific View," pp. 366–367.

26. . . . "today the stress is upon a more verifiable construct: the concept of rhyth-

mic, spontaneous, centrally proceeding pattern of nervous activity upon which peripheral stimulus configurations are superimposed and out of which authoritative effector commands emerge . . . so as to produce a delicately modulated pattern of behavior." (Clifford Geertz, "The Growth of Culture and the Evolution of Mind" *Theories of Mind*, ed. Jordan Scher [New York: Free Press, 1962] p. 725.)

27. von Weizsacker, *History of Nature.*

28. Geertz, "Culture and Evolution of Mind," pp. 722–723. See note 26 above.

29. *Ibid.*, p. 731.

30. Arthur Koestler, *The Ghost in the Machine* (New York: Macmillan Co., 1967).

31. *Ibid.*, pp. 281–282.

32. Calder, in *Mind of Man*, gives a journalistic report on a number of these experiments.

33. Livingston, "How Man Looks at His Brain," p. 68.

34. White, Introduction, p. xvii.

35. Rudolph Bultmann, "New Testament and Mythology," *Kerygma and Myth*, ed. Hans Werner Bartsch (New York: Harper & Row, Torchbooks, 1961), p. 3.

36. There are undoubtedly more; I kept getting interested and losing count! Thomas J. J. Altizer, "Word and History," in Thomas J. J. Altizer and William Hamilton, *Radical Theology and the Death of God* (New York: Bobbs-Merrill Co., 1966), pp. 121–139.

37. See the touching article by William Hamilton, "Thursday's Child," reprinted in Altizer and Hamilton, *Radical Theology.* See also my review/article on Ray Hart's, *Unfinished Man and the Imagination, Soundings.* vol. LIII pp. 323–338

38. As far as I am aware, the distinction was first made by Croce (1866–1952, Italian philosopher.—ED.) and, unfortunately for much subsequent art criticism, has been largely confined to Croceans. Benedetto Croce, *Aesthetic*, trans. by David Ainslee, (New York, Noonday Press, 1922 and 1956), pp. 15–16; and Theodore Greene, *The Arts and the Art of Criticism* (Princeton, N.J.: Princeton University Press, 1940) 31–

39. See Herbert Butterfield, *The Whig Interpretation of History* (New York: Scribner's, 1951), pp. 83–89.

40. Quoted in I.A. Richards, *Coleridge on Imagination* (Bloomington, Ind.: Indiana University Press, 1960), p. 122.

41. Phillip Fehl, "Mass Murder, or Humanity in Death," *Theology Today*, vol. 28, no. 1 (April 1971), 51–71.

42. The therapeutic implications of the Abraham-Isaac relation are set out in Erich Wellisch, *Isaac and Oedipus.*

43. Olson, *Human Universe*, p. 3.

44. Elizabeth Sewell, *The Human Metaphor* (Southbend, Ind: University of Notre Dame Press, 1964), p. 45.

45. Albert Einstein and Leopold Infeld, *The Evolution of Physics* (New York, Simon and Schuster, 1961), p. 294.

Bibliography

The problem of delineating a bibliography for a work of this kind is acute. Its preparation required a very large amount of reading over many years. A listing of all that material would result only in an extensive bibliography which would have no use except to impress the unwary reader with the author's industry. In lieu of that, the only adequate bibliography would be an essay that would recount the function of each important writing in the development of the book. This would extend the length of the book unduly.

Therefore I have chosen those books to list which have been formative in the development of the book or to which I would point as containing evidence or arguments which are its necessary foundation. Insofar as I can, I have included the works that have been functional, the ones I would want to base my case on.

Inevitably, I owe an apology to those on this list who might not care for the use I have made of their work. I owe another kind of apology to those who have contributed ideas that I have so absorbed that they have dropped out of consciousness.

I have omitted the names of some material referred to in the text but which did not have a formative influence on its development beyond providing an apt quotation. Similarly I have included many people not referred to directly in the text, but who did provide something fundamental.

The degree and kind of my indebtedness to these people varies widely. Some of these writings I have read and meditated on for years. Others acted suddenly to crystallize a series of ideas. For example, I could not master G. Spencer Brown's *Laws of Form* if I wanted to. Yet, two pages of his introduction quoted in a book catalogue acted like the crystal dropped into a supersaturated solution. This book might never have developed had it not been for that moment.

My major regret is that scholarly procedure does not make it possible to list works of art as authorities for ideas. Yet this book could not have existed had it not been for the many works of art that shaped its argument.

Arnheim, Rudolph. *Art and Visual Perceptions*. Berkeley: University of California Press, 1954.

Auerbach, Eric. *Mimesis*. Garden City, N.Y.: Doubleday, 1957.

Bachelard, Gaston. *The Poetics of Space*. New York: Orion Press, 1964.

Barfield, Owen. *Saving the Appearances*. New York: Harcourt, Brace & World, Harbinger Books, n.d.

Barr, James. *The Semantics of Biblical Language*. Oxford: Oxford University Press, 1961.

Bernanos, Georges. *Diary of a Country Priest*. New York: Macmillan, 1962.

Bertalanffy, Ludwig von. *Problems of Life*. New York: Harper & Row, Torchbooks, 1960.

Brandt, William. *The Shape of Medieval History*. New Haven: Yale University Press, 1966.

Broch, Herman. "The Style of the Mythical Age." Introduction to *On the Iliad*, by Rachel Bespaloff. New York: Harper & Row, Torchbooks, 1962.

Brown, G. Spencer. *Laws of Form*. New York: Bantam Books, 1973.

Butterfield, Herbert. *The Whig Interpretation of History*. New York: Scribner's, 1951.

Cassirer, Ernst. *An Essay on Man*. New York: Doubleday, Anchor Books, n.d.

———. 1946. *Language and Myth*. New York: Dover Publications.

Clark, Kenneth. *The Nude*. Garden City, N.Y., Doubleday, 1959.

Dante. *The Divine Comedy*. Baltimore: Penguin Books, 1949.

Dillistone, F. W.. *The Structure of the Divine Society*. Philadelphia: Westminster Press, 1955.

Dix, Dom Gregory. *The Shape of the Liturgy*. London: Daise Press, 1945.

Douglas, Mary. *Natural Symbols*. New York: Pantheon Books, 1970.

Ehrenzweig, Anton. *The Psychoanalysis of Artistic Vision and Hearing*. New York: George Braziller, 1965.

———. 1969. *The Hidden Order of Art*. New York: George Braziller.

Einstein, Albert. *Relativity.* New York: Crown Publishers, 1961.

Einstein, Albert, and Infield, Leopold. *The Evolution of Physics.* New York: Simon and Schuster, 1961.

Eliade, Mircea. *The Sacred and the Profane.* New York: Harper & Row, Torchbooks, 1961.

Faure, Elie. *The Spirit of the Forms.* Garden City, N.Y.: Garden City Publishing Co., 1937.

Fenellosa, Ernest. *The Chinese Written Character.* London: Stanley Nott, 1936.

Ferguson, Francis. *The Idea of a Theater.* Garden City, N.Y., Doubleday, Anchor Books, 1953.

_____. *Dante's Drama of the Mind.* Princeton: Princeton University Press, 1953.

Focillon, Henri. *The Life of Forms in Art.* New York: George Wittenborn, 1948.

Foucault, Michael. *The Order of Things.* London: Tavistock Publications, 1970.

_____. 1976. *The Archaeology of Knowledge,* New York, Harper & Row, Colophon Books.

Frankfort, Henri. *Before Philosophy.* Baltimore: Penguin Books, 1949.

Geertz, Clifford. *The Interpretation of Cultures.* New York: Basic Books, 1973.

Gibson, James. *The Senses Considered as Perceptual Systems.* Boston: Houghton Mifflin Co., 1966.

Giedion, Siegfried. *The Eternal Present: The Beginning of Art.* New York: Pantheon Books, 1962.

_____. 1964. *The Eternal Present: The Beginning of Architecture.* New York: Pantheon Books.

Gombrich, Ernst. *Art and Illusion.* Bollingen Series, vol. 40 no. 5. New York: Pantheon Books, 1960.

Greene, Theodore. *The Arts and the Art of Criticism.* Princeton: Princeton University Press, 1941.

Hall, Edward. *The Hidden Dimension.* Garden City, N.Y.: Doubleday, 1969.

_____. 1959. *The Silent Language.* Greenwich, Conn.: Fawcett Publications.

Hayek, Friedrich. *The Sensory Order.* Chicago: University of Chicago Press, 1952.

Ivins, William, Jr. *Prints and Visual Communication.* Cambridge: M.I.T. Press, 1953.

Jung, Carl. *Modern Man in Search of a Soul*. New York: Harcourt, Brace & World, 1933.

Kaschnitz-Weinberg, Guido von. *Ausgewahlte Schriften*. Berlin: Verlag Gebr. Mann, 1965.

Klee, Paul. *The Thinking Eye*. Edited by Jurg Spiller. London: Lund Humphries, 1961.

Koestler, Arthur. *The Ghost in the Machine*. New York: Macmillan Co., 1968.

———. 1969. *Beyond Reductionism*. Boston: Beacon Press.

Kubler, George. *The Shape of Time*. New Haven: Yale University Press, 1962.

Kuhn, Thomas. *The Structure of Scientific Revolution*. Chicago: University of Chicago Press, 1962.

Langer, Suzanne. *Philosophy in a New Key*. New York: Penguin Books, 1948.

Lashley, K.A. "The Problem of Serial Order in Behavior." In *Central Mechanisms in Behavior*. Edited by L. Jeffers. New York: John Wiley, 1951.

Levy, G. Rachel. *Religious Conceptions of the Stone Age*. New York: Harper & Row, Torchbooks, 1963.

Livingstone, Robert B.. "How Man Looks at His Own Brain." In *Biologically Oriented Fields. Psychology: A Study of a Science*. Edited by Sigmund Koch, vol. 4. New York: McGraw-Hill Book Co., 1962.

Maritain, Jacques. *Creative Intuition in Art and Poetry*. Bollingen Series, vol. 36, 1953. New York: Pantheon Books,

May, Rollo. "The Origins and Significance of the Existential Movement in Psychology," and "Contributions of Existential Psychotherapy." In *Existence*. Edited by Rollo May, Ernest Angel and Henri Ellenberger. New York: Simon and Schuster, 1958.

Merleau-Ponty, Maurice. *Signs*. Evanston, Ill.: Northwestern University Press, 1964.

———. 1962. *Phenomenology of Perception*. London: Routledge and Kegan Paul.

Nash, Arnold. *The University and the Modern World*. New York: Macmillan Co., 1944.

Neumann, Erich. *The Origins and History of Consciousness*. New York: Harper & Row, Torchbooks, 1962.

Nodleman, Sheldon. "Sixties Art." *Perspecta*, 11, 1967, 74–89

Olson, Charles. *Human Universe*. New York: Grove Press, 1967.

Ortega y Gasset, José. *Meditations on Quixote*. New York: W.W. Norton Co., 1961.

————. 1961. *The Modern Theme*. New York. Harper & Row, Torchbooks, (All of Ortega's translated works should be included.)

Otto, Rudolph. *The Idea of the Holy*. New York: Oxford University Press, 1958.

Otto, Walter. *The Homeric Gods*. Boston: Beacon Press, 1964.

Picard, Max. *Man and Language*. Chicago: Henry Regnery Co., 1963.

————. 1961. *The World of Silence*. Chicago: Henry Regnery Co.

————. 1947. *Hitler in Ourselves*. Chicago: Henry Regnery Co.

Platt, John. *Perception and Change*. Ann Arbor: University of Michigan Press, 1970.

Polanyi, Michael. *Personal Knowledge*. New York: Harper & Row, Torchbooks, 1963.

Portman, Adolph. *New Paths in Biology*. New York: Harper & Row, 1964. "Biology and the Phenomenon of the Spiritual." In *Spirit and Nature*. Edited by Joseph Campbell. New York: Princeton Books, Bollingen Series vol. 30 no. 1.

Read, Herbert. *Icon and Idea*. New York: Shocken Books, 1965.

Redfield, Robert. *The Primitive World and Its Transformations*. Ithaca: Cornell University Press, 1953.

Schroedinger, Ervin. *What Is Life?* Garden City N.Y.: Doubleday, Anchor Books, 1956.

Schwarz, Rudolph. *The Church Incarnate*. Chicago: Henry Regnery Co., 1952.

Sewell, Elizabeth. *The Human Metaphor*. South Bend, Ind.: University of Notre Dame Press, 1964.

Simson, Otto von. *The Gothic Cathedral*. New York: Pantheon Books, Bollingen Series vol. 48, 1956.

Steinberg, Leo. "The Eye is a Part of the Mind." In *Reflections on Art*. Edited by Suzanne Langer. New York: Oxford Press, 1961.

Strauss, Ervin. *The Primary World of Senses*. New York: Free Press of Glener, 1967.

Stokes, Adrian. *Colour and Form*. London: Faber and Faber, 1937.

Thompson, d'Arcy. *On Growth and Form*. Cambridge: Cambridge University Press, 1942.

Toulmin, Stephen and Goodfield, June. *The Architecture of Matter*. New York: Harper & Row, 1966.

Turbayne, Colin. *The Myth of Metaphor*. Columbia, S.C.: University of South Carolina Press, 1970.

Underhill, Evelyn. *Worship*. New York: Harper & Row, Torchbooks, 1957.

van der Leeuw Geradus. *Religion in Essence and Manifestation*. New

York: Harper Torchbooks, 1963.

Weizsacker, Carl Friedrich von. *The History of Nature.* Chicago: University of Chicago Press, 1947.

Wellisch, Eric. *Isaac and Oedipus.* London: Routledge and Kegan Paul, Ltd., 1954.

Westheim, H. *The Springs of Creativity.* New York: Atheneum, 1961.

Westheim, Paul. *The Art of Ancient Mexico.* Garden City, N.Y.: Doubleday, 1965.

White, Lynn. *Machina ex Deo.* Cambridge: M.I.T. Press, 1968.

Whitehead, Alfred North. *Science and the Modern World.* New York: Mentor Books, 1948.

Whyte, Lancelot. *Law: The Next Development in Man.* New York: Mentor Books, 1962.

_____. 1953. "A Scientific View of the 'Creative Energy' of Man." In *Eranos Jahrbuch 1952,* Zurich: Rhein Verlag.

_____. 1952. *Internal Factors in Evolution.* New York: George Braziller

Williams, Charles. *The Figure of Beatrice.* London: Faber and Faber, Ltd., 1943.

_____. 1956. *The Descent of the Dove.* New York: Meridian Books.

Whorf, Benjamin Lee. *Language, Thought and Reality.* Cambridge: M.I.T. Press, 1956.

Wittkower, Rudolph. *Architectural Principles in the Age of Humanism.* London: Alec Trianti, 1952.

Wolfe, Ivor. *The Italian Townscope.* New York: George Braziller, 1966.

Wolfflin, Heinrich. *Principles of Art History.* New York: Dover Publications, n.d.

Zener, Karl, and Gaffron, Mercedes. "Perceptual Experience: An Analysis of Its Relations to the External World through Internal Processing." In *Biologically Oriented Fields.* Psychology: A Study of a Science. Edited by Sigmund Koch, vol. 4. New York: McGraw-Hill Book Co., 1962.

Index

This index is intended to be useful and not exhaustive. Therefore, not every occurrence of terms or names is listed but only the ones that matter the most.